The Structure of Time

HUMAN COGNITIVE PROCESSING is a forum for interdisciplinary research on the nature and organization of the cognitive systems and processes involved in speaking and understanding natural language (including sign language), and their relationship to other domains of human cognition, including general conceptual or knowledge systems and processes (the language and thought issue), and other perceptual or behavioral systems such as vision and non-verbal behavior (e.g. gesture). 'Cognition' should be taken broadly, not only including the domain of rationality, but also dimensions such as emotion and the unconscious. The series is open to any type of approach to the above questions (methodologically and theoretically) and to research from any discipline, including (but not restricted to) different branches of psychology, artificial intelligence and computer science, cognitive anthropology, linguistics, philosophy and neuroscience. It takes a special interest in research crossing the boundaries of these disciplines.

Volume 12

The Structure of Time: Language, meaning and temporal cognition
by Vyvyan Evans

The Structure of Time

Language, meaning and temporal cognition

Vyvyan Evans

University of Sussex

John Benjamins Publishing Company
Amsterdam/Philadelphia

Cover image: *The structure of time* © 2005, Angela Evans.

The Library of Congress has already cataloged the hardcover edition as follows:

Evans, Vyvyan
    The structure of time : language, meaning and temporal cognition /
    Vyvyan Evans.
      p. cm. (Human Cognitive Processing, ISSN 1387–6724 ; v. 12)
      1. Space and time in language. 2. Semantics. 3. Cognition. I. Title. II.
    Series.

    P37.5.S65E93   2004
401'.43-dc22   2003062997
ISBN 90 272 2364 5 (Eur.) / 1 58811 466 X (US) (Hb; alk. paper)
ISBN 90 272 2367 X (Pb; alk. paper)

John Benjamins Publishing Co. · P.O. Box 36224 · 1020 ME Amsterdam · The Netherlands
John Benjamins North America · P.O. Box 27519 · Philadelphia PA 19118-0519 · USA

For Angela
Time spent with you is my most precious possession

Sonnet XII

When I do count the clock that tells the time,
And see the brave day sunk in hideous night;
When I behold the violet past prime,
And sable curls, all silvered o'er with white;
When lofty trees I see barren of leaves,
Which erst from heat did canopy the herd,
And summer's green all girded up in sheaves,
Borne on the bier with white and bristly beard,
Then of thy beauty do I question make,
That thou among the wastes of time must go,
Since sweets and beauties do themselves forsake,
And die as fast as they see others grow;
    And nothing 'gainst Time's scythe can make defence,
    Save breed, to brave him when he takes thee hence.

William Shakespeare

Table of contents

Acknowledgements

In writing this book I have amassed a number of debts, intellectual and otherwise. This book has its roots in doctoral research undertaken at Georgetown University. Hence, I owe an immense debt to the members of my doctoral committee, Andrea Tyler, Mark Turner and Joseph Grady, all of whom I worked with closely during the various stages of that early research period. Andrea Tyler, my former supervisor, and now colleague and co-author, provided the institutional support for me to explore Cognitive Linguistics. My debt to her is immense, not least for her friendship, support and insight into all things linguistic. Together we undertook joint research into lexical semantics which has culminated in the 'principled polysemy' approach detailed throughout this book. This forms the basis of the methodology introduced in Chapter 6 and the data analysis in Part II. Needless to say, I take responsibility for the version of the model presented here and my application of it to the abstract noun *time*. Mark Turner originally encouraged my interest in temporal cognition for which I am indebted. I would also like to express my gratitude for his illuminating work, his never failing support and his encouragement. Additionally, Joe Grady's own revealing research on the distinction between image and response concepts and on time as a primary metaphor provided the impetus for the line of research which has culminated in the present work. I am grateful for Joe's encouragement and friendly criticism, and for always challenging me to clarify my ideas.

This book was largely written in the two years I spent as a faculty member in the School of Cognitive and Computing Sciences (COGS), at the University of Sussex, from 2001–2003. In that time I amassed a number of further debts which need acknowledging. First and foremost I am grateful to the Dean of COGS, Professor Richard Coates, for institutional support of every kind. I am also indebted to Dr. Nicola Woods, chair of Linguistics during this period, for gracious and redoubtable support in times of change and upheaval. In addition, I am grateful to two linguistics colleagues, Drs. Lynne Murphy and Melanie Green, with whom I co-founded the Sussex Meaning and Grammar Group (SMAGG). This group has provided a research forum at Sussex for, amongst other things, Cognitive Linguistics. I am grateful to Lynne and Melanie for assisting in facilitating this. I was fortunate to have Wallace Chafe as a reviewer for this book. His thoughtful questions and extensive comments made me re-think many aspects of my analysis and presentation. I hope that I have done justice to his comments and his own impressive work on the nature of language and time. Needless to say, any remaining errors, particularly in a work as necessarily speculative as this, are my own.

My greatest debt of all is to my wife Angela. She has been my companion as I have travelled through the mysteries of time, and across the globe. I thank her for her grace, her good humour and her insight. She has spent literally hours discussing with me many of the issues dealt with in this book, and further hours finding and compiling quotations, references and thinking up linguistic examples. I really could not have written this book without her. Finally I would like to acknowledge the support of the editors of the Human Cognitive Processing Series, Marcelo Dascal, Ray Gibbs and Jan Nuyts.

PART I

Orientation

CHAPTER 1

The problem of time

> Of all the scientific intangibles that shape our lives, time is arguably the
> most elusive – and the most powerful. As formless as space and being, those
> other unseen realms of abstraction on which we are helplessly dependent, it
> nonetheless affects all material things...Without it we could barely measure
> change, for most things that change on this Earth and in the universe happen
> in time and are governed by it. Stealthy, imperceptible, time makes its presence
> known by transforming our sense of it into sensation. For though we cannot
> see, touch, or hear time, we observe the regularity of what appears to be its
> passage in our seasons, in the orchestrated shift from dawn to dusk to dark,
> and in the aging of our bodies. We feel its pulsing beat in our hearts and hear
> its silence released in the precise ticking of a clock.   (Langone 2000: 7)

Time adds an important and necessary dimension to our understanding of the
world and our place in it – it seems almost impossible to conceive of what our
world of experience might be like in the absence of time; after all, events happen *in* time. This has resulted in physicists treating time, along with space, as a
theoretical and an empirical primitive (Akhundov 1986; Coveney & Highfield
1990; Davies 1995; Einstein 1961, [1916] 1950; Sklar 1974). The view that time
constitutes, at some level, part of the physical fabric of the cosmos, and as such
is physically real, accords with what I will term the COMMON-PLACE VIEW of
time. According to Langone (2000), most people believe in this view of time, a
'true' time, a time that actually exists in a physical sense; on this account, time
is objectively embedded in the external world, as reflected in the physical laws
which govern the environment we inhabit. While time may itself be "incercep-
tible", it is nonetheless real, manifesting tangible consequences. Without time's
"passage" there could be no succession and thus no experience of duration, as
noted in the quotation above.

Not only does the common-place view of time accord with modern
physics, it also resonates with mythological views of time. A number of scholars
have observed that in ancient mythologies, for instance in the Persian, Greek
and Indian traditions, time was deemed to be one of the foundational principles of the cosmos (see Coveney & Highfield 1990; Lipincott et al. 1999;

Whitrow 1988). In the Platonic dialogue *Timaeus*, Plato presents a speculative cosmology, based on earlier Greek mythology, in which he describes time as the "moving image of eternity". On this account, time reflects physical attributes of the cosmos, namely the celestial spheres which are eternal in nature. This view is in some respects apparent in both classical physics (e.g., Newton's view of 'absolute time' in his *Principia Mathematica*), and in post-Einsteinian physics. In Einstein's ([1916] 1961) theory of general relativity time is seen as constituting part of the physical makeup of the cosmos, embedded with space in a physical spacetime manifold.

Yet, in the quotation above we see the tension apparent when we confront the nature of time. On the one hand, we have the common-place view and the view of modern physics which has built a theoretical edifice on the foundational axiom of the reality of time. Yet, on the other hand, time is "elusive", "intangible", "stealthy" and "imperceptible". Moreover, if time were in some sense objectively real, we might expect to be able to actually perceive it. However, there does not appear to be neurological apparatus which enables us to perceive global time (Lakoff & Johnson 1999). This has led a range of scholars to suggest that time may not be objectively real in the literal sense imagined by the common-place view. Indeed, while we intuitively experience time, beyond the physical periodicities (e.g., the daily passage of the sun across the sky, or the oscillation of quartz crystals in a digital watch) we harness in order to represent time, there appears to be nothing tangible in the world which can actually be pointed to and identified as time. This tension gives rise to the metaphysical problems which have been associated with time by philosophers, scientists and other scholars in the western tradition since pre-Socratic times.

1.1 The metaphysical problem and the linguistic problem

This book is primarily concerned with addressing what I will call THE META-PHYSICAL PROBLEM OF TIME. This can be stated as follows: if we are aware of time, and yet cannot be said to actually perceive it without, for instance, "the precise ticking of clocks", which serve to measure its "silence", what is the nature and status of time? Is time a primitive, an attribute of the physical cosmos, as suggested by modern physics, or is time dependent on the relations between events such as our experience of motion events, and hence not primarily an attribute of the world, but a consequence of it, an abstraction derived from comparing events, as suggested by, for instance, Lakoff and Johnson (1999), and by the psychologist James Gibson (1975, 1986)? Or is time neither a physical attribute of the world, nor a relation between external events, but rather something internal in nature? That is, is our awareness of time primarily phenomenological, deriving from internal cognitive and other perceptual processes, as suggested by phenomenologists such as Husserl ([1887] 1999) and Bergson ([1922] 1999)?

There is a second tension apparent in the quotation with which we began. While time seems to be fundamental to our understanding of other events (including motion), we ordinarily think and talk about time not in time's own terms, whatever these may be, but rather in precisely those terms which derive from the events, which according to modern physics, time structures – after all we talk about the 'passage' or the 'flow' of time and about being 'located in' time. In so doing we spatialise time. This represents THE LINGUISTIC PROBLEM OF TIME: why do we use language pertaining to motion through three-dimensional space and locations in three-dimensional space in order to think and talk about time? Is there something which is literally temporal beyond the language of motion and space we employ to describe it?

The ultimate goal of this book is to establish the nature and structure of time, in essence to resolve the metaphysical problem. One important way in which I will address the metaphysical difficulties associated with time will be by tackling the linguistic problem. In this book I will suggest that the manner in which temporal concepts are ELABORATED, which is to say structured by conceptual content from other (i.e., non-temporal) domains, provides important insights into the nature and structure of time. I will argue that this elaboration can be effectively studied via an examination of the linguistic problem. As language reflects conceptual structure in important ways, it accordingly represents a crucial window into the human conceptual system. By examining the way in which language lexicalises time, we will gain important insights into the conceptualisation of time and the nature and organisation of time.

However, as we will see, how we model time at the conceptual level does not tell the whole story, if we are to uncover the nature and structure of time. Phenomenological experience and the nature of the external sensory world to which subjective experience constitutes a response, give rise to our pre-conceptual experience of time, and so contribute to our conceptualisation of time in important, complex, and subtle ways. As we will see, a metaphysics for time cannot be solely physicalist, or cognitivist or phenomenologist. Time is not a unitary phenomenon restricted to a particular layer of experience. Rather, it constitutes a complex range of phenomena and processes which relate to different levels and kinds of experience. A balanced view is one which takes seriously this complexity and adopts a suitably responsible approach to the study of TEMPORAL COGNITION.

1.2 Temporal cognition

This book deals with temporal cognition. I am assuming a suitably broad definition of COGNITION which covers all aspects of conscious and unconscious mental function. Temporal cognition is that aspect which concerns the mental function responsible for temporal (and temporally-framed) experience (such as, for instance, perceptual processing – see Chapter 2) at the pre-conceptual level (prior to re-presentation in conceptual structure), as well as the organisation and structuring of temporal concepts (= re-presentations) at the conceptual level, i.e., within the CONCEPTUAL SYSTEM. The conceptual system, as I will understand it, is that attribute of mind which organises and stores information which has achieved REPRESENTATIONAL STATUS. Information which has achieved representational status can be recalled, modelled, employed for purposes of reasoning, projection, abstraction, etc. (see Barsalou 2003). Hence, the content of the conceptual system is available to symbolic processes such as language, which pairs a physical symbol (e.g., a sound) with a meaning element which I term a CONCEPT – language then symbolises information to which we have conscious access. That subset of concepts which are paired with linguistic symbols (e.g., words), I refer to as LEXICAL CONCEPTS.

From this two claims follow. First, to study linguistic meaning constitutes a study of the conceptual system (albeit in a form conventionalised for expression via language). Second, as lexical concepts represent only a subset of the range of concepts which inhere in the conceptual system, the linguistic-semantic system cannot be equated with the conceptual system (Brisard 1999; Heine 1997). Nonetheless, the view that the meanings paired with linguistic symbols are (a particular 'species' of concepts) entails that the study of linguistic semantics offers a direct way of investigating the human conceptual system.

I will argue that the nature of the metaphysical and linguistic problems derives, in essence, from a bifurcation in the conceptual system. That is, there is a fundamental distinction in the nature of concepts (Grady 1997a; Langacker 1987; Tyler & Evans 2001a). It is this bifurcation – between concepts of subjective origin as opposed to concepts of sensorimotor, i.e., external origin – that results in the nature of time appearing to be so paradoxical and mysterious. Once the distinction in concepts has been properly understood, it will become clear that temporality is a phenomenon which, while ultimately internal in nature, constitutes a response to the external world of sensory experience to which we have adapted as a species, and to which we continue to adapt over the course of a lifetime.

Consequently, my central thesis is that time is not ultimately an empirical primitive, in the sense of being a physical feature of an objective world, as in modern physics; nor is time at base a mental achievement, an abstraction derived from the relations holding between external events in a tradition going back to the philosophy of Leibniz (Turetzky 1998). Rather, I will argue in detail that temporality is fundamentally internal and hence phenomenological in origin.[1]

However, this is not to say that time does not reach its apotheosis in the cultural models we construct in order to co-ordinate everyday life by virtue of this ultimately subjective temporal experience. Indeed, much of this book will be concerned with such models. Nor does this conclusion serve to undermine the importance of sensory experience as a set of phenomena necessitating temporal awareness, and as a means of providing structure for cognitive models of time.

Based on the analyses to be presented, it will be possible in the final chapter to advance a metaphysics of time, in which the internal provenance of time, as well as its nature and organisation, are adduced. This metaphysics will take account of our cognitive model(s) for time evidenced via language, their subjective or phenomenological provenance, and their relation to our external world of sensorimotor experience.

1.3 Why should we be interested in investigating time?

One of the most intriguing issues which confronts a theory of conceptual structure concerns the nature of temporal representation. As time has often been held to be the example of a so-called 'abstract' concept par excellence, an investigation of how time is represented in the human conceptual system gives rise to a number of problems of central concern for the cognitive sciences. If concepts derive from the redescription of perceptual input, as suggested by the developmental psychologist Jean Mandler (1992, 1996), then what is the input which gives rise to conceptions of time? This question gives rise to the metaphysical problem discussed above. Time is one of the most mysterious and baffling of entities. While we 'feel' its 'passage' we cannot actually observe the 'flow' of time without the physical experience of succession and change which time appears to bring about. What then is the nature and status of the experience which provides the input for perceptual redescription? A further difficulty is that although we intuitively apprehend the concept of time, it's not at all clear how time is represented at the conceptual level. While I will examine linguistic evidence, and take this as representing, in some form, conventionalised conceptual content, it remains unclear how far such patterns of concept elaboration can be taken as evidence for conceptual structure. Moreover, while there is evidence from a number of modalities, including language, that at the conceptual level time is organised in terms of corporeal spatio-physical experience, this still fails to explain what is temporal beyond the spatial structure, and indeed, why temporal concepts should be elaborated in this way.

As work in the cognitive sciences progresses, it is increasingly becoming clear that human cognition is a highly complex phenomenon. The world we perceive to be out there is as much a product of cognition in a human body as it is the result of an external reality (Lakoff 1987; Torey 1999; Tyler & Evans 2003; Varela, Thompson & Rosch 1991). Hence, our world-view as human beings is exactly that, a view from one possible ecologically viable perspective among many possible perspectives (Varela et al. 1991). The world we have conscious access to is itself a product of embodied cognition, and moreover, this consciously accessible portion only constitutes one small aspect of the cognitive product (Dennett 1991; Edelman 1992; Jackendoff 1983, 1990, 1992). A study of time, or more properly temporal cognition (in the sense defined), allows us to begin to glimpse beyond the constraints imposed upon any investigation by consciousness. We are therefore able to reject the view that concepts such as time are difficult to define in their own terms because they are intellectual constructs; as we will see, they are difficult to define because they form part of the bedrock of our cognitive architecture. We are therefore also able to reject the view that time must be at some level an artefact of the world. A study of temporal cognition is important because it reveals the hidden depths of the human mind and how dependent our perceived world is on the nature and organisation of the cognition which happened to evolve in a human body.

1.4   Introduction to the rest of the book

The central proposal of this book is that time does in fact constitute a phenomenologically real, internally-derived experience. Drawing on findings in social and cognitive psychology, in neuroscience and utilising the perspective and methodology of cognitive linguistics, I argue that our experience of time cannot be equated with an objectively real entity inhering in the world 'out there'. Nor can it be equated with a second-order concept parasitic on 'more basic' kinds of experiences, such as external sensory experience. Rather, I argue that time appears ultimately to derive from perceptual processes which in fact may enable us to perceive events. As such, temporal experience may be a pre-requisite for abilities such as event perception and comparison, rather than being an abstraction based on such phenomena.

The investigation proceeds by tackling the linguistic problem of time. As linguistic structure, and particularly patterns of elaboration, reflect conceptual organisation conventionalised into a format encodable in language, the study presented here serves to investigate the human conceptual system for time. Such a study will reveal how we conceptualise and so structure our concepts for time. As conceptualisation must reflect, to a certain extent at least, the nature of (pre-conceptual) subjective experience (although see Dennett 1991), an investigation of time at the conceptual level provides a means of investigating the nature of temporal experience and so tackling the metaphysical problem. Hence, the book presents an examination of the nature of temporal cognition with two distinct foci: (i) an investigation into (pre-conceptual) temporal experience and (ii) an analysis of temporal structure at the conceptual level (which derives from temporal experience).

The book is divided into three parts. Part I is orientational in nature. In the next chapter I begin with a discussion of the linguistic problem: the fact that temporal concepts are conceptualised and lexicalised in terms of semantic content from the domain of motion and three-dimensional space. I review and reject the position that this constitutes evidence for concluding that temporal concepts are abstract in the sense of 'mental achievements', 'constructed' from 'more concrete' kinds of experiences and concepts, notably the comparison between events. Evidence is reviewed from neuroscience, psychology and linguistics which suggests that time may ultimately derive from fundamentally subjective experience, possibly deriving from perceptual processing, which relates to antecedent pre-conceptual experiences.

While time is of internal provenance, the linguistic evidence nevertheless indicates that it is structured at the conceptual level in terms of content which relates ultimately to sensory domains which are not primarily (or at least not wholly) temporal in nature. Accordingly, Chapter 3 considers why time should be elaborated at the conceptual level in non-temporal terms.

Chapter 4 presents a survey of the theoretical assumptions which inform and underpin the methodology and analyses to be presented in later chapters. Specifically, this chapter provides an experientialist account of the nature of meaning, relating linguistic semantics to the nature of conceptualisation and embodied experience. It argues that human embodied experience is itself an

outcome of evolutionary natural drift, in phylogenetic terms one viable outcome among many such possible outcomes in the particular ecological niche
occupied by humans.

In Chapter 5 I consider an account of time which has attempted to employ language to uncover conventional patterns at the conceptual level. This
constitutes the Conceptual Metaphor framework associated with scholars such
as Lakoff and Johnson (1980, 1999), Lakoff and Turner (1989), Gibbs (1994)
and Grady (1997a). A review of metaphors for time in this framework throws
up a number of problems for analysing temporal cognition. In particular, it
is argued that a more revealing account of temporality at the cognitive level
should focus on lexical concepts, in the sense defined. As some lexical concepts associated with temporality may relate to phenomenological experience
and so constitute plausible conceptual primitives, it is argued that such an approach offers a promising way of studying how larger-scale cognitive models
for temporality may derive.

Finally, Chapter 6 provides a methodology for investigating temporal lexical concepts. This approach is a development and an extension of the PRIN-
CIPLED POLYSEMY framework of Tyler and Evans (2001b, 2003; Evans & Tyler
2004a, b).

Part II presents an analysis of some of the lexical concepts associated with
time. In so doing I employ the criteria developed in part I for determining the
range of distinct temporal lexical concepts. In the first instance I consider lexical concepts conventionally paired with the lexeme *time* (Chapters 7 to 14).
These can be divided into those which relate directly to basic phenomenological temporal experiences (Chapters 7 through 10), and those which are more
derivative in nature, relating to (shared) socio-cultural experience (Chapters 11
through 14). The former I term PRIMARY temporal concepts and the latter SEC-
ONDARY. In Chapter 15 I turn to a consideration of the lexical concepts Present,
Past and Future.

Part III concerns larger scale cognitive models and theories of temporality,
which often make use of and integrate smaller-scale lexical concepts. Chapter 16 considers the role of motion in the development and elaboration of temporal concepts. It is argued that due to our perceptual apparatus, motion is
one of the most salient manifestations of change and hence suggests itself for
the elaboration of a number of temporal lexical concepts. Moreover, the correlation between motion and agency is considered, which may motivate the
integration of such lexical concepts in larger-scale cognitive structures.

Chapter 17 re-considers the well-known Moving Time and Moving Ego
models of temporal representation. In light of the findings adduced in the

book, it is argued that these two mappings constitute large-scale cognitive models, which integrate a range of distinct temporal lexical concepts. Moreover, evidence is presented for distinguishing between the two levels of conceptual representation: lexical concept vs. larger-scale cognitive model.

Chapter 18 discusses a third complex cognitive model for temporality, in which temporal events are related not to an ego, which corresponds to our experience of the present, but rather to a sequence of temporal events related with respect to each other. It is argued that this complex model, together with the two discussed in chapter seventeen, give rise to our common-place view of time.

In the light of the phenomenological provenance of time developed, Chapter 19 considers the view of time in modern physics. Once the metaphysical consequences of time in special and general relativity have been reviewed, it is argued that properly construed the theory of relativity predicts a single subjective experience of time, rather than a multiplicity of 'relativistic' times. This approach attempts to reconcile the paradoxical nature of time in modern physics with the subjective provenance of time.

In view of the major findings developed in the book, Chapter 20 serves to adduce the structure and structuring properties of time. In so doing, the discussion takes account of the subjective experience of time grounded in perceptual processing, the external world to which temporality is an adaptive response, and the conceptual and cultural levels, wherein temporality reaches its pinnacle of creativity and invention.

Chapter 2

The phenomenology of time

The point of departure for this investigation constitutes the following version of the linguistic problem: Why is time lexicalised in terms of space and motion through three-dimensional space and not in its own terms (whatever these might be)? It has long been recognised by theorists that linguistic expressions for time utilise linguistic structure pertaining to motion events and locations in three-dimensional space (e.g., Alverson 1994; Brisard 1999; Clark 1973; Fillmore 1982; Fleischman 1982; Gell 1992; Grady 1997a; Jackendoff 1983; Lakoff 1993; Lakoff & Johnson 1980, 1999; Lakoff & Turner 1989; Miller & Johnson-Laird 1976; Moore 2000; Radden 1997; Shinohara 1999, 2000a; Talmy 1983, 2000; Traugott 1975, 1978; Tyler & Evans 2001a; Yu 1998). It has been further observed that it is virtually impossible to talk about time without invoking motion and spatial content to do so (Lakoff & Johnson 1999). For instance, we conventionally elaborate the elapse of time by appealing to motion events[1] as attested by the following examples:

(2.1) a. The **passage** of time
       b. Time **flows on** forever
       c. The time for a decision has **arrived**

On the face of it, expressions such as the sentences in (2.1) appear to be perfectly ordinary, without need for explanation or cause for puzzlement. However, upon reflection it is paradoxical that a concept widely acknowledged as being abstract (see Einstein 1961: 155–178; Gibson 1975, 1986; Lakoff & Johnson 1999) – a higher level construct – should have motion (a phenomenon which derives from the three dimensional physical world) ascribed to it in language. In the expression in (2.1a) the elapse of time is understood in terms of its *passage*, which derives from the domain of physical motion. In (2.1b) the manner of motion verb *flow* is being ascribed to time. In (2.1c) a specific temporal moment, *the time for a decision*, is being lexicalised as having *arrived*, which presupposes that it is capable of motion. Ordinarily, only those entities which have physical substance, e.g., rivers, objects, people etc. are thought of as being capable of motion, whether self- or other-initiated. If time could undergo veridical locomotion this would entail that it did physically exist and could be directly observed and identified. Such a result is clearly at odds with (at least) one prominent view that time is a construct of the intellect.

Moreover, the ascription of motion to time is not an aberrant fact of English, but, on the contrary, is a cross-linguistic phenomenon. A wide cross-section of genetically and geographically unrelated languages, including Japanese (Shinohara 1999), Chinese (Yu 1998) and the Niger-Congo language Wolof (Moore 2000), follow this pattern. From this we might speculate that the ascription of motion to time constitutes a likely candidate for being a linguistic universal (in those languages which lexicalise the concept of time).[2]

Some other examples of the way in which time is elaborated in terms of space are given below:

(2.2) a. The relationship lasted a long time
      b. He could only concentrate for short periods of time

In these sentences the temporal concept of duration is conventionally elaborated in terms of physical length. While a *long* time is a time of greater duration, a *short* time is a time of lesser duration. Similarly, in the examples below durational experience is elaborated in terms of motion. For instance, when we experience PROTRACTED DURATION – the sensation that time is 'dragging', as in (2.3a), the temporal experience is elaborated in terms of motion relative to the observer. Similarly, in (2.3b), TEMPORAL COMPRESSION[3] – the sensation that time has 'speeded up' – is elaborated in terms of the rapidity of time's motion.[4]

(2.3) a. Time seemed to stand still
      b. The time flew by

Indeed, if we consider other temporal concepts such as hours, minutes, days, and even temporally-framed events such Christmas, etc., it seems almost impossible to elaborate such notions without recourse to language concerning space, and motion in space, as the following expressions attest: 'Christmas is *approaching*'; 'We're *moving up* on the big game'; 'She finished the exam *in* two hours'; 'The train arrived *at* two o'clock'; etc.

2.1 Temporal concepts and event-comparison

One of the most elaborate and influential frameworks which explicitly focuses on the language used to lexicalise concepts such as time is associated with the conceptual metaphor theory pioneered by Lakoff and Johnson (Johnson 1987;

Lakoff 1987, 1990, 1993; Lakoff & Johnson 1980, 1999), and scholars such as Gibbs (e.g., 1994), Kövecses (e.g., 2000), Sweetser (e.g., 1990) and Turner (e.g., 1987, 1991, 1996; Lakoff & Turner 1989).

Lakoff and Johnson in particular have developed the view that we employ lexical content from the domain of motion because this reflects how we conceptualise and, hence, experience time. On their view, motion and spatial concepts metaphorically structure temporal concepts. A consequence of this is that temporality is constituted by concepts from the spatial domain, thereby enabling us to experience time. Hence, conceptualisation precedes experience (as far as abstract concepts such as time are concerned). This does not deny, they argue, that there is nothing literal about time, but rather that without the constitutive metaphoric structuring we would not be able to adequately conceptualise and hence experience time.

For Lakoff and Johnson, "Literal time is a matter of event comparison", the events in question being "certain canonical events... [such as]...the movement of the hands of an analog clock or the sequential flashing of numbers on a digital clock. These in turn are defined relative to other events – the movement of the sun, a pendulum, or wheels, or the release of subatomic particles" (1999:139). Hence, the concept of time is constituted by virtue of the motion events which serve to facilitate event-comparison.

This view of time is consonant with that of James Gibson, pioneer of ECO-LOGICAL PSYCHOLOGY.[5] Gibson (1975, 1986) has argued that while events are perceived, time itself is not. Accordingly, time results from abstracting relations between events (e.g., by comparing them), and consequently, constitutes an "intellectual achievement".

Common to both the view of Gibson and of Lakoff and Johnson is that time itself is derived from the comparison of external events which inhere in the world. Hence, the concept of time is abstract in the sense that temporal experience is not itself directly perceived.

While evidence from language and indeed from other modalities (e.g., gesture) does strongly suggest that spatial concepts may, in part (or even largely), constitute our conceptions of temporality, from this it does not follow that time is not also constituted by other kinds of (perhaps subjective) experiences. Nor does it follow from this that time is not itself directly experienced or perceived.

If it turns out that subjective states (and the subjective concepts which arise from them) (i) do constitute direct experience in the sense that we are actually aware of such states, moreover, (ii) if such experiences can be traced to specific physiological processes and apparatus and finally (iii) if such physiological processes have reflexes in what Chafe (1994) has termed the "flow" of talk, then there remains no reason to suggest that subjective concepts such as temporality are mental achievements derived from the comparison of external events.

Of course, such a phenomenological view does not, in principle, deny that temporal mechanisms and processes have evolved as an adaptive response to the nature of the world. Hence, temporal experience may, in large-measure, constitute a response to sensory experience. Moreover, such an approach does not deny that cognitive models for time may require elaboration in terms of content derived from sensory experience, for reasons that will be explored in the next chapter. However, the view to be developed suggests that while temporal experience may constitute a response to external sensory experience, and may be represented at the conceptual level in terms of experience relating to sensory domains, this does not in itself deny that temporality is of internal provenance. That is, temporality at base may be a subjective, albeit real, experience, which is as basic and fundamental as sensations due to perception of external sensorimotor experience. Indeed, this position accords with Grady's (1997a, n.d.) influential claim that, based on the linguistic evidence, there is a bifurcation in conceptual structure between concepts derived from sensory experience (which he terms IMAGE concepts), and those derived from subjective experience (which he terms RESPONSE concepts).[6]

Accordingly, this chapter will survey a range of evidence which points to the conclusion that temporality is fundamentally subjective in nature, constitutes a real experience and is (at least partially) accessible to conscious awareness. Accordingly, I will argue that we should be sceptical of views which purport that time is ultimately derived solely (or largely) from external sensory experience, and may not constitute a basic experience, absent externally-derived sensory awareness. Indeed, I will argue that sensory experience is processed by virtue of the perceptual mechanisms responsible for temporal awareness.

2.2 The phenomenological basis of time

A robust range of studies conducted by psychologists and cognitive neuroscientists supports the contention that, although subjective in nature, the experience of time is indeed a real experience, that it is perceived and that it can be traced to cognitive structures and processes.

A large literature gives rise to the view that humans directly perceive and experience duration and simultaneity, both of which must contribute to the concept of time. Moreover, these experiences can be closely related to physiological processes such as the periodic rhythms in the visual cortex and other parts of the brain. A number of studies appear to suggest (i) that organisms do directly experience time in the sense that it can be investigated experimentally and subjects can make systematic judgements about it – we are aware of time, and (ii) that there are physiological structures and processes to which temporal experience can be traced. Evidence from language, specifically from discourse (see Chafe 1994, in particular), suggests that temporal processing, which may serve to structure conscious experience, shows up in language. Taken together these general findings provide evidence for the view that temporal experience is a real and direct experience rather than being an intellectual construct derived from, for instance, the comparison of external events. Accordingly, in the next few sections we will review a number of lines of evidence providing support for the view of temporal experience as phenomenological in nature.

2.3 Studies investigating the experience of duration

We begin with the experience of duration, which is presumably related to our concept of time. Based on a series of elaborate experiments, Ornstein ([1969] 1997) showed that the perception of the duration of an interval, as reflected in subjects' estimates of the length of time taken to complete various tasks, is affected by the complexity of the task that subjects undertake rather than the duration of the task per se, as measured by a clock. That is, shorter tasks may be experienced as having lasted longer if they were more complex than longer tasks. Moreover, 'complexity' was found to be a relatively subjective phenomenon, involving among other things, the degree of familiarity a subject had with completing a particular task.

Ornstein exposed subjects to a raft of different tasks, which included stimuli of graded complexity. The stimuli were both aural and visual ranging from tape recordings of different kinds of sounds, such as, for instance, tones produced by an audio oscillator, to pictures of more and less complex shapes (e.g., geometric figures of greater and lesser complexity). Subjects were exposed to stimuli of this kind for a set interval and then asked a series of questions including one which elicited an assessment of magnitude of duration. Other subjects were asked to perform more interactive activities in which they learned to complete particular tasks. Given that tasks which are performed habitually are routinised, and hence performed with less difficulty than those in which subjects have less mastery, tasks of the latter kind were experienced as being more complex. After completion of a set of tasks, each subject was again asked to rate the magnitude of duration for each. Ornstein found that tasks which involved greater stimulus complexity, either because the stimulus array was inherently more complex (e.g., a greater number occurrences of a particular stimulus, such as a greater frequency of tones on the audiotape), or due to the fact that a particular subject had less experience with completing a particular task, received a rating of greater duration.

Based on these findings, Ornstein suggested that the correlation between task complexity and experience of duration may be due to the amount of storage space in memory required for a particular stimulus array. He stated his hypothesis in the following way, "In the storage of a given interval, either increasing the number of stored events or the complexity of those events will increase the size of storage, and as storage size increases the experience of duration lengthens" (Ibid.: 41). This is suggestive that duration constitutes a judgement of temporal quantity and is related to our physiological subjective response to particular stimuli, rather than being an objective property of the stimulus-events themselves.

2.4 Investigations of temporal experience as "felt"

We now turn to evidence which suggests that we actually consciously "feel" the passage of time. The social psychologist Michael Flaherty (1999) argues in detail that humans experience what he terms PROTRACTED DURATION. This constitutes the experience that temporality is proceeding more 'slowly' than usual. Flaherty suggests that:

> [P]rotracted duration emerges within the context of so-called empty intervals (e.g., solitary confinement) as well as intervals which are full of significant events (e.g., interpersonal violence)... [this is because these]...intervals are in fact filled with cognitive and emotional responses to one's predicament. A sharp transition from normal interaction to "empty"... [or "full"]...time ignites a preoccupation with aspects of self and situation that would have been overlooked in ordinary encounters. In particular, we often find that the person becomes more caught up in the rhythms of his or her own physiological existence.   (Ibid.: 96)

Some examples of protracted duration include the following:

'Empty' intervals
(2.4) The days passed with a terrible, enervating, monotonous slowness, the tomorrows blending into weeks and the weeks blending into months.

"We were about a year in Auschwitz," says Menashe, "but in Auschwitz, one day – everyday – was like 10 years.   [Flaherty][7]

'Full' intervals

(2.5) My first thought was, "Where did that car come from?" Then I said to myself, "Hit the brakes.". . . I saw her look at me through the open window, and turn the wheel, hand over hand, toward the right. I also [noticed] that the car was a brown Olds. I heard the screeching sound from my tires and knew . . . that we were going to hit. . . I wondered what my parents were going to say, if they would be mad, where my boyfriend was, and most of all, would it hurt. . . After it was over, I realized what a short time it was to think so many thoughts, but, while it was happening, there was more than enough time. It only took about ten or fifteen seconds for us to hit, but it certainly felt like ten or fifteen minutes.   [Flaherty][8]

For duration to be experienced as protracted it is evident that there must be a normative experience against which durational experience can be judged as abnormal. Flaherty terms this form of temporal experience SYNCHRONICITY.

Within the field of social psychology it is generally held that temporal awareness is acquired via interpersonal interactions which are temporally coordinated. As such, synchronicity is, "a skill acquired in the course of primary socialization. Gradually, one learns not to cut encounters off too quickly or drag them out beyond their proper length. The regimentation of temporal experience is based upon one's awareness of social expectations" (Ibid.: 99). From this it follows that synchronicity, what counts as normative temporal awareness, is culture-specific.

Against this backdrop, internal physiological states such as increased self-awareness in situations which are abnormally intense (as in solitary confinement, i.e., 'empty' intervals, or interpersonal violence, i.e., 'full' intervals) give rise to duration appearing to be protracted, vis-à-vis typical temporal awareness.

In addition to protracted duration, Flaherty discusses the experience of TEMPORAL COMPRESSION. As he puts it, while "[p]rotracted duration is experienced when the density of conscious information processing is high. . .temporal compression is experienced when the density of conscious information processing is low" (Ibid.: 112–113). The density of conscious information can be said to be high when the subject is attending to more of the stimulus array. The density of conscious information can be said to be low when the subject is attending to less of the stimulus array. Flaherty provides a taxonomy of the various kinds of experiences which give rise to high and low densities of conscious information processing. For instance, experiences which give rise to a higher density of information processing, and hence in which time appears to pass more slowly (protracted duration), include suffering and intense emotions, violence and danger, waiting and boredom, concentration and meditation, and shock and novelty. As the subject is consciously attending to the stimulus array, a greater density of information processing occurs. Given that our experience of duration appears to correlate with the amount of memory taken up (Ornstein [1969] 1997), then if more of the stimulus array is attended to, more memory is required to store and process what is being attended to, and consequently it is to be expected that we should actually experience the duration as being more protracted, which is what we find.[9]

Flaherty suggests that experiences which produce a lower density of information processing, and hence in which time appears to 'pass more quickly' (temporal compression), include those which involve ROUTINE COMPLEXITY. This relates to the idea that activities, which while potentially complex, through routine practise give rise to "an abnormally low level of stimulus complexity brought on by the near absence of attention to self and situation" (Ibid.: 108). Habitual conduct results in little of the stimulus array being attended to, resulting in low density of information processing. Accordingly, time seems to have passed "quickly".

Flaherty's findings regarding temporal compression and routine complexity are remarkably consonant with Ornstein's conclusions. Ornstein (1997) described the routinisation through repetition of a complex task or activity and the impact of this on temporal experience in the following way:

> One way that the awareness of a given stimulus situation is changed is by its repetition. When we drive to work over the same route everyday, we notice less and less of our surroundings as we continue driving over the same route. We 'automatically' respond to the stimulus situation. Even though is clear that we are responding to the total stimulus situation (since we always arrive safely), when we perform a well-learned series of actions we are responding to the stimulus array in a different way than the first time we performed the action.
> (Ibid.: 73–74)

What is clear from situations such as the daily drive to work described by Ornstein is that the event itself does not somehow have its temporal structure altered. The journey still takes (roughly) the same amount of time from one year to the next. What does alter, however, is, as observed by Ornstein, that through repetition the activity becomes 'automatic'. This results in a subject attending less to the activity being engaged in as the complexity becomes routinised (and thus less memory is taken up, resulting in the experience of temporal compression). Hence, such activities appear, in retrospect, to have 'flown', precisely because we respond to different activities in different ways, depending on our familiarity with them.

The work by Flaherty and by Ornstein is suggestive that the experience of duration constitutes a physiological response to both self and situation, which is, in principle, independent of any objective temporal attributes of a particular event or situation. For instance, the phenomenon of protracted duration – the experience that time is 'slowing down' – appears to constitute a response to situations in which the subject's awareness of his or her situation and environment is heightened. However, not only is there no single commonality across the range of events and situations which appear to prompt such a subjective response, situations can be 'empty' or 'full', the resultant protracted duration is purely subjective, a consequence of the subject attending to more of the stimulus array than usual (Ornstein [1969] 1997).

As Flaherty argues, it is patently not the case that there is anything objectively different about the temporal structure of such situations and events which causes them to be experienced in terms of different kinds of duration; indeed, many of these situation types are markedly different from each other (cf. violence and danger versus waiting and boredom). Rather, it is due to our response to situations of this kind, and how much experience we have of and with such situations, that causes them to be experienced in terms of, for instance, protracted duration. This represents good evidence that temporality derives not from objective properties of events and the relations between them, but rather constitutes a subjective response to such events.

Similarly, as temporal compression results from the routinisation of potentially complex experiences, this phenomenon will then affect different subjects in different ways. This follows as different subjects will have routinised various kinds of experiences to different degrees, depending on issues such as familiarity and so forth. Again, this supports the contention that temporal experience is a subjective response rather than a consequence of the given temporal structure of external events.

2.5 Temporal processing

There is mounting evidence from cognitive neuroscience that perceptual processing is underpinned by neurologically instantiated temporal codes or rhythms (Crick 1994; Crick & Koch 1990, 1998; Davies 1995; Dennett 1991; Edelman 1992; Engel, König, & Scillen 1992; Engel, König, Kreiter, Schillen, & Singer 1992; Pöppel 1994; Stryker 1992; Varela et al. 1991). A temporal code represents a neurological mechanism whereby perceptual information is integrated in order to form a coherent percept.

In terms of neurological structure, the brain does not have a central node where perceptual input derived from different modalities, or even information from within the same modality, can be integrated. That is, there is no one place where colour, shape, texture, smell, etc., are integrated in order to produce the percept of an object such as a piece of fruit, for instance. The brain has not evolved to the designs of a predetermined blueprint, but rather has evolved opportunistically, exploiting and building upon slight advantages. A consequence of this is that spatially distributed sensory information associated with the different perceptual processing areas of the brain must somehow be integrated without the advantage of a centralised integration site.

A temporal code consists of a temporal interval characterised by the correlated oscillation of neurons, which lasts for a short period of time. This phenomenon has been termed a PERCEPTUAL MOMENT. Each perceptual moment appears to be bounded by a silent interval before re-occurring (Engel, König & Schillen 1992). It seems to be the case that integration of sensory information into percepts is enabled by the phenomena of periodic perceptual moments. Clearly, if spatially dislocated information is integrated by virtue of in which perceptual moment it is registered, i.e., 'when' it occurs, then the brain is able to solve the difficulty of having no 'where' in which to perform integration.

Neuroscientists refer to the phenomenon whereby information from different parts of the brain is integrated, so as to provide a coherent percept, as BINDING. As is well-known, in each modality, for instance in the visual system, "the sensory representations of the various qualities of an object are arrayed over an enormous expanse of cortex" (Stryker 1991:252). The problem is to discover how the brain manages to integrate the sensory information associated with spatially-dislocated neuronal assemblies into a coherent percept, given that there is no single place in the brain where such sensory stimuli are integrated. This has been termed the BINDING PROBLEM.

Recent experimental findings suggest that spatially-dislocated neurons associated with distinct sensory information may fire in correlated fashion, oscillating in a 20–80 hertz range (Crick 1994; Crick & Koch 1990; Engel, König, & Schillen 1992; Engel, König, Kreiter, Schillen, & Singer 1992; Pöppel 1994; Stryker 1991). The synchronous firing of neurons allows information which is spatially-distributed to be correlated into what Crick and Koch (1990) term a "temporary global unity" (Ibid.: 263), enabling binding to occur. Hence, synchronised oscillation of neuronal assemblies represents an effective means of solving the binding problem.

However, as Engel, König and Schillen (1992) note, a consequence of synchronised oscillation is that "these multiunit bursts occur in sequence alternating with silent intervals" (Ibid.: 333). If there were no silent intervals then it would be impossible to determine which neurons were being synchronised. The synchronised oscillations, bounded by silent intervals, last for a fraction of a second, giving rise to the correlation of sensory qualities, i.e., object perception.

Perceptual moments appear to be ubiquitous at the neurological level, i.e., they occur at all levels of processing. These range from a fraction of second up to an outer limit of about three seconds (Davies 1995; Pöppel 1994). In the visual-cortex, for instance, the dominant temporal rhythm (the so-called alpha rhythm), has a frequency of around 10 pulses per second (Ornstein 1997; Varela et al. 1991).[10] Varela et al. (1991) report that if two lights are shown with an intervening interval of less than 0.1–0.2 seconds, they will be perceived (and reported) as being simultaneous (the phenomenon of 'apparent' simultaneity); if the interval is increased slightly they will be perceived (and reported) as being sequential. However, if the two lights are set so that there is an equal chance of them being seen as simultaneous or as sequential, what is perceived depends on the point at which, in the subject's own cortical rhythm, the subject is subjected to the experiment.

The foregoing represents strong evidence that humans do have physiological processes which are closely associated with aspects of temporal perception. At one level then, the perceptual moment would appear to serve an important and indispensable function. Such a mechanism enables us to perceive, in that the nature of our percepts are in an important sense "constructed" by virtue of a neurologically instantiated temporal code. Hence, perception may be fundamentally temporal in nature, and, underpinned by temporal intervals or perceptual moments.

On this basis, we must question the view that the concept of time is *derived from* event perception and that cognitively temporal experience is less basic than sense-perceptory experience. On the contrary, a consideration of the neurological evidence suggests that a temporal code, cognitively instantiated, may ultimately ground event perception.[11]

2.6 Perceptual moments as the basis for the experience of duration

In terms of human perceptual experience, the occurrence of a neurologically instantiated temporal interval, the perceptual moment, is not alone sufficient to account for what James ([1890] 1950) termed the "stream of consciousness". The sensation of succession and so duration imbues human experience, providing it with its unique character. We are able to compare the present held in memory with the present as currently experienced. This ability to distinguish between the perceptual moment before from the perceptual moment which comes after provides the basis of succession, and, by virtue of relating the two perceptual moments, may contribute to our experience of duration, and so, temporal experience as we perceive it. This constitutes liberation from the 'straight-jacket' of a perceptual moment forever replayed, an updated now but without an awareness of duration.

As observed by a number of philosophers, psychologists and neuroscientists (e.g., Bergson [1922] 1999; Husserl [1887] 1999; Miller & Johnson-Laird 1976; Pöppel 1994), the crucial means of relating two perceptual moments requires memory. As Bergson puts it, "Without an elementary memory that connects the two moments, there will be only one or the other, consequently a single instance, no before or after, no succession, no time." He continues by noting that, "it is impossible to distinguish between the duration, however short it may be, that separates two instants and a memory that connects them, because duration is essentially a continuation of what no longer exists into what does exist" (Ibid. [1922] 1999: 33). That is, with a memory able to relate two perceptual moments, the before (held in memory) with the after (currently being perceived), is derived the experience of an interval relating the two, and so our fundamental experience of time.

A number of scholars, both from the phenomenological tradition in philosophy and within psychology have proposed accounts of temporal experience which are compatible with the view that temporal experience derives ultimately from the neurological phenomenon of successive perceptual moments integrated by a rudimentary memory, i.e., that temporality is fundamentally durational and internal in nature. Saint Augustine (354–430) was the first thinker in the western tradition to attribute the concept of time to human conscious experience (Turetzky 1998). In his *Confessions* ([circa 397] 1907), he suggested that perception can be divided into three parts: *continuitus*, 'on-going perception', *memoria*, 'memory', and *expectatio*, 'expectation'. *Continuitus* represents actual perception and hence direct experience of the current moment. As each new moment is updated, it passes into memory, which gives rise to expectations of the future being formed.[12] In this way, temporal experience derives from the nature of consciousness (cf. Chafe 1994; discussed below).

Husserl ([1887] 1999), in his phenomenological theory of internal time-consciousness, attempts to elucidate the nature of the human experience of time. Husserl notes that time-consciousness seems to consist of a dynamic continuum of present, past and future. He suggests that the present moment, which I will term A, constitutes the perceptual starting point of time experience. This moment A, which once was future, gives rise to a retained present, A', which is held in memory when A is superseded by moment B. When B is superseded by moment C, then the retention A' is superseded by the retained present B', resulting in the retention A' giving rise to a new retention A". When moment D supersedes C, B' is superseded by C', and gives rise to B" being held in memory as a retention of B'. Accordingly, B" supersedes A" causing A"' to be held in memory as a retention of A". In this way, the past is constantly being modified as the future becomes the present, and the present becomes the past. On this view, the past, present and future, as experienced, constitute a dynamic durational continuum. Moreover, this entails that a change anywhere in the continuum will effect changes elsewhere. As C becomes the present, this entails that B gives rise to the retention B' and A' gives rise to A" etc.

Within cognitive psychology, perception is often treated as an active and constructive process (Gell 1992; Miller & Johnson-Laird 1976; Rock 1984). For instance, Miller and Johnson-Laird suggest that experience derives from an on-going perceptual process (the present), which integrates perceptual input with, and hence modifies, schemata stored in memory (the past). The modified schemata are in turn used in order to generate expectations (the future), and hence to anticipate new perceptual experience. This represents a continuous perceptual process of updating successive perceptual information to which an organism has access. Gell (1992) has noted that such a tri-fold division in perceptual processing into current perception, memory and anticipation, and the view of these distinctions as constituting an on-going and dynamic process, is remarkably consonant with the human experience of time. Gell posits that:

> [P]erception is intrinsically time-perception, and conversely, time-perception, or internal time-consciousness, is just perception itself...That is to say, time is not something we encounter as a feature of contingent reality, as if it lay outside us, waiting to be perceived along with tables and chairs and the rest of the perceptible contents of the universe. Instead, subjective time arises as an inescapable feature of the perceptual process itself, which enters into the perception of anything whatsoever.   (Ibid.: 231)

In the foregoing I have proposed that the perceptual moment, which underpins perceptual processing, constitutes a possible (and indeed plausible) cognitive antecedent of temporality. However, a perceptual moment alone is unable to furnish the experience of temporality. For this to emerge a rudimentary memory is required which relates the perceptual moment just experienced with the updated perceptual moment. The relation between the two provides a before-after relation, an interval, and, at a very local level, provides an awareness of a change in the world-state or alternatively of a maintenance in the world-state. While the perceptual moment may prove to constitute the basic unit of perceptual experience, and moreover (as I will argue below) may ultimately constitute the cognitive antecedent of the concept of the present or now, the succession between a perceptual moment held in memory and the current perceptual moment giving rise to the experience of duration, constitutes, I suggest, a relation which forms the basic unit of temporal experience.

2.7 The perceptual moment and the experience of now

Pöppel (1994) has argued that two kinds of perceptual moment can be distinguished. The first, PRIMORDIAL EVENTS, which last for a fraction of a second, serve in effect as a 'linking activity', to integrate or bind spatially distributed information in the brain between and within different modalities. This facilitates the integration of spatially-distributed sensory information as primordial events, e.g., the perception of an object in which visual input, auditory input and information from other modalities are integrated into a coherent percept. The second kind, the perceptual moment with an outer range of 2–3 seconds, serves to link these primordial events into a coherent unity, which, he argues forms the basis of our concept of the present.

According to Pöppel, perceptual moments in the 2–3 second range involve what he terms TEMPORAL BINDING (as opposed to the binding of spatially-distributed activities). He proposes that it is the perceptual moment of approximately 2–3 seconds to which the concept of the present (our experience of now) can be traced.

Brisard (1999) echoes this view, suggesting that:

> The cognitive function of... [the perceptual moment]...appears to be focused on the temporary maintenance of an experiential event in the center of attention. Every two or three seconds, there is an apparent biological necessity of shifting attention to some other percept, or at least of reestablishing current relevance of a previous percept for an updated attention span.   (Ibid.:115)

This position is also consonant with detailed evidence presented by Chafe (1994), which is reviewed in the next section.

Davies (1995) makes the same observation regarding the outer 2–3 second limit. To illustrate this he provides the following example:

> Take the familiar "tick-tock", of the clock. Well the clock doesn't go "tick-tock" at all; it goes "tick-tick", every tick producing the same sound. It's just that our consciousness runs two successive ticks into a single "tick-tock" experience – but only if the duration between ticks is less than about three seconds. A really big pendulum clock just goes "tock...tock...tock...", whereas a bedside clock chatters away.
> (Davies 1995:265–266)

The evidence for a perceptual moment having an outer limit up to a 2–3 second range is persuasive. Ambiguous figures such as Necker cubes[13] have a reversal rate of about 2–3 seconds. Consequently, each perspective is perceived for about 3 seconds before reverting to the other perspective. This suggests that perceptual mechanisms re-analyse incoming input in a holistic way every 2 to 3 seconds. Similarly, there is good evidence from experiments on short-term memory that stimuli can only be retained for approximately 3 seconds if rehearsal is not permitted (Pöppel 1994). In addition, there is evidence that human music, poetry and language is segmented into intervals of up to 2–3 seconds irrespective of a speaker's age (Chafe 1994; see also Davies 1995; Pöppel 1994).

In sum, the perceptual moment constitutes a cognitive mechanism to which our experience of duration and temporality can be plausibly related.

2.8 Discourse, consciousness and time

In a remarkable study Chafe (1994) has argued in detail that temporal mechanisms and processes which are intrinsic to the ongoing "flow" of conscious experience show up in language.[14] Based on detailed analyses of spoken discourse, Chafe suggests that conscious experience has an active focus of about 2 seconds, termed FOCAL CONSCIOUSNESS, before shifting to a new focus. Chafe describes this focus as follows, "At any given moment the mind can focus on no more than a small segment of everything it 'knows'.... Consciousness is an active focusing on a small part of the conscious being's self-centered model of the surrounding world" (Ibid.:28). Moreover, he argues that this focus is embedded in a surrounding area of PERIPHERAL CONSCIOUSNESS of longer duration. Consciousness is thereby dynamic, such that events which are in fo-

cal consciousness can move into peripheral consciousness (from an active to a
semi-active state). Moreover, it is a distinction between the richness of detail
associated with focal consciousness, and the relative paucity of detail associated with peripheral consciousness, which distinguishes the two states. Chafe
has further suggested that, "it is above all this constant flow of events from focal to peripheral consciousness that constitutes the human experience of time"
(personal communication).

Chafe presents detailed evidence that the distinction between focal and
peripheral consciousness is reflected (and evidenced) by language. Based on
the analysis of discourse, Chafe posits what he terms an INTONATION UNIT
(which corresponds to focal consciousness). Spoken language appears to be
constituted in terms of intonation units which can be distinguished based
on prosodic criteria such as "breaks in timing, acceleration and deceleration,
changes in overall pitch level, terminal pitch contours and changes in voice
quality" (Ibid.:69). For instance, the following transcription, excerpted from
Chafe (1994:61–62), illustrates the way in which discourse is segmented into
intonation units. An individual intonation unit, identified by virtue of the
aforementioned features, are indicated by virtue of placement in a separate
line of the transcription. Different speakers are indicated by the notations (A),
(B) and (C):

(2.6) a. (A)   ...(0.4) Have the .. ánimals,
       b. (A)   ...(0.1) ever attacked anyone ín a car?
       c. (B)   ...(1.2) Well I
       d. (B)   well Í hèard of an éléphant,
       e. (B)   .. that sát dówn on a V̀Ẁ one time.
       f. (B)   ...(0.9) There's a gìr
       g. (B)   .. Did you éver hear thát?
       h. (C)   ...(0.1) No,
       i. (B)   ...(0.3) Some éléphants and these
       j. (B)   ...(0.1) they
       k. (B)   ...(0.7) there
       l. (B)   these gáls were in a Vólkswagen,
       m. (B)   ...(0.4) and uh,
       n. (B)   ...(0.3) they uh kept hónkin' the hórn,
       o. (B)   ...(0.2) hóotin' the hóoter,
       p. (B)   ...(0.6) and uh,
       q. (B)   ...(0.4) and the .. éléphant was in frónt of em,

     r.   (B)   so = he jùst procèeded to sìt dòwn on the V̇Ẇ.

     s.   (B)   ... (0.3) But thèy .. had .. mànaged to get óut first.[15]

Moreover, not only do intonation units have a duration of up to around 2 seconds, which is close to that of perceptual moments, they also appear to be constrained in terms of the nature of information which can be conveyed by any given intonation unit. That is, any given intonation unit can only convey one new idea, what Chafe terms the ONE NEW IDEA CONSTRAINT (see Chafe 1994: Ch. 9 for a range of examples and discussion). Thus, an intonation unit appears to convey a particular event, forming a sequence of intonation units such that through a "process of successive activations language is able to provide an imperfect bridge between one mind and another" (Chafe 1994: 63). Chafe suggests that this reflects a fundamental characteristic of focal consciousness, which appears to be only able to focus upon a relatively limited stimulus at any one time. The dynamic quality of consciousness appears to be, therefore, a function of the continual shift from one focal state to another, with previous focal states constituting semi-active information, namely peripheral consciousness.[16]

The foregoing is highly suggestive that an intonation unit may correspond to focal consciousness, providing the means of verbalising whatever is active in consciousness at the start of the intonation unit. As focal consciousness (in the sense of Chafe) appears to correspond quite closely to the notion of a perceptual moment, as evidenced by language, it appears that the "flow" of conscious experience from focal state to new focal state, with the previous focal state moving into peripheral consciousness, may give rise – or contribute to – our experience of time. In this sense, temporal experience constitutes an ongoing succession. Yet, by virtue of being constituted of specific focal states, temporal experience is structured. Hence, evidence from psychology, neuroscience and linguistics provide converging evidence that perceptual mechanisms, which structure and give rise to the ongoing flow and succession of conscious experience, may give rise to our phenomenological experience of time.

2.9 The primacy of subjective experience

In §2.2 I briefly discussed views associated with conceptual metaphor theory (CMT). Scholars within the CMT tradition have often emphasised the importance of sense-perceptory experience in structuring mental representations of subjective concepts such as time. Indeed, scholars in this tradition have constructed careful and elaborate arguments suggesting that concepts grounded in, what they have termed, CONCRETE EXPERIENCE, relating to the external world of sensory experience, serve to structure concepts which are more subjective in nature. That is, concepts from the domain of motion, for instance, *constitute* concepts for time.

However, it has sometimes been implied or suggested (as was the case with Lakoff and Johnson's treatment of time, discussed briefly above), that because such 'target' concepts may be constituted by concrete concepts, there is nothing that constitutes these 'abstract' concepts beyond the concrete experience in which they are grounded. That is, our experience of time can only emerge once it has been metaphorically structured in terms of the inter-subjective concepts which constitute it.

Indeed, scholars in the conceptual metaphor tradition have argued in an analogous way for a wide array of subjective concepts. For instance, Kövecses (2000), which presents a survey of over a decade and a half of research on emotion concepts, argues that concrete concepts constitute and so "create emotional experience for us" by metaphorically structuring emotion concepts (Ibid.:xii). This view follows as Kövecses assumes that language "corresponds to what human beings actually feel when they experience an emotion" (Ibid.:xiii).

However, we need to be very careful to qualify this position. After all, while I can consciously be aware of anger and other emotions, language is representational, in that it attempts to re-present what we feel and thus relates to off-line processes (see Barsalou 2003). That is, the form thought takes when re-presented in language is not necessarily the same as the experience itself of which I am consciously aware when I experience a particular feeling. For a number of reasons, explored in the next chapter, experiences which are internal in origin, such as emotional experience, may lend themselves to being represented within the conceptual system metaphorically. Yet, metaphorical structuring does not entail that there is nothing inherently emotional beyond the metaphorical structuring, a position sometimes implied in versions of CMT which present the utility of metaphor as a mapping from the concrete onto the abstract (see Grady 1997a for an insightful and influential critique of such a position).

The evidence presented in this chapter regarding time suggests both that metaphoric language, which presumably reflects conceptual structure, constitutes temporal concepts (recall the examples in (2.1) through (2.3)), and that temporal concepts relate to subjective experience which is just as basic and fundamental as experiences such as motion which metaphorically structure time.

These findings lead to the following hypothesis. Subjective experiences are consciously experienced (at least in part) prior to metaphoric structuring, but rely
on such structuring in order to be represented, in the sense of re-presented,
and in order to be modelled conceptually, symbolised (via language) and so
understood.

Subjective experiences, such as emotions, are among the earliest experiences we have. Indeed, they often precede the 'concrete' concepts which
Kövecses argues constitute them (see Ortony 1988). Damasio (2000) notes that
while emotion is based in biological functions essential for maintaining home-
ostatic mechanisms, nevertheless "we can feel our emotions consistently and
we know we feel them. The fabric of our minds and of our behavior is woven
around continuous cycles of emotions followed by feelings that become known
and beget new emotions" (Ibid.: 43). That is, emotions are related to specific
neurological mechanisms and processes, they constitute real experiences, we
perceive these experiences and are "aware" of these experiences via consciousness. However, being conscious of a subjective experience such as an emotion,
or indeed temporality, does not entail that it can be adequately represented
once the experience is no longer in focal consciousness.

From this perspective it becomes clear why we must be careful to distinguish between conceptual patterns which 'constitute' emotion concepts and
so 'create' our ability to experience them (the position apparently presented
by Kövecses), and the modified perspective being developed here. At the conceptual level, subjective concepts are constituted by conceptual projection and
metaphoric structuring, but a concept is a means of modelling an experience to
which we have (at least partial) conscious access. Hence, we are aware of subjective experiences prior to being able to structure them in terms of 'concrete'
concepts. Once we have achieved mental representations of subjective experiences, allowing us to transcend the ephemeral nature of conscious experience,
we are thus able to express, model and externalise such mental representations
in language. This perspective is consonant with that described in the following way by Damasio (2000), "I am suggesting that "having a feeling" is not the
same as "knowing a feeling", [and] that reflection on feeling is yet another step
up" (Ibid.: 284).

This situation is equally so with temporal experience. Temporality is a real
and directly perceived subjective experience, which, as we have seen, can be
plausibly traced to neurological states, processes and structures. We are aware
of the experience of temporality, as attested by the fact that subjects can report on their 'experience' of duration, for instance, in a consistent way. However, what the metaphoric structuring adds is our ability to model, extend,

express and understand the subjective experiences which we are consciously aware of. This ability ultimately facilitates the development of highly intricate and elaborate models of temporality (developed in Part III of the book).

2.10 Conclusion

In this chapter I have argued that the essence and origin of temporality is crucially internal in nature. This being so, our temporal awareness is projected outwards from within, rather than deriving from external phenomena. Temporal experience, like affect (e.g., anger, jealousy, fear, pain, love, etc.), and consciousness, etc., constitutes a subjective state. There are a number of reasons for thinking this. First, as already noted, there is nothing physical in the external world which can be unambiguously identified as time. Although some scholars have attempted to identify time as the relation holding between external events (a salient example being the periodicity exhibited by 'clocks', ranging from the regular rising and setting of the sun to the periodic behaviour of caesium atoms in modern atomic clocks), this view treats time as not being distinct from the properties and inter-relationships of external events. On such a view, our conceptualisation of time as an entity which can be measured is derived by abstracting temporality away from the relational properties holding between events, 'creating' the abstract concept of time. However, this view of time, as with all treatments which attempt to derive temporality from external phenomena, fails to explain where the temporality which imbues temporal measurement comes from.[17] Second, this relational approach fails to recognise that we are directly aware of the subjective nature of time (subjects can report on temporal experience in a relatively reliable and consistent way). Crucially, we 'feel' the passing of time, whether we have perceptual access to external events or not. As noted, Flaherty (1999) provides evidence that subjects are aware of the passing of time in solitary confinement with no external stimuli.[18] Third, such experiences can be traced to neurological mechanisms (e.g., the perceptual moment).

CHAPTER 3

The elaboration of temporal concepts

If temporal concepts are derived from experiences which are as basic as concepts derived from sensorimotor experiences such as motion, this still does not explain why temporal concepts are elaborated in terms of, for instance, motion concepts. Although I have been arguing that temporal experience is neither illusory nor that it depends upon a prior conceptualisation (we do not have to first conceptualise time before we can experience it), this is not to deny the fact that temporal experience is extremely difficult to define in its own terms.

Moreover, as I have suggested that temporal experience constitutes an internal subjective state, this difficulty in defining time is an instance of the more general difficulty we have in verbalising internal states and feelings.[1] In this chapter, then, I briefly explore two approaches which attempt to account for the elaboration of subjective concepts, such as time, in terms of other kinds of concepts related to sensory experience.

3.1 Intermodal connections and cognition

Jackendoff (1992, 1996) has argued that our relative inability to verbalise what we feel may be a function of how the various cognitive processing centres responsible for experience from different modalities are connected. As he puts it, "our relative great ability to talk about what we perceive out in space compared to our relatively poor ability to talk about the state of our bodies is a function of the ways in which the central representations are able to communicate with one another" (Ibid. 1992: 16). He suggests that mental communication, or the central representations of the mind, take the form of what he terms CENTRAL FORMATS. A central format is a modality-independent means of encoding information, which allows different modalities, e.g., vision and language, to communicate with one another. He posits that without such central formats we would not be able to talk about what we see, for instance, as the mind would have no means of 'translating' visually encoded information into input which the linguistic modality could understand, and hence verbalise.

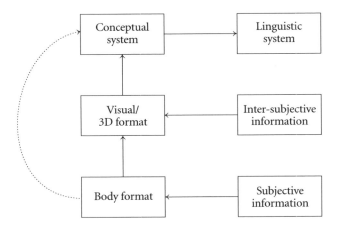

Figure 3.1. Possible relations between mental representations (adapted from Jackendoff 1992: 14)

Jackendoff hypothesises that there are at least three central formats. These consist of the conceptual format, which provides information in a form ready for linguistic encoding (i.e., lexical concepts), a 3D or visual format, which encodes visual-spatial information from the external world, and a body format, which encodes information pertaining to internal states, including emotions etc. Jackendoff suggests that our ability to verbalise visual-spatial information, what I will term INTER-SUBJECTIVE INFORMATION, and our relative inability to articulate internal states, what I will term SUBJECTIVE INFORMATION, may be due to the 3D format being directly linked to the conceptual format (the conceptual system in present terms), while the body format may be only indirectly linked to the conceptual system.

A simplified representation, adapted from Jackendoff (1992: 14), is given in Figure 3.1. The dashed line between the body format and the conceptual system is meant to indicate the relatively weak encoding of subjective information that occurs in the conceptual system, while the unbroken lines indicates a strong connection, e.g., between the visual format and the conceptual system.

In evolutionary terms, it makes sense that inter-subjective information should be better connected to the conceptual system. As the conceptual system provides an important venue for off-line modelling, which facilitates adaptive strategies such as learning, categorisation and anticipation, as well as symbolisation via language, it is clearly crucial that experiences deriving from the external world should be readily available to conceptual processes. However, as subjective processes may be less well connected, by virtue of subjective states being elaborated in terms of inter-subjective information, such experiences may become more accessible to the conceptual system. This assumes that the body state format is connected to the visual format, as indicated by the unbroken arrow in Figure 3.1.

Accordingly, it is plausible that the human conceptual system has been able to circumvent the lack of sufficient 'hardwiring' between subjective information and the conceptual system by selectively appropriating concepts which relate to inter-subjective information in order to structure subjective concepts and hence make them accessible to the conceptual system. This process is extremely efficacious as it allows access to otherwise (at least partially) inaccessible internal subjective experience. Hence, by elaborating temporal concepts in terms of external sensory experience to which the conceptual system has much better access, the range of concepts available has been enhanced.

Concept elaboration of this kind has a number of obvious benefits. Not least, if we assume that language enhances evolutionary viability, then the wider the array of concepts available, and the more highly elaborated they are, the greater the expressive and communicative power of language.

3.2 Subjective concepts and levels of cognitive processing

A related proposal has been advanced by Grady (1997a, n.d.). Grady argues that (an important subset of) subjective concepts may relate to cognitive processes and mechanisms which produce assessments, judgements and evaluations which enter into focal consciousness, while the mechanisms themselves which produce the evaluations seldom do. This suggests that the concepts which relate to such processes and mechanisms operate at a level of cognitive processing which fail to enter into focal consciousness.

To make this point, Grady provide the example of the subjective concept of similarity:

> Similarity is a relation which we perceive immediately and effortlessly in many cases, and which plays a role in all our categorizations. When we recognize a dog, for example, it is because of features which make it similar to other dogs we have seen. Furthermore, it seems unlikely that we learn how to recognize similarity; instead the ability to do so would seem to be an innate feature of our cognitive apparatus, without which various common behaviors, linguistic and otherwise, would be impossible.   (Grady 1997a: 156)

The point is that the concept of similarity relates to a cognitive process which may well be back-grounded, in terms of its accessibility to conscious awareness. Equally, as temporality may relate to perceptual processing, and hence the ongoing flow of conscious experience (in the sense of Chafe 1994) – an operation which occurs unconsciously – and may constitute one of the most basic components of mental experience, the mechanisms which produce temporal awareness are seldom, if ever, accessible to focal consciousness. This is not to say, of course, that assessments due to temporal processing are not subject to focal consciousness. As we saw in the previous chapter subjects can report on their experience of duration, which suggests that such an experience is in focus. However, the mechanisms responsible for this subjective experience remain part of the background.

On this account, the elaboration of subjective concepts in terms of concepts derived from external sensory experience, what I am referring to as inter-subjective information, may provide a means of foregrounding otherwise back-grounded mechanisms and experiences. Hence, by appealing to external sensory experience, the back-grounded mechanisms and experience associated with temporal cognition can more readily enter into focal consciousness.

Of course, it is important to emphasise that from this it does not follow that temporal experience cannot be communicated directly. Put another way, the encoding of temporal experience in language can be accomplished in the absence of elaboration (i.e., metaphor). After all, we can consciously focus on assessments of temporal magnitude, simultaneity, and other aspects of temporal experience (e.g., the experiments conducted by Ornstein [1969] 1997). Moreover, there are lexical items which directly encode concepts derived from such experiences, e.g., *time, now, duration, simultaneity*, etc. However, as temporal experience enters into our experience of anything, and indeed everything, even when we are not actively focusing on (an aspect of) temporality itself, temporal experience is omnipresent at a relatively low level of conscious processing. Hence, patterns of elaboration serve to enrich temporal concepts which relate to a fundamental and otherwise back-grounded, for the most part, aspect of human cognition.

3.3 Conclusion

In this chapter I have considered two accounts for the observation that concepts such as time are extra-ordinarily difficult to define in their own terms without recourse to elaboration in terms of external sensory experience. One reason for the elaboration of time in terms of inter-subjective concepts (i.e., concepts which relate to external sensory experience), may relate to neuronal connections, with subjective information being relatively less well connected to the conceptual system. This may be due to evolutionary pressures in the formation of neuronal connections, in which certain experiences which are subject to higher-order processing such as decision-making, learning, etc. are more useful when they can be represented by the conceptual system.

A second account, due to work by Grady, suggests that temporal processing and experience may constitute one of the most basic aspects of our cognitive architecture. As such, it enters into many aspects of cognitive function and therefore operates at a level of cognitive processing which may not readily become accessible to focal consciousness. On this view, the elaboration of temporal concepts in terms of external sensory experience serves to foreground otherwise back-grounded processes and experiences.

CHAPTER 4

The nature of meaning

Having considered the nature and scope of the problem to be addressed, the purpose of this chapter is to present the theoretical assumptions and perspective which will inform the examination of temporal cognition. As this book is primarily addressing the linguistic problem associated with time in order to circumvent the metaphysical problem, it accordingly represents a linguistic analysis of the conceptual system. Hence, it constitutes an investigation of the relationship between language and meaning. The expression of meaning is presumably the reason why language has developed at all – the symbolic nature of language and the mental faculties responsible represent the means whereby meaning can be encoded and externalised. It would therefore be surprising in the extreme if language and linguistic structure failed to reflect this primary motivation. Consequently, the present approach assumes that our understanding of language cannot be advanced in a significant way without taking seriously the nature and central role of meaning.

However, my concern in this chapter is not just to approach the nature of linguistic meaning; in addition, I consider how anything can be meaningful at all. The reason for adopting this more ambitious tack is that it is meaning broadly conceived – that is, the nature of our environment and on-going changes to which an organism must respond in an appropriate way if it is to be ecologically viable[1] – which presumably must ultimately give rise to the nature of mental representation in the conceptual system. It is upon this mental representation that language depends.

In addition to offering a more general view of meaning, this chapter will also focus on the nature of the conceptual system itself and how it is constituted. In Chapter 1 I defined the CONCEPTUAL SYSTEM as that attribute of mind which encodes, organises and structures information which has achieved REPRESENTATIONAL STATUS. As I noted, representational status relates to the ability to represent, model and thus recall an experience, qua a CONCEPT, even when the experience is no longer accessible to focal consciousness. Hence, concepts are mental representations, which can potentially serve as the semantic pole (in the sense of Langacker 1987) of a linguistic expression.[2] The subset of con-

cepts which perform this latter function I identified in Chapter 1 as LEXICAL
CONCEPTS, a theoretical construct which will be of central importance in the
rest of the book.[3] Henceforth, in order to distinguish the phonological pole associated with linguistic expressions from our conceptualisation of time, I will
employ italics to refer to the phonological pole, e.g., *time*.

The conceptual system is of fundamental importance for a number of
reasons. Not least, it seems reasonable to suggest that a relatively sophisticated conceptual system must have co-evolved with language (Deacon 1997;
Edelman 1992; Jackendoff 1992, 2002). This is entailed if one accepts the
premise that language, at base, constitutes the means of encoding and hence externalising conceptual structure (Evans & Green 2006; Jackendoff 1992; Lakoff
1987; Langacker 1987; Talmy 2000; Tyler & Evans 2003; Wierzbicka 1996).
This conclusion leads to the assumption that the conceptual system will ultimately constrain and delimit the nature of representation by language. We
would therefore expect to see the conceptual system leave its mark on the
linguistic system.

A number of scholars take quite seriously the notion that linguistic organisation reflects conceptual considerations. For instance, Jackendoff (1983, 1990,
1992, 2002), Langacker (1987, 1991a, 1991b, 1999), and Talmy (2000) illustrate
in detail how conceptual categories, e.g., THING, PATH, PROCESS[4] etc., are mirrored syntactically by Noun, Adposition and Verb. Edelman (1992), and especially Langacker (1987, 1991a, 1991b) have suggested that even word order may
ultimately be the result of conceptual/semantic and usage-based considerations
(see also Croft 2001; Tomasello 2003). For instance, Edelman hypothesises that
a syntax may have evolved as follows:

> When a sufficiently large lexicon is collected, the conceptual areas of the brain
> categorize the *order* of speech elements, an order that is then stabilized in
> memory as syntax. In other words, the brain recursively relates semantic to
> phonological sequences and then generates syntactic correspondences, not
> from preexisting rules, but by treating rules *developing in memory* as objects
> for conceptual manipulation.   (Ibid.: 130; original emphasis)

Some evidence for this has begun to emerge as work progresses in the gram-
maticalisation framework (e.g., Bybee et al. 1994; Hopper & Traugott 1993;
Svorou 1994; also see the 'cognitive' typological studies of Heine, e.g., 1993,
1997; and usage-based approaches to grammar of Croft 2001; Goldberg 1995;
Langacker 1987, 1991a, 1991b 1999[5] and first language acquisition, notably the
work associated with Michael Tomasello (e.g., 2003)).

4.1 Meaning, experience and the nature of evolution

If meaning, broadly conceived, can be traced to the nature of human experience, then an important aspect of that experience will constitute the nature of the physical world 'out there'. It is an organism's physical environment, after all, which has non-trivial consequences for survival, and prompts behaviour choices and selections. Where regularities and predictable patterns occur, an organism's response can become 'hard-wired'. In this sense, evolution represents and reflects the behaviour responses, choices and habits adopted by a particular species.

Dennett (1991) makes the same point in the following way:

> We all assume that the future will be like the past – it is the essential but unprovable premise of all our inductive inferences, as Hume noted. Mother Nature (the design-developer realized in the processes of natural selection) makes the same assumption. In many regards, things stay the same: gravity continues to exert its force, water continues to evaporate, organisms continue to need to replenish and protect their body water, looming things continue to subtend ever-larger portions of retinas, and so on. Where generalities like these are at issue, Mother-Nature provides long-term solutions to problems: hard-wired, gravity-based which-way-is-up detectors, hard-wired thirst alarms, hard-wired duck-when-something-looms circuits.   (Ibid.: 182)

There are other regularities which do involve change, although the change is cyclical and hence predictable. A good example of this concerns the Earth's 24 hour rotation upon its axis, which affects the amount of light and dark organisms are exposed to. For organisms which require periods of low activation, sleep, and have evolved physiological apparatus for activity by daylight (i.e., diurnal as opposed to nocturnal animals), the Earth's day-night cycle is meaningful, and, has prompted an important evolutionary response. The Earth is, in effect, a geo-physical clock constituting a 24 hour day-night cycle as it rotates upon its own axis. The human organism has internalised this highly predictable cycle enabling humans to become more ecologically viable in a PERIDOIC ENVIRONMENT (Winifree 1987).

The biological instantiation of the Earth's periodicity is a series of biological cycles, which constitute the circadian rhythms, from the Greek *circa* 'about' and *dies* 'a day'. The master circadian rhythm, or 'body-clock', is the wake-sleep cycle, which controls the length of time a person is asleep and awake. It is interesting to note that the wake-sleep rhythm runs on a 24.8 hour cycle, closely mirroring the 24 hour day-night cycle of the Earth (Coveney & Highfield 1990; Winifree 1987). Winifree notes however that, "An uncorrectable biological clock would be almost useless unless the match between its period and that of the earth's rotations were perfect" (ibid.: 47), as the human 24.8 hour wake-sleep cycle would gradually become out of step with the Earth's day-night cycle. Hence, humans have evolved a mechanism for maintaining their own biological rhythm in synchronicity with the Earth's, a process termed ENTRAINMENT.

The wake-sleep cycle in humans is regulated by the detection of light, and controlled by the suprachiasmatic nuclei, located above the crossing of the optic nerve in the mid-brain. Clearly, a wake-sleep cycle, which closely parallels the Earth's own day-night rhythm, and moreover, which has a physiological mechanism for ensuring the internal cycle remains entrained with the geo-physical cycle, allows a diurnal organism to sleep when there is no light and function when there is. The point is that the nature of the environment which an organism inhabits necessitates responses from the organism in order to function more effectively (and hence ensure survival). These behavioural responses which can lead to physiological responses (i.e., evolutionary change which enhance biological morphology), are, in this sense, meaning-based.

However, to suggest that evolution constitutes a response to the environment does not entail that there is a single optimal response. As pointed out by Varela et al. (1991), it is difficult to argue that evolution constitutes a process which is based on best suiting the organism to the environment. Such a view would treat adaptation as a process which leads to optimal physiological systems, a teleological tendency, in which evolution is driven by some ultimate goal (or cause). As Toulmin and Goodfield (1965) observe, the doctrine of functional teleology, prevalent until as late as the nineteenth century, was undermined by the discoveries made by Darwin. As they put it:

> The Darwinian theory called in question all teleological interpretations of the History of Nature – theistic and naturalistic alike. It did not deny that organic structure and animal behaviour were adaptive. But it did deny that these functional aspects of Nature came into existence as the end-results of processes specifically aimed at their production.   (Ibid.: 228)

Varela et al. (1991) argue that the diversity of physiological structures in different organisms strongly suggests that evolution proceeds by virtue of producing ecologically viable organisms, rather than optimal ones. For instance, they observe that human vision is trichromatic, which is to say, it utilises three types of photoreceptors and three colour channels. More importantly, a consequence of having trichromatic vision is that three dimensions are required for representing the range of colour distinctions that we are able to make. Yet, some organisms are dichromats (e.g., squirrels, rabbits and possibly cats, two dimensions), while some animals have tetrachromatic vision (four-dimensions, e.g., goldfish and pigeons), while still others are pentachromats (five dimensions). As Varela et al. put it, "We can safely conclude that since our [human] biological lineage has continued, our color categories are *viable* or *effective*. Other species, however, have evolved *different* perceived worlds of color on the basis of different cooperative neuronal selections" (Ibid.: 181). They continue by noting that, "Our perceived world of color, is rather a result of one possible and viable phylogenetic pathway among many others realized in the evolutionary history of living beings" (Ibid.: 183). This view of evolution, then, suggests that evolutionary fitness does not so much constitute adaptation in the sense that there is some pre-given property of the world that can be adapted to. Rather, successful evolutionary change entails a viable response to diverse ecological niches, by developing effective, as opposed to optimal, means of exploiting regularities in the world. Moreover, once a species has happened to embark upon a particular phylogenetic pathway, continued development along the route selected takes place (i.e., a species with tetrachromatic vision is unlikely to evolve trichromatic vision but rather is more likely to enhance its existing neuronal connections to make the existing system more viable, and by so doing, it further integrates and develops the existing system). This process they refer to as EVOLUTIONARY NATURAL DRIFT.

In terms of a broadly-situated view of meaning, the foregoing has important consequences as, in essence, the world we experience, i.e., our perceived world, and ultimately the world to which we have conscious access, is not pre-given in the sense of being mind-independent. Rather, it is constructed by virtue of our particular evolutionary history and the nature of our embodiment, a subject to which we now turn.

4.2 The embodiment of meaning

If evolution represents an ecologically viable response to the environment, which can be characterised by evolutionary natural drift, then it follows that the world we as humans perceive is radically different from the perceived world of other organisms. In this sense, our world, and indeed our reality, is largely determined by the nature of our physiology and our evolutionary history. The fact that we see in three colour dimensions, as opposed to two, four or five, means that our experience of the world will be very different from another organism's. In this way, what is meaningful for us is determined by our embodiment, as this, in part, constructs the world we perceive and respond to. Put another way, organisms such as human beings will always experience the world as mediated by the nature and structure of their bodies which includes biological morphology (e.g., the fact that humans have arms rather than wings, walk upright rather than on all fours, etc.), their sense-perceptory apparatus (e.g., the kind of the vision they have), and their neuro-anatomical architecture (which is to say the structure of the brain and the neuronal connections therein).

For instance, the experiential vertical axis can be distinguished by the notions of up and down. Given that the world is ultimately an unlabelled place (Edelman 1992), how is it that we can distinguish up from down? These notions are distinguishable presumably because they have consequences for the nature of our interaction. In short, they constitute a meaningful distinction. The distinction is meaningful because we experience gravity (presumably a property of the world), which effectively distinguishes up from down, and hence renders the vertical axis experientially asymmetric. How we experience the world is clearly a function of the world 'out there', or at least one aspect of it, as attested by the internalisation of the Earth's 24 hour cycle.

Nonetheless, it is not sufficient that gravity is a property of the world for gravity to represent a meaningful way of distinguishing up from down. There are, after all, a large number of physical properties of the world which are not meaningful for us in our everyday lives. For instance, the fact that we cannot detect colours in the infra-red range, while some organisms can, does not mean that the world is incomplete for us, but merely reflects the fact that our reality is, in part, a result of the nature of our visual apparatus and hence our embodiment (Jackendoff 1992: 162).

Hence, what is meaningful for us as human beings is not necessarily the same as for another organism. That gravity should be a property of the world which is meaningful for us, in that it distinguishes up from down, is a consequence of the nature of our physiology which mediates our experience of gravity. As such, gravity is not meaningful in a mind-independent, so-called 'god's-eye', way, as clearly it must have different consequences for different physiological structures which have evolved in different ecological niches. Hummingbirds, which can hover, and fish, whose environment reduces the effect of gravity, presumably experience and perceive gravity in a different way than humans do for instance. In essence, to say that meaning is embodied is to suggest that it is the nature of our bodies which mediates and hence determines the nature of our experience, and the manner in which it is meaningful. On this account, meaning becomes a function of the nature of the totality of our physiology, not just the explicitly cognitive (i.e., mental) aspects.[6]

4.3 The experiential basis of conceptual meaning

Having related how things can be meaningful at all to the nature of our embodiment, we must now see how this relationship is connected with the development of conceptual structure which forms the basis of the meaning conveyed symbolically (e.g., utilising language). This section will accordingly relate the notion of experiential or embodied meaning to the notion of conceptual meaning.

Given that the conceptual system is unable to fully encode subjective information (e.g., we do not elaborate time purely in its own temporal terms), but rather employ other kinds of concepts relating to external sensory experience, why is the inter-subjective information which comes to be associated with particular subjective concepts appropriate, in lieu of other kinds of inter-subjective content? In effect, this entails establishing why time is associated with motion events (as in examples such as: *Time flows/goes/runs on forever*) and not something else: why temporal duration is associated with physical length (as in sentences such as: *The exam only lasted a short time*), and so forth. Is the choice of which sets of inter-subjective concepts are associated with particular subjective concepts arbitrary, or is it predictable in some way?

The research programmes associated with Lakoff and Johnson (1980, 1999), Jackendoff (1983, 1990) and many others strongly suggest that the choice is highly predictable. However, there is disagreement as to whether the particular inter-subjective information that comes to be associated with the subjective concepts is due to experience, or is innately prescribed.

For instance, Jackendoff, influenced by the rationalism of the generative tradition in linguistics, argues that the structuring of concepts such as time in terms of space does "not appear to be based on experience... [but is due to]...the machinery available to the human mind to channel the ways in which all experience can be mentally encoded" (1992:43). Hence, THEMATIC STRUCTURE, the organisational scheme which 'channels' the encoding of new experience and hence selects the nature of the inter-subjective information to structure subjective concepts, is innately given. While it is highly likely that some conceptual associations will be due to innate prescription, there is good reason to believe that some conceptual associations are entailed by correlations between sets of experiences.

4.4 Experiential correlation

Joseph Grady (1997a) has investigated in detail the nature of what he terms EXPERIENTIAL CORRELATION. Grady has studied sets of conceptual associations which seem to be highly conventionalised and productive. Consider some illustrative examples:

(4.1) a. The stock prices went up
       b. His test score wasn't as high as he had hoped for

In these sentences there is a conventional reading pertaining to quantity of a certain kind. In (4.1a) the sentence refers to an increase in stock prices. In (4.1b) it refers to a test score result which constitutes a numerical quantity. Although each of these readings is perfectly conventional, the lexical items which provide these readings, *went up*, and *high*, literally refer to vertical elevation. Examples such as these provide good evidence that quantity and vertical elevation are associated in some way at the conceptual level. What then should motivate such associations?

Grady observed that in experiential terms quantity and vertical elevation are often correlated, and that these correlations are ubiquitous in our everyday lives. For instance, when we increase the height of something there is typically more of it. If an orange farmer puts more oranges on a pile, thereby increasing the height of the pile, there is a correlative increase in quantity. Similarly, water poured into a glass results in a correlative increase in both height or vertical elevation of the liquid, and quantity. Accordingly, it is plausible that this tight and recurring correlation in experience gives rise to an association being formed at the conceptual level, as attested by the linguistic examples. Grady (personal communication) has suggested that there may be in the order of several hundred such conceptual associations based on analogous instances of foundational correlations in experience.

What is particularly attractive about the notion of experiential correlation is that it constitutes quasi-universal experiential correspondences which all human beings, given their shared physiology and the nature of the world, would experience. This is suggestive that there may be a corresponding number of conceptual associations which are cross-linguistic in nature, a hypothesis being borne out by on-going investigation (see Grady 1999b; Svorou 1994). This view has been echoed in the typological work of Heine (e.g., 1997), who observes that:

[H]uman beings irrespective of whether they live in Siberia or the Kalahari Desert, have the same intellectual, perceptual and physical equipment; are exposed to the same general kinds of experiences; and have the same communicative needs. One therefore will expect their languages and the way their languages are used to be the same across geographical and cultural boundaries.

(Ibid.: 11)

It is also interesting to note that evidence is beginning to emerge that correlation is a fundamental operation at all levels of cognitive processing. As noted in Chapter 2, at the neurological level evidence suggests that integration or 'binding' of perceptual information results from the correlated firing of the relevant neurons (Crick 1994; Crick & Koch 1990; Pöppel 1994; Stryker 1991). That is, the particular neurons associated with the sensory qualities constituting the perception of an object are fired in correlated fashion. This synchronous firing serves to integrate the various spatially-distributed sensory qualities into a coherent percept, without requiring that the information be transmitted to, and hence integrated at, a single site in the brain.

Similarly, C. Johnson (1999) has found that experiential correlation plays an important part in the development of conceptual structure as evidenced by child language acquisition. He studied the polysemy of the lexeme *see*, which in adult speech is distinct from the lexeme *know*. Grady (1997a) has argued that the concepts of seeing and knowing are related by virtue of a tight experiential correlation in which seeing that something is the case correlates with also knowing that it is the case. This correlation has given rise to an association at the conceptual level, as evidenced by expressions such as: *I see* [=*know*] *what you mean*. Johnson's findings, which are presented in terms of what he calls the CONFLATION HYPOTHESIS, suggest that in first language acquisition children begin with a single concept, e.g., seeing, which subsumes both seeing and knowing. During a process of separation, or deconflation, the child begins to distinguish two aspects (i.e., seeing *and* knowing) of the developmentally earlier single concept (i.e., seeing). These two aspects emerge as two distinct, albeit related, concepts. It may be for this reason, he suggests, that in the adult linguistic system, the lexeme *see* encodes both meanings. Importantly, the notion of conflation provides a tentative hypothesis for understanding how the phenomenon of experiential correlation produces meaning from experience.

The notion of experiential correlation will prove to be important for two reasons. As we will see, tight correlations in experience can give rise to implicatures associated with particular lexical concepts. If conventionalised, such implicatures can become instantiated in the conceptual system as distinct concepts associated with the same lexical form. Hence, experiential correlation plays an important role in the development of new lexical concepts (see Chapter 6). The second way in which this mechanism is important is that patterns of experiential correlation can facilitate the elaboration of lexical concepts. As we saw above, quantity is elaborated in terms of content relating to vertical elevation due to experiential correlation (also see Chapter 6, and Part II).

4.5 Perceptual resemblance

There is also another mechanism which appears to play an important role in concept elaboration. This is PERCEPTUAL RESEMBLANCE.[7] Perceptual resemblance (or analogy) has been widely studied by psychologists, cognitive scientists and philosophers of language. Unlike experiential correlation, this is a process that establishes connections between concepts based not on experiential givens (such as an increase or decrease in quantity or height), but rather as a result of perceived similarities. That is, two entities, which are perceived as resembling each other in some way (e.g., perceived physical resemblance, or the perception of shared qualities or characteristics or function) come to be associated at the conceptual level. Consider the following example:

(4.2) She's just a twig

In (4.2), the perceived resemblance between the physical appearance of a person and a twig, namely the fact that in both cases there is a lack of excess outer material to cover the structural material beneath, prompts the speaker to elaborate the person designated by *she*, in terms of *a twig*. Perceptual resemblance differs from experiential correlation in that it is not (patterns of co-occurrences in) experience per se which gives rise to the resemblance, but rather our perception of shared characteristics. Hence, perceptual resemblance provides a means of comparing, and in turn perceiving similarity or dissimilarity between, distinct entities. As such, it constitutes an active process of comparison.

Within the cognitive linguistics tradition it has been common to employ the term METAPHOR in order to describe conceptual associations mediated by both experiential correlation and perceptual resemblance. However, as pointed out by Grady (1997a, 1999a) such studies have largely failed to realise that their use of this term encompasses associations which appear to be formed by (at least) two qualitatively distinct processes.

For present purposes, perceptual resemblance will be seen to be an important process for the elaboration of concepts. Based on the findings to be adduced in Part II, perceptual resemblance appears to play a role primarily in the elaboration of secondary temporal concepts; that is, those temporal lexical concepts which relate to socio-cultural knowledge and experience, rather than due to presumably universal subjective experiences.

4.6 Perception and 'reality'

In the foregoing I suggested that meaning is fundamentally embodied, in the sense that our perceived world is, in part, a consequence of the nature of our physiology. However, this view needs to be qualified as the 'reality' to which we have conscious access is also constructed, in part, by perceptual processes and mechanisms to which we may not have conscious access (see surveys in Dennett 1991; Jackendoff e.g. 1983, 1992: Ch. 8; Rock 1984).

As Dennett (1991) observes, "The brain's task is to guide the body it controls through a world of shifting conditions and sudden surprises, so it must gather information from that world and use it *swiftly* to "produce future" – to extract anticipations in order to stay one step ahead of disaster" (Ibid.: 144). The difficulties are compounded by the fact that the processes which the brain employs to carry out this task are spatially distributed, and as Dennett observes, communication within the brain which employs electrochemical impulses is relatively slow compared with light or even with electrical signals along wires. Hence, the brain must "utilize ingenious anticipatory strategies that feed on redundancies in the input" (Ibid.). The startling consequence of this is that the reality we are consciously aware of is not necessarily the same as what may objectively be the case.

For instance, Dennett (1991) describes an experiment in which two or three tappers were located along a subject's arm, at the wrist, elbow and upper arm. A series of taps were administered such that the subject experienced several taps at the wrist, followed by the elbow and then upper arm. The time between individual taps was between 50 and 200 milliseconds, so that the total series of taps lasted less than a second. Dennett reports that, "The astonishing effect is that the taps seem to the subjects to travel in regular sequence over equidistant points up the arm" (Ibid.: 143). Of course, in this experiment, the taps are not objectively equidistant, yet the subjects "experience" them as such.

Experiments such as this reveal that what is actually experienced, non-equidistant taps on the arm, is available to consciousness as equidistant taps. Put another way, the nature of mental images[8] to which we have conscious access is derived from unconscious processes which serve to construct our reality for us.

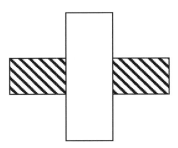

Figure 4.1. A partly occluded rectangle (drawn from Jackendoff 1992:163)

Jackendoff (1992:Ch. 8) presents some striking pieces of evidence to support the contention that conscious experience involves structure and organisation imposed by perceptual processes which is not available in the input itself. He observes that in a diagram such as that in Figure 4.1, "one vividly sees the shaded portions of the figure as a unified object, partly occluded by a rectangle in front of it" (Ibid.:163). However, in purely objective terms we cannot be said to see a partly occluded rectangle, as there is no such rectangle available which can be so perceived. Rather, our unconscious cognitive processing presents a view of 'reality' in which there is a partly occluded rectangle. This indicates that perceptual input has organisation imposed upon it which does not derive from the input itself; that is, the nature of conscious experience is structured by cognitive processes below the level of consciousness with the result that that of which we are directly aware, our conscious experience, does not necessarily equate with what may objectively be there. Indeed, the notion of an objectively 'real' world, as revealed by our perceptual apparatus, is called into question by findings such as these.

The foregoing casts doubt on the naïve view that the information referenced and mediated by language is about the real world. Indeed, I suggest that in so far as language 'refers', it refers to lexical concepts,[9] the mental representations which may or may not reflect an objective world 'out there'. Moreover, given that we have no conscious access to such a world, but only the world of representation, then it makes no sense to posit that language can be about the world, in a pre-given 'god's-eye' sense (see in particular Lakoff 1987). Accordingly, language, and meaning, which it serves to express, must, on this view, be fundamentally conceptual in nature.

The general position that there cannot be a mind-independent view of reality to which humans have direct access has been stressed by a number of philosophers, cognitive scientists and linguists (e.g., Fauconnier 1997;

Jackendoff 1983, 1987, 1990, 1992; Johnson 1987; Lakoff 1987; Lakoff & Johnson 1999; Langacker 1987, 1991a; Marmaridou 2000; Putnam 1981; Torey 1999; Tyler & Evans 2003; Varela et al. 1991). As Jackendoff (1983) puts it, "We have conscious access only to the projected world" (Ibid.: 29); for Jackendoff, the PROJECTED WORLD is that level of information which has achieved mental representation via the perceptual processes which organise such raw sensory input (see Dennett's 1991, Multiple Drafts Model of consciousness for one view of some of these unconscious processes).

4.7 Perceptual analysis

Having argued that sensory input constitutes a different level of cognitive processing from perception, I will now address how perception (in the sense of the perceptual categorisation of objects) may give rise to concepts.

The developmental psychologist Jean Mandler (e.g., 1988, 1992, 1996) has studied the nature of the interaction between perceptual experience and the development of the immature conceptual system. Mandler makes a clear distinction between perception and conception. She identifies perception as the ability to form percepts, or perceptual categories, by "learning to abstract the central tendencies of perceptual patterns" (Mandler 1992: 588). Hence, an infant's ability to distinguish animals from vehicles, for instance, results from perceptual categorisation. However, according to Mandler, perceptual abilities while allowing certain kinds of discrimination, do not enable a theory of what an animal or a vehicle is, nor the ability to use such information "for purposes of thought" (Ibid.: 588).

Mandler suggests that concept formation results from a process she terms PERCEPTUAL ANALYSIS. Perceptual analysis enables perceptual information to be reanalysed, such that a new kind of information is abstracted, resulting in concept formation.[10] In essence then, early concepts constitute 'redescribed' sensorimotor information. Mandler suggests that the rudimentary concepts infants develop result primarily from the redescription of "spatial structure and of the structure of motion that is abstracted primarily from vision, touch, and one's own movements" (Ibid.: 591). Hence, in developmental terms, early concepts include the concepts object, animate, inanimate, etc., and relational concepts such as containment.[11]

Scholars such as Gibson (1975, 1986), and Einstein ([1916] 1961) have made the same point regarding the concept of space. Like containment, it appears that the concept of space derives from the redescription of various geometric properties and attributes of the perceived world. According to Einstein, the concept of space:

> is suggested by certain primitive experiences. Suppose that a box has been con- structed. Objects can be arranged in a certain way inside the box, so that it becomes full. The possibility of such arrangements is a property of the mate- rial object "box", something that is given with the box, the "space enclosed" by the box. This is something which is different for different boxes, something that is thought quite naturally as being independent of whether or not, at any moment, there are any objects at all in the box. When there are no objects in the box, its space appears to be "empty".   (Ibid.: 157)

The foregoing suggests that while space and containment are not things in themselves, through perceptual analysis – the redescription of various per- ceived experiences – these concepts represent 'theories' concerning how ob- jects of perception are related to one another and are conceptualised. More- over, there is evidence that infants have developed the concept of containment as early as 5.5 months of age (Mandler 1992).

If perceptual analysis (in the sense of Mandler) is responsible for the re- description of external sensory experience into conceptual structures, it may be that similar processes result in the redescription of subjective experience, resulting in subjective concept formation.

4.8 On the meaning of words

One of the problems that linguists have traditionally encountered is the dif- ficulty in attempting to provide definitions for words, i.e., to give an account of the meanings associated with words. According to Wierzbicka (1996) this problem led linguists in the American Structuralist tradition to largely exclude the study of meaning from linguistics. She suggests that Bloomfield "was afraid of meaning, and was eager to relegate the study of meaning to other disci- plines such as sociology or psychology. The reason he was afraid of it was that he wanted to establish linguistics as a science and that he thought that mean- ing couldn't be studied with the same rigour as linguistic sounds and forms" (Ibid.: 3). This diffidence towards meaning has been inherited in modern lin- guistics by theories (e.g., the generative tradition associated with the work of Chomsky) in which the separation of meaning and form is a central axiom, with the emphasis being placed on the study of form.

One of the difficulties which has hindered attempts to define the meanings of words has been the assumption that definitions should be (and perhaps are) solely linguistic (or propositional) in nature. This has led theorists to attempt to define meanings in terms of semantic features (see Jackendoff 1983:Ch. 7 for a review). However, while language is symbolic (pairing a physical symbol with a meaning), meanings themselves are sub-symbolic. That is, meanings (or lexical concepts) are not primarily linguistic, but rather derive from perceptual analysis and are hence redescribed perceptions (i.e., they are embodied; see Barsalou 2003). In addition, they are informed by our interaction and experience with the entities they represent, and a whole welter of other background knowledge, such as knowledge gleaned through cultural transmission. It is for this reason, I suggest, that we often intuitively 'know' what a word means, and yet only with difficulty, and painstaking work (as lexicographers will attest), can produce definitions which even come close to their intuited meaning.

Jackendoff (1987:Ch. 10, 1992:Ch. 2) makes a similar point suggesting that, for instance, geometric differences (e.g., size, shape, etc.), between the meanings of words such as *duck* and *goose* or *chair* and *stool*, derive from perceptual-visual information which must at some level inform the lexical entries (i.e., meanings) of these words. If we allow that the conceptual system has access to such information (e.g., via perceptual analysis described above), then we avoid the inevitable difficulty in attempting to define word-meaning in terms of semantic features or some other propositional approach. That is, the meanings associated with words cannot simply be captured in propositional terms, precisely because they constitute more than the sum of the conventionalised conceptual substrate which constitutes their definition in this simplistic sense. Clearly, definitions of the following kind are hopelessly inadequate in terms of capturing all of the embodied information that we actually have access to in term of ducks: *Duck, any bird of the family Anatidae, characterised by short webbed feet, and a quacking sound.*

4.9 Dictionaries versus encyclopaedias

The distinction between viewing words as indexing precise definitions, and the view that lexical forms prompt for complex conceptualisations with access to potentially vast repositories of information, has been framed in terms of a distinction between a dictionary versus encyclopaedic view of word-meaning (see Haiman 1980; Langacker 1987; Tyler & Evans 2003). On such a view, linguists subscribing to the dictionary view of word-meaning identify a fi-

nite and restricted set of specifications with a particular lexical form. As both
Haiman and Langacker point out, such an enterprise is flawed on grounds of
practicability alone.

Tyler and Evans (2003) observe that, "The mistake in adopting a dictionary view of lexical items has been to view words as 'containing' meaning, a
naïve view of communication, which Reddy (1979) argued was to fall prey to
what he termed the conduit metaphor" (Ibid.:17). Rather than viewing words
as 'containing' anything, it is more felicitous to treat lexemes as prompts for
meaning construction. Langacker (1987) has summarised this position as follows, "[L]inguistic expressions are not meaningful in and of themselves, but
only through the access they afford to different stores of knowledge that allow
us to make sense of them" (Ibid.:155).

The encyclopaedic view, then, treats words as POINTS OF ACCESS (in Langacker's terms) or PROMPTS, not tied to isolated and restricted specifications,
but rather, to the totality of knowledge we possess concerning a particular entity or experience, reflecting both our knowledge of the way in which a particular lexical item is used, and that aspect of our projected reality which the
entity prompted for occupies (see Fauconnier 1994, 1997; Fauconnier & Turner
2002; Turner 1991). An important consequence of adopting the encyclopaedic
view of word-meaning is that the traditional distinction between semantics and
pragmatics falls away (Marmaridou 2000). Rather than semantics being clearly
distinguishable from pragmatics, on this view, these two 'types' of knowledge
form a complementary and equally indispensable partnership in providing an
understanding of how and what words mean.

One way in which I will attempt to capture the encyclopaedic knowledge
prompted for by the lexeme *time* is to model the meaning associated with
this form in terms of a SEMANTIC NETWORK. A semantic network constitutes a
model of the putative association of related meanings prompted for by a single
lexical item, in this case *time*. The particular meaning prompted for by a lexeme will depend on its use in context. Hence, interpretation can never, on this
account, be divorced from situated language use. As our semantic knowledge
cannot be separated from our pragmatic knowledge, it is a mistake to attempt
to identify semantic information independently of pragmatic information. In
other words, both semantics and pragmatics constitute the study of linguistic
meaning properly conceived.

4.10 Meaning and truth

In view of the foregoing, we are forced to conclude that theories of meaning which assume that the information conveyed by language is about an objectively verifiable world must be erroneous. After all, if we do not have conscious access to an objective mind-independent reality, and moreover, 'reality' is constructed by virtue of an organism's embodiment, then we cannot define meaning in terms of an external verifiable reality. Yet, truth-conditional and model-theoretic approaches to meaning, as presented in texts such as Bach (1989), Cann (1993) and Chierchia and McConnell-Ginet (2000), define 'core' meaning in terms of TRUTH, a putatively objective property of the world. As we have no access to such a property, then clearly such approaches are fatally flawed (Fauconnier 1997; Jackendoff 1983; Lakoff 1987; Langacker 1987, 1991b; Putnam 1981; from a neuroscience perspective see Edelman 1992; Torey 1999).

A related problem with such so-called 'formal' approaches to meaning is that they are not concerned with meaning properly conceived. If meaning constitutes an attribute of the embodied mind, as advocated here, the study of meaning should constitute a true 'cognitive' semantics (e.g., Evans & Green 2006; Fauconnier 1997; Jackendoff 1983, 1990; Lakoff 1987; Langacker 1987, 1991a; Marmaridou 2000; Sweetser 1990; Talmy 2000; Tyler & Evans 2003; Wierzbicka 1996). As Wierzbicka observes, an explication of the cognitive significance of meaning is not the goal of theories based on the notion of truth. She states that, "Despite its name, "formal semantics"...doesn't seek to reveal and describe the meanings encoded in natural language, or to compare meanings across languages and cultures. Rather, it sees its goal as that of translating certain carefully selected types of sentences into a logical calculus. It is interested not in meaning (in the sense of conceptual structure encoded in language) but in the logical properties of sentences such as entailment, contradiction, or logical equivalence" (Ibid.:8).

4.11 Conclusion

In this chapter I have discussed the nature of meaning, how anything can be meaningful at all. I suggested that meaning is fundamentally a reflection of our embodied experience, itself a function of the regularities and predictable irregularities in the physical world 'out there', and evolutionary natural drift. The purpose of language, I suggested, is in part to symbolise and hence externalise conceptual structure, and hence to facilitate communication. Thus, considerations of meaning are of central importance for the study of language, and those theories which fail to take seriously the cognitive significance of meaning should be rejected. In analysing the way in which language, and so words, become meaningful, I have set the scene for a frontal assault on the linguistic problem of time.

CHAPTER 5

The conceptual metaphor approach to time

We begin to approach the linguistic problem of time by considering how this issue has been addressed within Conceptual Metaphor Theory (CMT). The purpose then of this chapter will be to re-examine the CMT approach to time. This will pave the way for the theory of word-meaning to be presented in Chapter 6, and the identification and analysis of distinct temporal lexical concepts, developed in Part II of the book.

In recent versions of CMT (e.g., Grady, Taub, & Morgan 1996; Grady 1997a, 1997b; Lakoff & Johnson 1999), two kinds of metaphoric mapping have been distinguished based on their degree of experiential grounding. PRIMARY METAPHORS are held to constitute cross-domain mappings between sets of concepts which are directly and ubiquitously associated in experience. These contrast with more complex COMPOUND METAPHORS, which may be more culture-specific. As primary metaphors are hypothesised to be universal, they presumably constitute a relatively small and finite set (Grady 1999b). Hence, an important goal of current research within CMT, and one objective of this chapter, is to provide criteria for excluding those conventional mappings which do not relate to primary metaphors.

To this end, the present chapter constitutes a reanalysis of the well-known Moving Time mapping, e.g., *Christmas is fast approaching* (*us*), and the Moving Ego mapping, e.g., *We're fast approaching Christmas*. While it has been claimed that these two mappings constitute instances of primary metaphor (Grady 1997a), criteria are adduced for evaluating this. It is concluded that these mappings in fact constitute instances of compound not primary metaphor. This finding will have important consequences for the approach we take to the analysis of temporal concepts in the rest of the book

The view that the Moving Time and Moving Ego mappings are primary metaphors is based on two basic claims: (1) that the primary source concept in each variant relates to a relatively 'simple' IMAGE CONCEPT,[1] e.g., the motion associated with objects, and (2) that the primary target concept, i.e., time, relates to a phenomenologically 'simple' concept, termed a RESPONSE CONCEPT.[2] This chapter presents three problems for the position that these mappings constitute primary metaphors: (i) the problem of unelaborated time, (ii) the problem of cultural concepts, and (iii) the problem of complex concepts.

While CMT constitutes a theory of conceptual projection, it seeks and values generalisations which are as broad as possible (see Gibbs & Steen 1999; Grady 1997b; Lakoff & Johnson 1999). For instance, as temporal concepts appear to be structured in terms of concepts derived from the domain of MOTION,[3] the conceptual metaphor framework utilises mnemonics such as TIME IS OBJECTS IN MOTION (Moving Time) and TIME IS (MOTION ALONG) A PATH (Moving Ego) in order to capture this pattern of conceptual projection. However, although such putative patterns capture the structure of thought at a certain level of generality, the linguistic evidence suggests that there is a further more specific level of analysis which offers more detailed and revealing patterns in the way concepts are structured and organised. This level of organisation relates not to conceptual domains, but rather to individual lexical concepts. Based on the linguistic evidence presented, the second objective of this chapter is to demonstrate that the Moving Time and Moving Ego mappings are not primary metaphors, in the sense envisaged, but rather are sophisticated and complex models of time, comprised of more elementary temporal concepts, which are integrated in a way which gives rise to two coherent but complex cognitive models for time. This position will be substantiated in Part III of the book.

5.1 Primary and compound metaphors

Grady (1997a) constitutes a landmark study in the development of CMT, not least for providing a methodology for distinguishing between primary metaphor and compound (or complex) metaphor.[4]

According to Grady, primary metaphor constitutes "a special case – though a foundational one – of the varied phenomenon of figurative thought and language" (Ibid.: 199). A primary metaphor constitutes an association at the cognitive level between a PRIMARY TARGET CONCEPT and a PRIMARY SOURCE CONCEPT.

A primary target concept is determined as follows. First, concepts of this kind are subjective in that, "they refer to aspects of cognitive experience that organize sensory stimulus into a meaningful representation of the world" (Grady, n.d.: Ch. 5–14). And second, "they refer to basic units or parameters of cognitive function, at or just below levels to which we have direct conscious access" (Ibid.). This view of primary target concepts stipulates concepts which are fairly simple, and unlikely to be imagistically rich. Grady gives the example of the concept 'theory', which due to its complex nature would be unlikely to serve as a primary target concept.[5] However, as "primary target concepts are, in some sense, responses to sensory stimulus and sensations – judgements, assessments, evaluations, inferences and so forth" (Ibid.:Ch. 5–15), they are familiar, simple (in the sense of not being complex), and relate to directly perceived phenomenological experience. Due to this characterisation they are likely to constitute universal experiences and hence universal concepts (rather than culture-specific notions such as, for instance, Christmas).[6]

Like primary target concepts, primary source concepts relate to what Grady terms "'simple' experiences" (Grady 1997a:139). However, unlike primary target concepts, primary source concepts relate to sensorimotor experience and perception and are inter-subjective in nature.[7]

As with the earlier work in CMT upon which he builds, Grady's theory assumes that the cognitive associations or metaphors between sets of concepts are grounded in experience. However, in Grady's theory there must be a clear experiential motivation. Primary metaphors are grounded by virtue of being correlated in a tight and recurring fashion. As the experience of grasping something correlates with the experience of controlling and hence understanding, Grady argues that at the cognitive level the concepts of 'grasping' and 'controlling' become associated.[8]

The correlation between primary target and primary source concepts is motivated naturally and inevitably by virtue of what Grady terms PRIMARY SCENES. These constitute, "recurrent patterns of experience, in which simple dimensions of perception are associated with simple dimensions of meaningful interpretation or response." Grady continues by observing that it is primary scenes which "tie particular concepts together and ground the primary metaphorical associations that ultimately contribute important structure and content to subjective mental experience" (Grady, n.d.:5–31, 5–32).

The ensuing association results in structure from, for instance, the concept of 'grasping' being mapped onto the concept of 'controlling', facilitating structure from the primary source being applied to the primary target, as evidenced by the following sentences drawn from Grady (1997a:148):

(5.1) a.   I've got a firm grip on the situation
       b.   She has a solid grasp of microcellular biology

In this way, structure from the concept of 'grasping' can be applied to that of 'controlling' *by virtue of* the conventional metaphoric mapping. Hence, we understand and lexicalise the concept of 'controlling' in terms of the concept of 'grasping'.

As the experiential grounding relates relatively 'simple' concept types due to correlation, this predicts that there can be no 'gaps' in the metaphoric association. That is, there should be a straightforward correspondence between the primary source concept and the primary target concept. Where some aspects of a source fail to map, then such a mapping 'gap' suggests a more complex metaphoric association rather than a primary one, what Grady terms a compound or complex metaphor. Moreover, Grady suggests that compound metaphors may be 'constructed' from primary metaphors.

For instance, in his re-analysis of Lakoff and Johnson's (1980) THEORIES ARE BUILDINGS metaphor, as illustrated by the following:

(5.2)   Some of the arguments are well **put together**, but in its overall **design**, this is a very **weak** theory   [Grady][9]

Grady (1997b) observes that characteristics of the conceptual domain of BUILDINGS include windows, tenants and rent. Yet, these components fail to map onto the target concept:

(5.3) a.   ?This theory has French windows
        b.   ?The tenants of her theory are behind in their rent   [Grady][10]

According to Grady, this 'poverty' of mapping, along with a lack of a clear experiential basis (buildings and theories are not tightly correlated in our experience), is suggestive that the THEORIES ARE BUILDINGS metaphor does not constitute a primary metaphor.[11] Grady proposes that primary metaphors can be UNIFIED, such that two or more distinct primary metaphors can give rise to more complex metaphors, of which the THEORIES ARE BUILDINGS metaphor is an instance.[12]

5.2 The moving time and moving ego mappings

In the conceptual metaphor literature it has been common to assume that there are two sets of mappings in terms of which time is metaphorically structured by motion. These are the MOVING TIME mapping and the MOVING EGO (or OBSERVER) mapping.[13] In both patterns the Observer or Ego faces the future. In the Moving Time mapping the Ego is conceptualised as stationary, and moments of time move from the future towards the Ego before going past, disappearing behind the Ego. The Moving Time mapping accounts for linguistic examples such as those in (5.4).

Moving Time

(5.4) a.   The time for action has **arrived**
b.   The deadline is **approaching**
c.   Christmas is **coming up** on us
d.   The summer has just **zoomed by**
e.   Time **flies** when you're having fun
f.   Time **drags** when you're bored
g.   Time **flows on/by**
h.   His time [=death] **has come**

In this pattern, time is being conceptualised in terms of an entity or object in motion. In the Moving Ego pattern by contrast, moments of time are conceptualised as landmarks. In this pattern the Ego moves towards a particular moment. The Moving Ego pattern would account for sentences such as those in (5.5).

Moving Ego

(5.5) a.   We're **coming up** on Christmas
b.   We're **getting close** to Christmas
c.   We **passed** the deadline
d.   We've **reached** June already
e.   We're **close** to the start of the new year

In this pattern time is being conceptualised in terms of the Ego's motion along a path or across a landscape.

Grady suggests that these two patterns can be analysed as primary metaphors. In both cases the primary target concept is time. As we have seen, for this to constitute a candidate target concept it must be relatively 'simple' and readily experienced at the phenomenological level. Grady concludes that in phenomenological terms "time is a simple, if abstract, [in the sense of difficult to define] concept rather than one which is constructed from more basic elements of understanding" (1997a: 121). Hence, according to Grady, time does indeed appear to qualify as a primary target concept. As motion, according to Grady, meets the criteria for being a primary source concept, the cognitive association resulting between the two concepts constitutes a primary metaphor.

Further evidence for treating the Moving Time and Moving Ego patterns as primary metaphors derives, Grady suggests, from their clear experiential basis, which motivates the structuring of time in terms of motion. As he puts it, "Our experience of motion is clearly correlated with our experience of time – it is difficult even to conceive of motion that takes place without the passage of time. This fact holds for both our own motion and the motion of objects in our environment" (Ibid.: 120). Grady formalises the primary metaphors based on the Moving Time and Moving Ego patterns as, TIME IS THE MOTION OF OBJECTS and TIME IS (MOTION ALONG) A PATH respectively.[14]

5.3   Evaluating moving time and moving ego as instancs of primary metaphor

There are three potential problems for conceptual metaphor theorists in claiming that the Moving Time and Moving Ego mappings are primary metaphors. These constitute what I will term: (i) the problem of unelaborated time, (ii) the problem of cultural concepts, and (iii) the problem of complex concepts.

The problem of unelaborated time can be characterised as follows. In recent versions of CMT it is assumed that primary target concepts constitute a literal (what I am terming UNELABORATED) subjective concept (e.g., time), which comes to be structured in terms of content deriving from a distinct concept (e.g., motion), by virtue of a cross-domain mapping.[15] While metaphor theorists assume that what is literal and inherent about time relates to an awareness of change (there are two variants of this hypothesis, explicated below), evidence of the kind presented in Chapter 2 suggests that the subjective experience of time may in fact ultimately relate to our experience of duration. The problem of unelaborated time is dealt with in §5.3.1.

The problem of cultural concepts relates to the nature of the linguistic evidence employed in order to support the contention that Moving Ego and Moving Time are primary metaphors. Many of the temporal concepts indexed by the linguistic examples appear to be cultural constructs. Given that a primary target concept is claimed to relate to a universally-available phenomenological experience, evidence of this kind is clearly problematic, as we will see in § 5.3.2.

The third issue, the problem of complex concepts, will be dealt with in §5.3.3. The difficulty for CMT here is that it is not at all clear that the linguistic examples, such as (5.4) and (5.5), do relate to a relatively simple phenomenological experience of time. There are four lines of evidence for this: (a) the issue of distinct meaning, (b) the issue of mapping gaps, (c) the issue of patterns of elaboration and (d) the issue of grammatical distinctions (all explicated below).

5.3.1 The problem of unelaborated time

As already observed, for recent versions of CMT a metaphoric association must have a clear experiential basis. In practice this means that primary metaphors must be related by virtue of tight correlations in experience as discussed above. For this to hold, the primary source and target concepts must be equally as basic, in the sense that they both relate to antecedent experiences (although of different kinds), which can thus be correlated.[16] That is, while primary target concepts may be abstract, in the sense of difficult to apprehend and define, they do appear to be phenomenologically real, and, in some sense basic. After all, we really do feel that we 'experience' time, even if it less obvious what our experience of time and hence our concept of time is.[17]

If then we really do experience time, an important question for CMT in general, and primary metaphor theorists in particular, concerns what constitutes the primary target concept in the putative Moving Time and Moving Ego primary metaphors. In other words, what constitutes the literal or unelaborated concept of time prior to its metaphoric structuring in terms of motion?

The basic position in CMT appears to be that temporal experience relates to an awareness of change. There are two variants of this view, associated with Grady (1997a) and Lakoff and Johnson (1999) respectively. However, the problem for both of these hypotheses is that they do not appear to relate to the phenomenological experience of time as revealed by neuroscience, cognitive psychology and linguistic etymology, as we will see.

Lakoff and Johnson's view: The event-comparison hypothesis
As observed in Chapter 2, for Lakoff and Johnson time may not exist as a thing of and unto itself. Rather, our concept of time relates to an antecedent awareness of ongoing change exhibited by events in the world. In other words, what is literal and inherent about time relates to event comparison. To recap, they express this view as follows, "We cannot observe time itself – if time even exists as a thing-in-itself. We can only observe events and compare them. In the world, there are iterative events against which other events are compared" (Ibid.: 1999: 138).[18]

However, as I argued in Chapter 2 there are a number of reasons to suspect that it may rather be the experience of duration (rather than an awareness of change) which gives rise to foundational conceptions of temporality. First, an ability to experience duration is logically a prerequisite for an awareness of change, while an awareness of change is not a prerequisite for experiencing duration. This suggests that an awareness of change (or non-change) requires an ability to judge that the present moment is distinct from the previous experienced moment, and hence to compare them – the ability to perceive duration (as opposed to a present endlessly replayed). Thus, it seems likely that an awareness of change requires an antecedent ability to perceive duration, in order to assess whether a change has in fact occurred.

Second, we actually experience the 'passage' of time whether there has been a change in the world-state or not. That is, temporal experience does not appear to require an awareness of a change in the world-state. For instance, Flaherty (1999) found that in situations of relative sensory-deprivation (the absence of observable change in the environment as in windowless, sound-proofed cells employed in certain kinds of solitary-confinement), subjects are still aware of the 'passage' of time. Indeed, in such situations they appear to focus on time's elapse such that time appears to 'pass more slowly' than usual, the phenomenon of protracted duration.

Third, our experience of time appears to be independent of the nature of the external events we are exposed to, i.e., how much change is occurring. Flaherty found that just as protracted duration results from states in which the stimulus array is impoverished (e.g., boredom), this particular temporal experience can also result from events which are extremely rich in sense-perceptory terms, as in a near-death experience such as a serious car-crash – a rapidly changing world-state – in which a number of events are experienced extremely vividly, and appear to be presented to the senses in 'slow-motion'. The point is that an experience of duration seems to be, at least in principle, unrelated to the degree or manner change in a particular world-state, again suggesting that an awareness of duration antecedes an awareness of change.

Fourth, at the neurological level, synchronous firing of neurons with the same frequency, bounded by a "silent" interval may account for the so-called binding problem[19] (e.g., Crick 1994; Crick & Koch 1990, 1998; Davies 1995; Dennett 1991; Edelman 1992; Engel, König & Scillen 1992; Engel, König, Kreiter, Schillen, & Singer 1992; Pöppel 1994; Stryker 1992; Varela et al. 1991). This evidence suggests that neurologically instantiated temporal codes which are durational in nature provide the basis for perceptual processing and hence our awareness of a change (or maintenance) of a particular world-state (Pöppel 1994). Accordingly, the experience of duration may be a more plausible antecedent for our concept of time than that of change.

Finally, etymological evidence from linguistics suggests that it is 'duration' which may constitute the historically earliest sense associated with the lexical item *time*. For instance, a Duration Sense appears to have been among the earliest of meaning components associated with the archaic Old English form *tide*, and with *time*. Moreover, the modern form *time* is etymologically related to the reconstructed Old Teutonic verb root **ti*, which describes processes constituting spatial analogues of duration (see Chapter 7).

Taken together these findings are suggestive that what is literal and inherent about our concept of time may not relate to an awareness of change in an external world-state but rather to the subjective experience of duration.

In the final analysis, Lakoff and Johnson appear to assume that time does not relate to a first-order subjective experience, but rather constitutes a second-order construct. That is, for them the experience that gives rise to time is not directly perceived. Rather, it is only ever experienced indirectly, by virtue of more basic kinds of experiences, such as motion events, in terms of which our experience of time is grounded. This position does not fit well with the primary metaphor approach they claim to support. After all, on their view, time cannot be related to the kind of basic phenomenological experience which can be correlated with other sorts of experiences giving rise to primary metaphors.

Grady's view: The mental-state-comparison hypothesis

Being the architect of the primary metaphor approach within CMT, Grady (e.g., 1997a) is sensitive to the position that time must, at base, relate to a subjective experience. Hence, for time to participate in primary metaphors it *must be* something in and of itself (contra the position adopted by Lakoff & Johnson). Accordingly, he posits that a subjective awareness of a change in our mental-state gives rise to our concept of time. Grady expresses this view as follows, "Even if nothing in our environment has changed, the difference between our exact mental state now versus the one we experienced a moment ago...might be enough of a cue for us to feel we have experienced the passage of a moment of time" (Ibid.: 121).

Although this move attempts to render temporal experience subjective by replacing an awareness of a change in an external world-state with internal mental-states, this approach still falls foul of the same criticisms as Lakoff and Johnson's hypothesis. After all, Grady is positing that time in its unelaborated form relates to an antecedent awareness of change, rather than change being underpinned by a logically and empirically more basic experience such as duration.

5.3.2 The problem of cultural constructs

An important claim associated with the primary metaphor approach to CMT is that the kinds of concepts associated in primary metaphors are relatively simple, relating to salient and universal experiences. That is, they cannot be concepts which are in any way culture-specific. The problem of cultural constructs results from the nature of the linguistic evidence metaphor scholars have provided in support of their position. In order to make this point explicit consider some examples that Grady (1997a: Ch. 4) provides in order to illustrate the Moving Time and Moving Ego metaphors:

> Moving Time

> (5.6) a. The holiday season passed quickly this year
>   b. My favorite part of the piece is coming up

> Moving Ego

> (5.7) a. We're getting close to the start of the school year
>   b. She is past her prime

Grady appears to be assuming that phrases such as *the holiday season, my favourite part of the piece, the start of the school year, her prime* etc. index the primary target concept time.

However, this begs the question as to what makes the primary target concept temporal. After all, sentences which reveal a similar pattern, in which a change in a world-state is elaborated in terms of Motion, as in (5.8) and (5.9), are treated as evidencing the primary metaphor CHANGE IS MOTION (and not one of the two variants of TIME IS MOTION):

> (5.8) a. We're heading for disaster
>   b. That species is moving towards extinction

> (5.9) a. Disaster is approaching
>   b. I can feel a headache coming

Without operationalising and thus distinguishing the concepts of time and change it is difficult to see what warrants the claim that examples such as those in (5.8) and (5.9) relate not to the Moving Time and Moving Ego mappings associated with time, but rather the metaphor CHANGE IS MOTION. After all, the occurrence of a headache, or the extinction of a species, both represent changes in the world-state, and on this basis are presumably no different in kind from sentences such as: *Christmas is getting closer.*

It appears then, that Grady is assuming that sentences such as (5.6) and (5.7) employ concepts which are inherently temporal. That is, lexical phrases such as e.g., *her prime*, or indeed *Christmas* make use of 'temporal' frames of experience such as 'ageing' and 'the calendar' respectively. If we allow that such frames relate to change which can be conventionally measured by virtue of certain iterative events, which serve as temporal 'yard-sticks', whereas concepts such as disaster are not understood with respect to frames of this kind, we might allow that sentences such as (5.6) and (5.7) do relate to temporality, while those in (5.8) and (5.9) do not.

While this appears to be what Grady is assuming, the difficulty for a theory of primary metaphor is that temporal domains such as CALENDRICAL SYSTEM and AGE-SYSTEM are culturally relative. For instance, what constitute a person's prime in one culture may differ in another, etc. Equally, the start of the (school) year is relative to the particular (academic) calendar adopted, etc. Clearly, relying on data such as (5.6) and (5.7) does not appear to index a primary target concept for time. Accordingly, we must justify on what grounds lexical expressions as diverse as: *the start of the school year, the holiday season, my favorite part of the piece, her prime,* etc. are all to be related to the primary concept of time. Indeed, as most (if not all) of these notions are arguably cultural constructs, then we must conclude, as we did with the concept Christmas, that these concepts cannot be universal, and hence are not primary concepts.

5.3.3 The problem of complex concepts

The final problem in claiming that the Moving Time and Moving Ego mappings constitute primary metaphors relates to the notion of concept complexity. In this section I will argue that the range of lexical forms which are assumed to relate to a primary target concept of time in fact relate to a number of distinct lexical concepts. That is, the concept time described by Grady (1997a) does not relate to a 'simple' experience, in the sense he intends.[20]

There are four lines of evidence for this: the issue of distinct meanings, the issue of mapping gaps, the issue of distinct patterns of elaboration and the issue of grammatical distinctions. For the sake of consistency, I will, in this section, largely restrict my discussion to the lexical concepts indexed by the lexeme *time.* Accordingly, if it can be shown that *time* relates to a complex category of temporal lexical concepts, then it follows that the range of lexical items employed to invoke the primary target concept time (e.g., *Christmas, her prime, the future,* etc.) relate to a diverse and possibly heterogeneous set of temporal lexical concepts, each with a distinct set of background frames/domains of experience.[21]

Distinct meanings
Consider the following sets of examples, which are based on the kinds of linguistic examples employed by conceptual metaphor scholars to support their claims:

(5.10) a. The time for action has arrived
        b. The time to start thinking about irreversible environmental decay
            is here   [Lakoff and Johnson][22]

(5.11) a. Time flies when you're having fun
        b. Time drags when you have nothing to do

(5.12) a. The young woman's time [=labour/child-birth] approached
        b. His time [=death]had come
        c. Arsenal saved face with an Ian Wright leveller five minutes from
            time   [BNC]

(5.13) a. [T]ime, of itself, and from its own nature, flows equably without
            relation to anything external   [Newton]
        b. Time flows on forever

In each of these sets of examples a different reading is obtained. In (5.10) a discrete temporal point or moment without reference to its duration is designated. In (5.10a) the moment designated relates to the point at which a particular agent should act. In (5.10b) the designated moment relates to the point at which environmental issues should be considered. The sentences in (5.11) provide a reading of 'magnitude of duration'. For instance, (5.11a) relates to the sensation that time proceeds 'more quickly' than normal – the duration while objectively constant, i.e., as measured by a clock, 'feels' as if it is less than it actually is. This constitutes the phenomenon of temporal compression (Flaherty 1999). The sentence in (5.11b) relates to the experience of time proceeding 'more slowly' than usual – the duration 'feels' as if it is more than it actually is. This relates to the phenomenon of protracted duration. In (5.12) the reading obtained is of an event. In (5.12a) the event relates to the onset of child-birth while in (5.12)b the event designated relates to death. The event in (5.12c) relates to the referee blowing the whistle signalling the end of a game of soccer. In the sentences in (5.13) *time* prompts for an entity which is infinite (5.13a); and hence eternal (5.13b). Thus, in (5.13) the reading relates to an entity which is unbounded in nature.

The different readings associated with the lexeme *time* suggest that there may be a range of distinct lexical concepts associated with this form. For instance, while the examples in (5.10) relate to a discrete 'temporal moment', the examples in (5.11) relate to the notion of 'magnitude of duration'. Clearly, a Temporal Moment is a distinct kind of lexical concept from that of Duration. Similarly, particular events such as the onset of child-birth and death, etc., are understood relative to particular frames of experience, such as an entire pregnancy or a human life-span, rather than other aspects of temporality (cf. the lexical concepts of Temporal Moment and Duration). Finally, the examples in (5.13) relate to an unbounded entity, or infinite elapse. Hence, the entity designated, which I will term the temporal Matrix, is all-encompassing, constituting the entity within which experience unfolds.[23] Accordingly, the examples in (5.10) through (5.13) appear to highlight four distinct sets of lexical concepts associated with the lexeme *time*: a Moment Sense (5.10), a Duration Sense (5.11), an Event Sense (5.12), and a Matrix Sense (5.13) respectively.[24] These lexical concepts are further developed in Chapters 7, 8, 10 and 11.

The evidence presented in the foregoing has begun to suggest that the lexeme *time* may relate to distinct sets of lexical concepts. If this finding is substantiated, then this clearly undermines the claim that there really is a single, relatively simple temporal concept which constitutes the primary target concept in these putative metaphoric mappings. Further evidence of this kind is presented below.

Mapping gaps
According to Grady (1997a, 1997b) the hallmark of primary metaphor is that there are no so-called 'gaps' in the mapping. As we saw earlier, we are able to conclude that THEORIES ARE BUILDINGS constitutes a compound, rather than a primary, metaphor, precisely because while conceptual structure relating to buildings can often be applied to the concept of theories, there are salient aspects associated with our conceptual representations of buildings such as tenants, rent and French windows which cannot be readily applied to theories. Recall the examples in (5.3) above.

However, there also appear to be gaps in the nature of the motion content which can be projected onto time, as Grady himself has observed. After all, in terms of Moving Time, the motion ascribed to temporal concepts relates to the horizontal axis rather than the vertical, as attested by the oddness of the example in (5.14):

(5.14)   ?Christmas is falling   (Grady)[25]

Although we could presumably find a way of interpreting this example, it is not a conventional way of conveying the 'passage' of time.

In terms of the Moving Ego mapping, on the face of it, the following might be taken as evidence that time can be structured in terms of Ego's motion along the vertical axis:

(5.15)   We're moving up to/on Christmas (fast)

However, an informal survey of native speakers reveals that in this context, the verb particle constructions *to move up on/to something*, are taken to mean 'to approach something on the horizontal axis', rather than the vertical. Moreover, this reflects the fact that as we approach an entity, such that it gets closer to us, it comes to distend a larger area of the retina (Gibson 1986). This causes the ocular experience of entities which are approaching, or which we are approaching, to appear to 'move up', in our visual field. That is, (5.15) relates to motion along the horizontal not the vertical axis. Moreover, if the Moving Ego could be elaborated in terms of the vertical axis, we would expect sentences such as (5.16) and (5.17) to be readily interpretable. As they are not we must conclude that like Moving Time, it appears not to be possible, in English at least, to elaborate Moving Ego in terms of the vertical axis.

(5.16)   ?We're above/below Christmas

(5.17)   ?We're just south of Christmas   (Grady)[26]

We might preserve a primary metaphor account, in spite of these mapping gaps, by suggesting that, for instance, only the horizontal axis is relevant for the Moving Time and Moving Ego mappings. However, if we are to take seriously Grady's admonition that there can be no mapping 'gaps' if we are to conclude that we have a primary metaphor, then a 'gap' of the kind in evidence here is problematic.

Failure to predict specific elaborations
The third issue relating to the problem of complex concepts concerns the failure to predict specific patterns of conceptual elaboration. That is, the two variants of the TIME IS MOTION metaphor (Moving Time and Moving Ego) fail to predict why certain temporal lexical concepts can be elaborated in terms of certain kinds of motion events, but not others.

To make this explicit, let's re-consider the temporal lexical concepts in (5.10) through (5.13). Let's first examine the Moment Sense in (5.10) and the Event Sense in (5.11). In semantic terms these lexical concepts appear to be related. After all the Moment Sense constitutes an event, albeit of a restricted kind, namely the occurrence of a temporal moment.[27] This relatedness is reflected in the elaboration patterns exhibited by these lexical concepts, both of which are elaborated in terms of deictic motion.[28] Other kinds of motion produce semantically anomalous readings for these senses, as illustrated in (5.18):

(5.18) ?The time for action has flown/spun/turned around/flowed
         (cf. The time for action has come/arrived/reached us, etc.)

Just as the Moment and Event Senses can only be elaborated by certain kinds of motion event, the Matrix Sense also appears to restrict what kind of motion event it can be elaborated in terms of. For instance, it cannot be elaborated in terms of deictic motion, as illustrated in (5.19):

(5.19) ?Time is flowing towards us   [Temporal Matrix reading]
         (cf. Time flows on forever)

While the sentence in (5.19) is not uninterpretable, and we could no doubt construct a plausible reading for it, it is not a conventional or readily understandable way of describing the ongoing and infinite nature of our temporal Matrix conception.

Equally, 'protracted duration' readings (recall the example in (5.11b) above), require elaboration in terms of lack of motion (e.g., *Time stood still*), or else if there is motion, the manner of motion must be slow (e.g., "*How the time drags!*"). If the motion concept relates to rapid motion then the sentence becomes semantically anomalous, as illustrated in (5.20):

(5.20) ?Time raced by   ['protracted duration' reading]
         (cf. *Time stood still*)

Notice however that the sentence in (5.20) is readily interpretable if a 'temporal compression' reading is assumed (recall the example in (5.11a)). This follows as 'temporal compression' appears to require elaboration in terms of rapid motion (e.g., "*Hasn't the time sped by!*"), stealthy motion (e.g., "*It felt as if the time had slipped by*") or barely perceptible motion (e.g., "*Where has all the time gone?*"). Motion events which relate to slow motion or stationariness produce a semantically anomalous reading as evidenced in (5.21):

(5.21) ?The time seemed to stand still   ['temporal' compression reading]
         (cf. The time seemed to go by in a flash)

Table 5.1. The elaboration of temporal lexical concepts in terms of motion events

Temporal lexical concept	Motion event	Examples
1. (Magnitude of) Duration:		
(i) 'protracted duration'	Slow motion	*drag, move slowly, etc.*
	Stationariness	*stand still, stop, freeze, etc.*
(ii) 'temporal compression'	Rapid motion	*move fast, fly, whizz, zoom, etc.*
	Imperceptible motion	*disappear, vanish, has gone, etc.*
2. Temporal Matrix	Non-terminal motion	*flow, move on, go on, etc.*
3/4. Temporal Moment/ Temporal Event	Deictic/terminal motion	*come, arrive, approach, get closer, move up on, etc.*

Having highlighted these differences in conceptual elaboration, we would expect a theory of conceptual projection to be able to explain why temporal lexical concepts exhibit such differential patterning. However, the primary metaphor approach within CMT fails to do exactly this. It has no way of predicting that certain mappings appear to be licensed and others are not. If we assume that the different kinds of elaboration are licensed by virtue of there being a range of distinct lexical concepts which are being structured, this would account for the patterns observed. This position is summarised in Table 5.1. However, such a position serves to support the view that time is not a relatively simple concept, and moreover, that it is elaborated in terms of a diverse range of motion events (rather than a single motion concept), further undermining the view that Moving Time and Moving Ego involve 'simple' primary concepts.

Grammatical distinctions

Now let's turn to the issue of grammatical distinctions. I argued in Chapter 4 that formal properties of language have conceptual significance. Indeed, a number of scholars have argued that grammatical organisation and structure has evolved (at least in part) in order to support the encoding and externalisation of thought (e.g., Jackendoff 1983, 1992, 2002; Lakoff 1987; Lakoff & Johnson 1980, 1999; Langacker 1987, 1991b, 1999; Talmy 2000; Tyler & Evans 2001b, 2003). Accordingly, we would expect that formal distinctions in the lexeme *time*, should such exist, may pattern along the lines adduced using semantic criteria. Moreover, as semantic distinctions are also held to reflect conceptual distinctions, formal distinctions may provide converging evidence for the view that the lexical item *time* is conventionally associated with a range of distinct temporal lexical concepts.

There is a two way grammatical distinction apparent in the sets of examples in (5.10) through (5.13). For instance, standard syntactic tests (see Chapter 6)

suggest that the instances of *time* in sentences (5.11) and (5.13) are mass nouns, while the instances of *time* in (5.10) and (5.12) are count nouns. Accordingly, the lexical concepts referenced by *time* in (5.10) and (5.12) are sufficiently distinct from those in (5.11) and (5.13) that they receive a divergent syntactic characterisation. However, the fact that the instances of *time* in (5.11) and (5.13) are both mass nouns does not entail that these instances refer to the same lexical concept. Similarly, the fact that the instances of time in (5.10) and (5.12) are count nouns does not mean that these refer to the same lexical concept, as we will see.

Let's first consider the Duration Sense (5.11) and the Matrix Sense in (5.13). Although these are both formally mass nouns – for example, they cannot be determined by the indefinite article – there is other grammatical evidence that they are distinct. For instance, the Matrix Sense also appears unable to undergo determination by the definite article, as evidenced by the ungrammaticality of (5.22):

(5.22)   *The time flows on forever

This contrasts with the Duration Sense which can be determined in this way:

(5.23)   a.   Last night at the fair, the time seemed to fly by

['temporal compression']

  b.   Last night while waiting in the doctor's surgery, the time just seemed to drag   ['protracted duration']

What is interesting about the examples in (5.23) is that they provide specific reference, and the use of the definite article appears to play an important role in this. A reason why the Matrix Sense may be incompatible with the definite article, then, is that the Matrix Sense is already specific. That is, there is only a single unique temporal Matrix, which is conceived as constituting the event which subsumes all others. For this reason, the application of the definite article would simply serve to individuate an entity which is already individuated by virtue of being unique. It may be for this reason, then, that the Matrix Sense is incompatible with the definite article.

Now let's consider the way in which the examples in (5.10) and (5.12) are formally distinct. While the Moment Sense in (5.10) appears to undergo determination, and can have both specific and non-specific reference (e.g., *The time has come for action*, vs. *A time will come when we'll have to act*), the Event Sense exemplified in (5.12) is unusual in that while it can be premodified by an attributive possessive pronoun or a genitive NP with possessive enclitic -'s, as in (5.24a–b), it cannot undergo determination by the definite or indefinite articles, as is clear from (5.24c–d):

(5.24)   a.   His time [=death], as they say, had come
         b.   The young woman's time had come
         c.   The goal was scored 3 minutes before/from *(a/the) time
         d.   The bar-tender rang the bell to signal/call *(a/the) time

Moreover, unlike the Moment Sense which has specific or non-specific reference, the Event Sense appears to always have specific reference. Hence, in view of the foregoing, it appears that there are, at the very least, plausible reasons for thinking that syntactic patterning does follow along the lines adduced by a lexical-semantic analysis. These lines of evidence, together with those developed above are strongly suggestive that Moving Time and Moving Ego relate to distinct temporal concepts, and so do not constitute primary metaphors.

5.4   Implications for the primary metaphor approach

The findings presented in this chapter have a number of serious consequences for CMT as it searches for the finite set of universal primary metaphors. These are considered below.

As has been demonstrated, there appears to be a mismatch between what CMT takes to be a concept and the semantic pole associated with lexical items, at least in so far as temporality is concerned. As it is widely assumed in cognitive linguistics that the semantic representation associated with a lexical item constitutes a species of conceptual structure, i.e., what I have been referring to as a lexical concept, there is a methodological difficulty inherent in employing lexical concepts to uncover more general primary concepts. This follows as the primary target concept time, as assumed by Grady, does not appear to correspond to any of the lexical concepts employed to invoke this concept. Clearly then, it is crucial for CMT to stipulate exactly how lexical concepts relate to primary concepts. If primary concepts are more schematic, for instance, than lexical concepts, an important issue concerns path of derivation. Are (what I am calling primary) lexical concepts, i.e., those lexical concepts that appear to be phenomenologically basic, derived from primary concepts (in the sense of Grady), or are primary concepts abstracted from across a number of primary lexical concepts? Hence, what is the nature of the conceptual structure associated with primary concepts? And, how is this distinct from lexical concepts? These are questions that future research in CMT might consider addressing.

Related to this, given that primary concepts are not the same as lexical concepts, how can lexical concepts (as evidenced by language) provide evidence for the existence and nature of more abstract primary concepts? That is, methodological justification is required for employing language as a key tool in uncovering a level of conceptual organisation which may not be directly revealed by language.

Moreover, primary metaphors are held to relate to distinct concepts, albeit in distinct domains, e.g., TIME and MOTION, rather than constituting a set of mappings relating two entire domains (as in earlier versions of CMT, e.g., Lakoff 1990, 1993; Lakoff & Johnson 1980). Given the position to be developed in detail in later chapters, that Moving Time and Moving Ego may constitute instances of compound rather than primary metaphor (see Chapter 17), we require linguistic (and other) evidence for suggesting that primary metaphors hold between distinct concepts (rather than entire domains).

Finally, CMT has traditionally valued generalisations which are as broad as possible, a point that has been made by a number of scholars (see Gibbs & Steen 1999). The problem with the level of generalisation at which metaphor scholars have assumed cross-domain mappings can be stated is that it may simply constitute a post-hoc analysis due to the analyst. While the linguistic facts do support the view that there is a primary metaphor which might be stated as TIME IS MOTION (subsuming the two variants posited by Grady), there is no reason that just because such a pattern can be adduced by the analyst, that it must, ipso facto, have psychological reality for the language user. That such an analysis is plausible does not mean that it constitutes the correct level of generalisation (or specificity). Indeed, as empirical experimentation has begun to reveal (e.g., Rice, Sandra, & Vanrespaille 1999), language users appear not to have access to such a metaphor in key areas of meaning-extension where metaphor scholars have often assumed this metaphor plays a key role. While the study by Rice et al. does not in itself deny that such a pattern may exist, we are clearly in need of further empirical investigation to test the claims made by CMT.[29]

5.5 Implications for the present study

There are two preliminary conclusions which emerge from the foregoing re-analysis of Moving Time and Moving Ego. First, these mappings may actually constitute complex models of temporality, rather than being relatively simple sets of cross-domain mappings between unitary concepts (i.e., primary metaphors). Second, the most revealing level of linguistic analysis may lie at the level of the lexical concept, rather than at a more schematic level of conceptual organisation. Indeed, it is intuitively appealing that a perhaps finite set of lexical concepts may in fact constitute the more complex Moving Time and Moving Ego mappings. Hence, an analysis of the range of lexical concepts associated with the lexeme *time* may provide a way of uncovering the conceptual system for time (in English). Moreover, the criteria developed in §5.3 may provide a means of identifying distinct lexical concepts. Accordingly, in Chapter 6, and building upon insights arising out of the PRINCIPLED POLYSEMY framework I have developed elsewhere with Andrea Tyler (e.g., Evans & Tyler 2004a, b; Tyler & Evans 2001b, 2003, to appear), I advance a framework for identifying distinct temporal lexical concepts. In Part II I apply this framework to the lexeme *time*. Also considered are the lexical concepts Present, Past and Future. This will allow us, in Part III, to show how the range of lexical concepts uncovered are integrated into two distinct and high complex cognitive models of temporality.

5.6 Conclusion

In this chapter I have presented evidence which suggests that Moving Time and Moving Ego, as treated in recent versions of CMT, may not constitute primary metaphors. There are three potential problems for adherents of such a position. These constitute what I termed: (i) the problem of unelaborated time, (ii) the problem of cultural concepts and (iii) the problem of complex concepts. In terms of the first problem, while metaphor theorists have assumed that what is literal and inherent about time relates to an awareness of change, a broad range of evidence suggests that the subjective experience of time may in fact ultimately relate to our experience of duration. The second problem relates to the temporal concepts employed in the linguistic examples used to support the primary metaphor position. The lexical concepts invoked appear to be cultural constructs, rather than deriving from universal experiences. The third problem is that of complex concepts. The difficulty for CMT here is that it is not at all clear that the linguistic examples employed do relate to a relatively simple phenomenological experience of time. Four lines of evidence were surveyed: (a) the issue of distinct meaning, (b) the issue of mapping gaps, (c) the issue of patterns of elaboration and (d) the issue of grammatical distinctions.

In terms of the present study, the findings presented have two important consequences. First, Moving Time and Moving Ego may actually constitute complex models of temporality, rather than being relatively simple sets of cross-domain mappings. Second, the most revealing level of linguistic analysis may lie at the level of the lexical concept, rather than at a more schematic level of conceptual organisation. Hence, it is to the notion of a temporal lexical concept that we now turn.

CHAPTER 6

A theory of word-meaning
Principled polysemy

The analysis of *time* in Part II of this book will employ the PRINCIPLED POL-YSEMY approach to lexical concepts which was originally developed in order to model prepositions (Evans & Tyler 2004a, b; Tyler & Evans 2001b, 2003, to appear). The purpose of this chapter is, both, to outline the main tenets of this approach, and to indicate how, in the light of the previous chapter, it will be extended and developed to account for the abstract noun *time*. The frame-work will then be employed to investigate the range of distinct lexical concepts for *time* presented in Part II. Principled polysemy is an approach which seeks to account for the meanings associated with words as not being absolute and fixed, but rather as being capable of changing over time. Hence, in this quali-fied sense lexical concepts are treated as being mutable and dynamic in nature. Word-meaning derives from the way in which words are used, which facili-tates new lexical concepts or SENSES[1] becoming associated with a particular form (meaning-extension). This process results in new senses becoming con-ventionalised, such that they achieve mental representation independent of the antecedent sense which motivated their occurrence. Hence, 'new' senses can, over time, and through use, come to be reanalysed as being no longer re-lated to the original sense. Principled polysemy captures this dynamic aspect of meaning-extension by recognising that not all the senses associated with a particular form are recognised by the language user as being related at the synchronic level.

The importance of understanding the nature of, and relation between, distinct word-senses, and the way in which new word-senses are derived, can-not be underestimated. As Heine (1997) has observed, developing a coherent model of semantic structure, and how this interfaces with conceptualisation is both a central and a controversial issue for linguistic theory. The position taken not only affects how we model the semantics of individual lexical items and the architecture of semantic memory (the 'mental lexicon'), but also the rest of our model of language. Tyler and Evans (2003) state the position as follows,

> The lexicon represents the pivotal interface between syntax, semantics and pragmatics; the representation of the semantic component of lexical items has crucial implications not only for a theory of word-meaning but also for a theory of sentence-level meaning construction. At stake are issues concerning the source of the information that is necessary in the interpretation of an utterance and the appropriate location of the productive (rule-governed) elements of the linguistic system. Such issues bear on the interaction between words and the human conceptual system. In addition, establishing the semantic content of the lexical representations directly impinges on the distinction between our conventionalized linguistic knowledge and encyclopedic, general world knowledge in the process of meaning-construction, which is to say, the traditional distinction between pragmatics and semantics.   (Ibid.: 2)

The main tenets of the principled polysemy approach can be summarised as follows. A form such as *time* has, at the synchronic level, a number of distinct lexical concepts or senses independently stored in semantic memory. These derive in a principled way from a historically earlier sense (or senses). At the synchronic level the distinct senses can be analysed as being related by virtue of a semantic network. The senses are organised with respect to a SANCTION-ING SENSE, which typically (although not inevitably) has parallels with the diachronically earliest sense. This Sanctioning Sense is taken as prototypical in that it constitutes the 'citation' sense that language users would be most likely to produce in response to the question "What does the word X mean?"[2] The distinct senses are the result of a dynamic process of meaning-extension, which is a function of language-use and the nature of socio-physical experience, as will be seen. Finally, language users do not inevitably recognise that all senses associated with a particular form are synchronically related (although they may be genetically i.e., historically related, e.g., Heine's 1997 notion of GENETIC POL-YSEMY). Hence, the more peripheral members in the semantic network may be stored as independent entries associated with a particular form (recall the discussion in Chapter 4). Relations between senses are modelled in terms of a radiating-lattice structure, a 'network' of senses (e.g., Lakoff 1987; Langacker 1987; Tyler & Evans 2003). This approach allows us to identify degrees of relatedness, with more peripheral members being less-related to the Sanctioning Sense than more central senses.

In terms of methodology the present chapter has three over-arching objectives: first, to provide a means of identifying the distinct senses instantiated in the semantic network for *time*; second, to provide a way of identifying the Sanctioning Sense lexicalised by *time*; and third, to describe the mechanism whereby distinct senses come to be derived from the historical antecedent of the Sanctioning Sense. In view of the principled polysemy approach it is likely that the distinct senses will be related to one another to varying degrees. While some of the senses may not, in synchronic terms, be closely related (or related at all) in the adult conceptual system, I hypothesise (based on historical evidence) that the paths of development to be adduced may approximate diachronic developments.

6.1 Traditional views of lexical structure

In order to situate the present approach, I begin with a presentation of traditional views of lexical structure. The lexicon as traditionally viewed constitutes the repository of the arbitrary and idiosyncratic, with all regularity and productivity associated with language taking place in the syntax (Bloomfield 1933). From this perspective "[t]he lexicon is like a prison – it contains only the lawless, and the only thing that its inmates have in common is lawlessness" (DiSciullo & Williams 1987:3). Hence, the lexicon is seen as constituting "a fixed point of reference, interacting with other components of grammar in a predictable and well-defined way" (Pustejovsky 1995:38). This traditional view is alive and well today, having been recently reasserted by Chomsky, "I understand the lexicon in a rather traditional sense: as a list of "exceptions", whatever does not follow from general principles" (1995:235). Indeed, as Tyler and I have previously observed, a consequence of this traditional position is that lexical organisation amounts to "a static set of word senses, tagged with features for syntactic, morphological and semantic information, ready to be inserted into syntactic frames with appropriately matching features" (Tyler & Evans 2001b:725).

More recently, however, it has been realised by a range of lexical-semanticists that the traditional view is simply incompatible with the linguistic facts (e.g., Brugman & Lakoff 1988; Evans & Tyler 2004a, b; Lakoff 1987; Pustejovsky 1995; Tyler & Evans 2001b, 2003). This follows as there are (at least) three ways in which the traditional view of lexical organisation fails to match-up with the behaviour of words. That is, the view of the lexicon as constituting a set of static words senses is incompatible with the "dynamic" nature of word-meaning as outlined below.

6.1.1 The 'distributed' nature of word-meaning

The first way in which the traditional view of the lexicon is inadequate relates to what has been termed the 'distributed' nature of word-meaning (Evans & Tyler 2004a, b). That is, the same word can be used in a diverse range of contexts, in which novel meanings are derived. This constitutes what I will call the issue of on-line meaning contruction (see Tyler & Evans 2001b) or following Sinha and Kuteva (1995) DISTRIBUTED SEMANTICS. That is, word-meaning is context-sensitive drawing upon encyclopaedic knowledge as well as inferencing strategies which relate to different aspects of conceptual structure, organisation and packaging (see Sweetser 1999 for discussion and examples).

For instance, that the sentence in (6.1) means something different from (6.2) is in part a consequence of the different contributions of the conventional range of meanings associated with *safe* and *happy*.

(6.1) John is safe

(6.2) John is happy

However, the range of meanings associated with utterances involving, for instance, *safe* are also, in part, a consequence of the range of novel contexts in which *safe* can be employed, and how these contexts can be integrated with the conventional range of senses associated with this lexical item, in keeping with inferences based and contingent upon real-world knowledge. For instance, in their discussion of the role of conceptual blending in semantic composition Fauconnier and Turner (2002: 25) provide the following examples:

(6.3) a.   The child is safe
       b.   The beach is safe
       c.   The shovel is safe

While one (common) interpretation of (6.3a) is that the child will not come to any harm, (6.3b) does not mean – at least from the perspective of a parent allowing their child to play in the location designated by *the beach* – that it (=the beach) will not come to harm, but rather that the beach constitutes an environment in which the risk of the child coming to harm is minimised. Similarly, again from the parent's perspective, a shovel is safe in so far as it is blunt and can be played with by the child (as when digging on the beach), without causing harm to the child. What the meanings of these utterances reveal is that there is no fixed property that *safe* assigns to the nominal elements *child*, *beach* and *shovel*. The meaning of *safe* interacts with the sentential and the non-linguistic context in a way which prompts for a particular facet of experience with respect to which *safe* (and the utterance) is meaningful. After all, with a different frame, e.g., one in which an application by property-developers to build on a hitherto unspoilt beach has been refused, the contribution of *safe* to the meaning of the utterance in (6.3b), for instance, will also change.

The point then is that a theory of lexical structure requires a motivated account of how word-meaning is integrated with sentential and non-linguistic context. That is, a theory of *distributed semantics* is required (see Sinha & Kuteva 1995), a theory which recognises that utterance meaning is the result of the integration of word senses in a way which is coherent with and contingent upon real-world knowledge. As such, utterance meaning does not reside in individual lexical items, but rather results from their interaction, which serves to prompt for integration at the conceptual level (see Tyler & Evans 2001b, 2003), guided by a range of inferencing strategies.

6.1.2 Polysemy

The second way in which the traditional view of the lexicon is inadequate relates to the phenomenon of polysemy. Under the traditional view, conventional word-meanings associated with many lexical items sharing the same form are unrelated to one another (a homonymy position). Contrary to this stance, I argue that lexical items do not act like static bundles of features, but rather evolve and change, such that new senses are derived from pre-existing senses. Hence, lexical-items are treated as constituting categories made up of distinct but related senses (Lakoff 1987; Taylor 1995; Tyler & Evans 2001b, 2003).

Influential studies such as Brugman and Lakoff (1988) and Lakoff (1987), which examined the English preposition *over,* have demonstrated that senses as diverse as 'above', e.g., *The picture is over the mantle,* 'covering', e.g., *The clouds are over the sun,* and 'completion', e.g., *The relationship is over,* are related to one another, and thus provide evidence that word-meaning is neither a static phenomenon, nor is a homonymy perspective always plausible. Just as word-meanings can 'change' in context by virtue of their differential interaction with other sentential elements, so the inventory of word-senses conventionally associated with a lexical item can change, with new word-senses evolving. Hence, a theory of lexical-organisation requires a motivated account of the experiential and conceptual factors that facilitate the derivation of new conventional senses, and thus an account of the nature and origin of polysemy.

Related to this are two further issues. The first concerns whether polysemous senses are computed from a single underlying abstract sense, as assumed by what Cuyckens and Zawada (2001) have termed SINGLE-MEANING approaches. Such approaches, which include Ruhl's (1989) monosemy framework and Pustejovsky's (1995) Generative approach treat linguistic polysemy as merely a 'surface' phenomenon (discussed below).

The second issue concerns fallacious reasoning in attributing all distinctions in language usage to distinct mental representations. That is, while accepting that lexical items are polysemous, we must still distinguish between meaning which derives from the interaction between words in context – namely UTTERANCE MEANING, which falls out from our theory of distributed semantics – and the contribution of words due to the range of conventional meanings associated with them, namely WORD-MEANING. In the following sentences, due to Lakoff (1987):

(6.4) a.   Sam climbed over the wall
       b.   The bird flew over the wall
       c.   Sam walked over the hill

we might suggest that *over* has three distinct polysemous senses, which is what Lakoff in fact argues. Under Lakoff's (1987) analysis, these senses involve presence of contact between the trajector (TR) – the motile entity, e.g., *Sam* – and the landmark (LM) – the locating entity, e.g., *the wall* – as in (6.4a) and (6.4c), or absence of contact as in (6.4b), and presence of a horizontally extended LM (as in (6.4c)) or absence of an extended LM (as in (6.4a) and (6.4b)). According to Lakoff, these differences result from three distinct senses being conventionally associated with *over*, an approach to polysemy which he labels FULL SPECIFICATION.

However, to claim, based on these sentences, that there are three distinct senses associated with *over* downplays the information supplied by the TR.NP and LM.NP and the 'distributed semantics' of the entire utterance. The fact that LMs such as hills are extended while walls are not, and that birds can fly and hence need not come into contact with walls, while people cannot and so often must have contact with the LM, is a consequence of the properties associated with the LMs *hill* and *wall*, and the TRs *bird* and *Sam*. When interpreting these TRs and LMs, and the relationship prompted by *over* in utterances in which TRs and LMs with these varying properties occur, the various, nuanced, interpretations of the relationships between the TR and LM arise from the distributed semantics of the utterance, which crucially draw on background knowledge, rather than being due to distinct senses of *over* being represented in the mental lexicon. As noted by Kreitzer (1997), the relation encoded by *over* in these sentences is unchanged. What does change is the precise metric properties of the TRs and LMs. I therefore reject Lakoff's 'full-specification' view, as this equates (spatial) meaning with highly specific interpretations which crucially include metric properties of TRs and LMs, rather than allowing sentential context, and the interaction and integration of the preposition with the lexemes with which it collocates, appropriate significance. Hence, a full specification view fails to take seriously the role of distributed semantics in utterance meaning, placing the burden of meaning-construction (primarily) at the level of the word.

To fail to appropriately distinguish between the equally important but differential roles of word-meaning and context in meaning construction has been termed the POLYSEMY FALLACY (Sandra 1998). That is, just because differences in word-meaning can, in principle, be accounted for by positing highly granular word-senses, it does not follow that all word-meaning must be accounted for in this way. Given the observation that words are often associated with distinct conventional meanings, it does not follow that every novel context in which a word can appear requires a distinct sense. A consequence of committing the polysemy fallacy is that rampant polysemy is posited, a consequence which has been criticised by a number of scholars (Kreitzer 1997; Sandra 1998; Tyler & Evans 2001b, 2003; Vandeloise 1990).

Developing a means of curbing the potentially unwarranted excesses attendant on committing the polysemy fallacy involves positing clear 'decision principles'. Such decision principles serve to identify when a particular usage of a lexical item constitutes a distinct conventionalised lexical concept, instantiated in semantic memory, and when it constitutes a context-derived meaning constructed on-line for local purposes of understanding. I present such criteria in §6.3 below.

In contrast to representing lexical meaning in terms of discrete feature bundles, I follow the model developed within cognitive linguistics of representing lexical categories in terms of a radiating lattice structure, a semantic network, arranged with respect to a primary or Sanctioning Sense.[3] A consequence of this position is that the Sanctioning Sense must also be methodologically motivated. In §6.3 I also present criteria which provide clear decision principles for determining what counts as the Sanctioning Sense in the semantic network associated with the lexeme *time*.

6.1.3 Grammatical considerations

The third way in which the traditional view of the lexicon is inadequate relates to the phenomenon of the part of speech of lexical items. Traditionally, lexical items have been viewed as being tagged with a range of lexical, semantic and syntactic features. Hence, a word such as *time* is tagged as belonging to the lexical class noun, while the word *in*, for instance, is tagged as belonging to the lexical class preposition. However, lexemes can also appear in a range of different syntactic configurations associated with other word classes. For example, the lexeme *in* can appear in configurations in which it is clearly not preposed with respect to a noun. This is illustrated by its adverbial usage in (6.5a) with the copula, and its usage as part of a verb particle construction (or phrasal verb) in (6.5b):

(6.5) a.   The sun is in
      b.   The sandcastle caved in

Due to its view of word-meaning as consisting of static sets of features, the traditional approach is forced to conclude that a difference in lexical class is evidence for distinct lexical items. However, such an account fails to recognise that the meanings associated with *in* in a prepositional use such as (6.6) and the usages in (6.5a) and (6.5b) appear to be strongly related.

(6.6)   The kitten is in the box

Moreover, the traditional view of the lexicon is tied to a view of syntax being totally divorced from meaning. I concur with the arguments put forward by Langacker (1987, 1991a, 1991b, 1999), which hold that a particular part of speech provides a means of profiling similar (or at least related) semantic content, and that selection of a particular part of speech signals a distinct construal of thing or relation. Under this view, syntax is represented as having conceptual (i.e., meaningful) significance. Hence, as suggested in Chapter 5, I will assume that the use of the lexeme *time*, in different syntactic configurations, is motivated by conceptual factors.

    In the foregoing I have argued that a traditional approach to lexical-structure fails to provide an adequate account of the way in which words in natural language appear to behave and how they appear to be organised. That is, a proper consideration of the nature of lexical structure reveals that the lexicon, far from being the repository of the arbitrary and idiosyncratic is systematically organised with utterance meaning and extensions to word-meaning (the phenomenon of polysemy), being highly motivated. I also suggested that in order to study phenomena such as lexical concepts and polysemy, decision principles are required for adducing the central and extended senses that instantiate a lexical category. That is, one's approach to the study of the lexicon must also be a motivated one, employing clearly articulated criteria for distinguishing between conventionalised senses and for establishing which sense in the semantic network is primary or central.

6.2 Alternative approaches to lexical concepts

In Chapter 5 I suggested that sentences of the following kind relate to four distinct lexical concepts conventionally associated with *time*:

(6.7) The time for a decision has come   [Moment Sense]

(6.8) Time flies when you're having fun   [Duration Sense]

(6.9) The young woman's time [=labour/child-birth] approached
                                                                           [Event Sense]

(6.10) Time flows on forever   [Matrix Sense]

In attempting to account for the four different meanings associated with *time* above, we could assume that while they do constitute distinct senses they are unrelated. This, in essence, constitutes the homonymy approach to word-meaning. The fact that *time* has four different meanings associated with it, is, on this view, simply a bizarre accident with each meaning being completely un-related to each other. This treatment of *time* would parallel forms such as *tattoo*, which has two distinct meanings associated with it due to historical accident. According to the OED, the oldest meaning of *tattoo* pertains to a drum-beat or buglecall which was a signal to soldiers to return to their quarters at the end of the day. However, in some Polynesian languages such as Tongan, Samoan and Tahitian, the form *'tatau* had a meaning of an elaborate ink design perma-nently made in the human skin. This meaning was brought back to England by Captain Cook after his first voyage to Polynesia of 1769, who transcribed the form as *tattow*. The modern use of the form *tattoo* to reference both a military march and a permanent skin design is thus completely accidental.

While the homonymy approach appears to be justified when accounting for the two distinct meanings associated with a word such as *tattoo*, it has a number of significant problems when attempting to account for the distinct meanings associated with a word such as *time*.

First, such an approach gives rise to the claim that it is merely an acci-dent that these four meanings happen to be prompted for by *time*. This would ignore any commonality among the usages, and moreover, would seem to con-tradict the impressive body of work which claims that lexical organisation is highly structured and motivated (e.g., Brugman & Lakoff 1988; Cuyckens &

Zawada 2001; Goldberg 1995; Jackendoff 1983, 1990, 1992, 1997; Lakoff 1987; Langacker 1987, 1991b; Levin 1993; Pustejovsky 1995; Sweetser 1990; Tyler & Evans 2001b, 2003).

Second, to conclude that these four meanings exhibit homonymy would be to adopt a rather narrow synchronic perspective, and in essence deny that word-meaning (and language more generally) constitutes an evolving system whose changes are motivated and principled, as revealed by the growing body of research on grammaticalization (e.g., Bybee et al. 1994; Fleischman 1982; Heine 1993, 1997; Hopper & Traugott 1993; Svorou 1994; Sweetser 1988, 1990). It is reasonable to assume that at one point at an earlier stage in the language, *time* had fewer distinct meanings associated with it. Hence, some of the meanings, which at the synchronic level are conventionally associated with *time*, must have, at one time, been novel usages. The homonymy approach begs the very question as to why forms such as *time* should have become conventionally associated with these newer distinct meanings, rather than a new phonological form being employed.

Third, the homonymy approach fails to consider the fact that communication is inherently purposeful, in the sense of Gumperz (1982). It is clear that a speaker would not use a particular lexical form in order to reference a particular meaning unless he or she felt that the hearer had a reasonable chance of interpreting what the speaker intended. In order for a particular lexical form to be used to signal a new meaning it is reasonable to assume that there must have been something about the conventional meaning associated with the form which suggested itself to the speaker, as opposed to another, in order to convey the desired meaning.

In view of the foregoing, it is clear that genuine historical accidents excepted, the homonymy position denies any systematicity in the relationships between the distinct meanings associated with a single lexical form. This position thereby denies the principled nature of language change, the purposeful nature of communication and meaning-extension, and so misses important generalisations. In view of this, it appears that the homonymy position is probably inadequate to account for the four different meanings associated with *time* in the sentences above.

A second position, the monosemy approach has been proposed by Ruhl (1989). This position states that a lexical form (e.g., *time*) is paired with a single highly abstract sense. This single monosemous meaning is abstract enough that any of the usages associated with the form could be derived from it. A particular reading is derived by the abstract meaning being filled in by contextual knowledge. On this view, the various meanings associated with *time* would simply be explained in terms of contextually derived variants of a single monosemous concept.

There are two significant problems with a monosemy approach. First, a number of the meanings associated with *time* are demonstrably context-independent. Thus, although a range of the distinct senses associated with *time* might in principle be derivable from a single underspecified meaning, contextual knowledge, whilst important, in some cases is insufficient in predicting the conventional meanings ordinarily derived. For instance, as some of the senses associated with *time* are so distinct (as we will see in Part II), it is difficult to see what an underlying abstract meaning might consist of in order that context could fill-in the requisite semantic specificity.

The foregoing leads to the second difficulty associated with the monosemy approach. In essence, the underlying meaning for *time* would have to be so abstract in order to be able to give rise to the complete set of meanings potentially associated with this form, that it is difficult to see how the meanings associated with other forms such as *past, present, future, existence, eternity, consciousness, change, occurrence*, etc., could be mutually distinguished. In short, while context is clearly important in meaning-construction and interpretation, at least some of the meanings associated with words must derive from particular lexical concepts being paired in semantic memory with particular lexical forms. Put another way, some of the meaning derived from a particular utterance must be associated with words, as must be the case in examples such as: *John ran up the stairs*, versus, *John ran down the stairs*, in which a different meaning results when a particular lexical item is switched, in this case *up* for *down*.

While the monosemy approach might be termed a single meaning approach (Cuyckens & Zawada 2001), there is another type of model distinct from monosemy which also constitutes such an approach. This is the generative or derivational approach of Pustejovsky (1995).

Like the work of Ruhl, Pustejovsky is concerned to posit an underspecified abstract representation from which situated usages can be generated. However, while Ruhl's theoretical motivation was due to what he saw as the over-arching importance of context in producing meaning, Pustejovsky is primarily motivated by the rationalism of the generative tradition in linguistics which values economy of representation and generality. Pustejovsky terms the underspecified representations associated with lexemes 'meta-entries', and argues that these are instantiated in semantic memory as highly abstract LEXICAL CONCEPTUAL PARADIGMS (LCPS). His approach is further distinct from Ruhl's in that he posits a series of 'generative devices' which facilitate 'semantic transformations' (Ibid.: 61). These devices operate on the underlying LCPs resulting in the contextually correct meaning associated with a particular word being derived.

Pustejovsky's generative approach, like monosemy, is flawed in a number of respects. First, this model can be criticised in terms of the reasoning employed to adduce the model. As observed by Croft (1998), the generative model of word-meaning – Croft uses the label derivational model – is motivated by theoretical dictates such as parsimony, elegance, simplicity, and the desire to eschew redundancy. That is, irrespective of psychological evidence as to the amount of granularity with respect to word-meaning stored in the mind, Pustejovsky assumes that the 'right' model of word-meaning will be one which includes minimal 'meta-entries' from which contextually rich meanings can be 'generated'. While in principle not implausible, simply because a plausible model of word-meaning can be adduced, which posits underspecified LCPS, does not mean that this is how language users actually structure or derive the semantic representations associated with words. Indeed, a range of psycholinguistic experiments (e.g., Cuyckens & Zawada 2001; Sandra & Rice 1995; Rice et al. 1999) suggest that language users actually represent considerably more detail, with respect to word-meaning, than is assumed by the generative model.

A second problem with Pustejovsky's approach is that while he posits a number of levels of representation in order to capture the semantic structure associated with 'concrete' lexemes such as *man*, or *book*, it is more difficult to see how such representations would adequately capture the semantic structure associated with nouns such as *time* which relate to subjective concepts. For instance, one of the levels of representation Pustejovsky posits is what he terms QUALIA. Qualia structure relates to "our basic understanding of an object or a relation in the world" (Ibid.: 85). Qualia roles includes notions such as the relation between an object and its constituents such as material, weight, etc., its orientation, shape and magnitude, the purpose and function of the object and issues involved in bringing the object into being, such as how it is created. While such considerations might plausibly relate to conceptual representations for physical objects, it is less clear how such might account for the semantics associated with a notion such as temporality.

The third difficulty associated with the generative model is that in generating a range of different senses from a single LCP, the levels and nature of semantic representation posited by Pustejovsky are not justified or argued for but are simply asserted as constituting the requisite levels of representation. Hence, it is unclear, beyond the stated aims of parsimony of representation, why Pustejovsky's model should be preferred over ones which take a different approach to the levels and nature of semantic representations, etc.

Finally, as with the monosemy approach, even if an underspecified characterisation of the LCP for *time* could be provided, by attempting to pare down the semantic information associated with *time* it becomes unclear how this lexeme and its various senses could be distinguished from other lexemes such as *now, duration, moment, epoch, period, hour, era, present, future, eternity*, etc. In short, such an approach may radically underestimate the complexity prompted for by lexical items.

The position to be advocated here is that words such as *time* in (6.7)–(6.10) are not represented in the mind as single abstract meanings, but rather they constitute a network of distinct but related lexical concepts. In other words, the position to be developed is a model of polysemy situated at the level of mental representation. This view suggests that the four meanings associated with lexical forms such as *time* constitute four distinct senses at the conceptual level (criteria for judging when a sense is distinct will be explicated), and are related to one another in principled and motivated ways.

While there is now some empirical evidence to support the view that the meanings associated with words participate in polysemous relationships, (i.e., distinct word-meanings are related at the conceptual level, Sandra & Rice 1995; Rice et al. 1999), and thus to reject the wholesale application of homonymy and the single-meaning approaches of Ruhl, and Pustejovsky, it is not at all clear that at the synchronic level all the distinct meanings associated with a particular form are related to one another in equal ways. That is, some meanings may be synchronically more or less or even unrelated, reflecting the view that once a particular sense has become conventionalised, i.e., entrenched in semantic memory, such a sense can be employed in contexts of use other than those which originally gave rise to it. New ways of using distinct senses instantiated in memory can begin to obscure the original motivation for the sense being associated with a particular form in the first place. Thus, this serves to make the relationship between the derived sense and the central sense opaque, resulting in certain senses being reanalysed by native speakers as no longer being related to other senses associated with the same form (Rice et al. 1999).[4] However, this is not to deny that a central lexical concept for *time* was not historically responsible for the range of distinct concepts in the synchronic semantic network. An important consequence of this principled polysemy approach is that the representation of new senses by a lexical form is a highly motivated process, which develops and extends pre-existing senses resulting in further senses being derived.

6.3 Meaning-extension as a principled process

In this section I address the issues that a principled theory of polysemy must account for. Criteria are adduced for distinguishing distinct lexical concepts, and for determining the central lexical concept which will be applied to *time* in Part II.

6.3.1 The modelling issue

This concerns how the synchronic polysemy exhibited by a particular lexeme should be modelled, in this case *time*. Following scholars such as Lakoff (1987), Taylor (1995) and Tyler and Evans (2003), and the results of psycholinguistic studies such as Rice et al. (1999) and Sandra and Rice (1995), I will assume that lexical items constitute lexical categories consisting of form-meaning pairings. The semantic pole of the form-meaning pairing I model in terms of a semantic network, organised with respect to a Sanctioning Sense. A Sanctioning Sense need not, in principle, be the same as the ORIGINATION SENSE (discussed below), as the Sanctioning Sense is hypothesised to constitute the synchronic sense which language users intuitively feel is the most representative meaning associated with a particular lexical item (discussed further below). However, as the historically earliest attested meaning may still play an active part in the synchronic network associated with the lexeme *time*, the Origination Sense and the Sanctioning Sense may overlap.

The intuition behind positing a Sanctioning Sense is that language users appear to intuitively categorise senses with respect to some lexical prototype. A word's semantic network, i.e., the range of conventional senses associated with it, can be modelled or organised with respect to the Sanctioning Sense. As I will diagram the semantic network for *time* as a radial-like structure (see Chapter 7), I will follow the practice of referring to semantic networks organised with respect to a Sanctioning Sense as a RADIAL CATEGORY (Lakoff 1987).

One advantage of modelling a lexical category in terms of a radial structure is that this facilitates understanding degrees of relatedness between senses, and accounts for the appearance of CHAINING within categories (see Lakoff 1987). That is, while some senses will appear to be more closely related to the Sanctioning Sense, other senses may appear to be more closely related to other derived senses. This pattern of clustering suggests possible paths of derivation (see Evans & Tyler 2004a; Tyler & Evans 2001b, 2003), and provides predictions that can be assessed against what is known about the diachronic development of word senses from the historical record.

In spite of the foregoing, I am not claiming that the Sanctioning Sense for *time* will necessarily be the same across a community of speakers. Patterns of entrenchment may vary from language user to language user.

6.3.2 The methodological issue: Determining distinct senses

This issue falls into two parts. The first concerns the problem of distinguishing between entrenched meanings (stored in long-term memory), and contextually-derived meanings. This problem results from attempting to distinguish between the conventional meaning associated with a word, i.e., word-meaning, and the way words interact in context, resulting in distributed or utterance meaning. The second concerns the problem of providing methodology to motivate the correct choice for the Sanctioning Sense. In this section I address the first of these.

One of the problems noted by Sandra and Rice (1995) is that there appear to be as many different approaches of how best to model a semantic network as there are semantic network theorists. While I accept that all linguistic analysis is to some extent subjective, I propose here to introduce methodology in order to minimise the subjective nature of the present analysis, and hence provide a motivated methodological approach for investigating the lexical polysemy associated with *time* in Part II. Until work by Tyler and Evans (2001b, 2003) such a methodology had been lacking in previous attempts to identify what counts as a distinct sense. However, that work addressed the lexical class of prepositions. In the present work I advance new criteria in order to deal with the (abstract) noun *time*.

I propose three criteria for determining whether a particular instance of *time* counts as a distinct sense. These were introduced informally in the previous chapter. First, for a sense to count as distinct it must contain additional meaning not apparent in any other senses associated with *time*. This constitutes the MEANING CRITERION. It is concerned with the assumption that as a lexical concept relates to the semantic pole of a lexical item (or expression), for a lexical concept to be distinct it must evidence a distinct meaning.

Second, the putatively distinct lexical concept will feature unique or highly distinct patterns of concept elaboration. This constitutes the CONCEPT ELABORATION CRITERION. This concerns the selectional or collocational restrictions which apply to the lexeme *time*. For instance, we observed in Chapter 5 that while the Matrix Sense can be elaborated in terms of the manner of motion described by *flow*, e.g., *Time flows on forever*, the Moment Sense cannot be, but rather is elaborated in terms of deictic motion, e.g., *The time for a decision is ap-*

Table 6.1. Test table for noun classes (after Quirk et al. 1985: 246)

	(1)	(2)	(3)	(2 + 3)
(a)	Sid	*book	furniture	brick
(b)	*the Sid	the book	the furniture	the brick
(c)	*a Sid	a book	*a furniture	a brick
(d)	*some Sid	*some book	some furniture	some brick
(e)	*Sids	books	*furnitures	bricks

proaching. Semantic collocational restrictions of this kind can be observed in, for instance, patterns of modification (e.g., *a short time*), in the predicate (e.g., *The time sped by*), or in the adverbial (e.g., *The time went by very quickly*). That is, and as we shall see in Part II, the use of *long* to modify *time* can only apply to the Duration Sense; the use of *sped by* in the predicate can only apply to the 'temporal compression' reading, as can *very quickly* as an adverbial element (cf. Croft's 2001 discussion of what he terms COLLOCATIONAL DEPENDENCIES).

Third, a distinct lexical concept may manifest unique or highly distinct structural dependencies. That is, it may occur in unique grammatical constructions. This constitutes the GRAMMATICAL CRITERION, and concerns the nature of the grammatical profile adopted by the nominal. In practice this concerns whether the nominal is a count noun, a mass noun, or a proper noun and also, what kinds of grammatical constructions it can appear in. Idealised grammatical properties associated with different classes of noun are given in Table 6.1 based on Quirk et al. (1985). For instance, the column identified as (1) relates to proper nouns; (2) relates to count nouns; (3) relates to mass nouns; and (2 + 3) relates to a hybrid category which can be either count or mass.

As we will see when we apply the Grammatical Criterion in Part II, *time* does not always neatly fit into any one of the categories identified in Table 6.1. For present purposes, the test table, provided in Table 6.1, is useful in that it will assist in highlighting distinctions in grammatical behaviour which may be indicative of distinct lexical concepts.

For a lexical concept to count as distinct, I hypothesise that it must satisfy the Meaning Criterion and at least one other. The reason for this is that it is, in principle at least, sufficient that a usage of *time* satisfy the Meaning Criterion for it to count as a distinct concept. However, in practice the meaning associated with lexemes can be interpreted in various ways given different contexts. Cruse (1986) has termed this CONTEXTUAL MODULATION. The application of at least one other criterion is meant to safeguard judgements of meaning distinctiveness (on the part of the analyst), from the undue influence of context in identifying a particular usage as a particular lexical concept. After all, I am attempting to establish the range of lexical concepts associated with *time* instantiated as distinct units in semantic memory, independent of context, in so far as this is possible.

In order to provide an initial demonstration of how these criteria apply, consider the following sentences:

(6.11)   The romance fizzled out of the relationship after only a short time

(6.12)   Looking back on the evening of their first date, it seemed to the couple that the time had flown by

In the sentence in (6.11) *time* designates a duration, in this case short, before the romance fizzles out of a particular relationship. In (6.12) *time* also references a duration, namely, a period of time spent by two people out for the evening on a first date. What is interesting is that although the interpretation of duration is elaborated in (6.11) in terms of physical length, in (6.12) it is elaborated in terms of motion (satisfying the Concept Elaboration Criterion for these two instances of *time* constituting distinct lexical concepts). Hence, although the Concept Elaboration Criterion has been satisfied, as both usages of *time* have approximately the same meaning, the Meaning Criterion has not been satisfied. From this we can conclude that they constitute two instances of the same sense.[5]

Now let us consider another usage of *time*:

(6.13)   Time flows on forever

In this sentence *time* designates an entity which 'flows on forever' and as such constitutes an unbounded entity which is therefore infinite in nature. This adds meaning not apparent in the examples in (6.11) and (6.12). As we have seen, in those examples *time* references an interval of (in principle) bounded duration. Hence, based on the first criterion, the sense indexed by *time* in (6.13) would seem to constitute a distinct sense.

But for a particular usage to index a distinct lexical concept, it must also meet one of either the second or third criteria. In terms of the second criterion it appears that this meaning component, which corresponds to what I identified in the previous chapter as the Matrix Sense, cannot be elaborated in terms of length content, as in (6.14), (compare the example in (6.11)), nor can it be elaborated in terms of rapid deictic motion, as in (6.15), (compare the example in (6.12):

(6.14)   ?Time flows for a short period   [Temporal Matrix reading]

(6.15)   ?Time has flown (rapidly) by   [Temporal Matrix reading]

In neither (6.14) nor (6.15) do the patterns of elaboration allow us to understand *time* as prompting for an entity which is infinite in nature. In other words, by altering the way in which the lexeme *time* in (6.13) is elaborated, we appear either to obtain an utterance which cannot be readily interpreted as the Matrix Sense, as in (6.14),[6] or else one which indexes a different lexical concept, for instance the 'temporal compression' reading in (6.15).

Hence, as the Meaning and Concept Elaboration Criteria are met, we can conclude that *time* in (6.13) indexes a distinct temporal lexical concept. This lexical concept I refer to as the Matrix Sense (see Chapter 11).

Taken together, application of the criteria presented above may preclude meanings which do constitute distinct senses from being included in the semantic network associated with a particular noun such as *time*. Ultimately, however, determining which meanings associated with particular forms constitute distinct senses remains an empirical question. Future psycholinguistic work in the vein of Sandra, Rice and their colleagues (e.g., Rice et al. 1999; Sandra & Rice 1995), will yield important insights into the way in which language users represent and relate distinct meaning components associated with a particular lexical form. Moreover, such work may reveal that some senses, legitimately instantiated in memory, have been excluded by the foregoing criteria. It may also transpire that while some language users derive certain meanings contextually, others may have already conventionalised these particular meaning components. Nonetheless, the advantage of the criteria proposed is that they offer a rigorous and relatively consistent (i.e., inter-subjective) methodology for assessing what constitutes a distinct sense. Given that prior to Tyler and Evans (2001b, 2003) such methodology had been largely absent from previous theoretical analyses of the polysemy exhibited by words, this approach, which extends those earlier insights to the nominal lexeme *time*, represents, I suggest, an important step in the right direction. These criteria, then, will form the basis of the lexical semantic analysis of *time*, which is the subject of much of Part II.

6.3.3 The methodological issue: Determining the Sanctioning Sense

Following my suggestions for adducing distinct senses associated with a semantic network, I also advance a set of criteria that provides a more principled, and hence motivated, method of determining the appropriate Sanctioning Sense for *time*. As with my criteria for determining distinct senses, I see this set of criteria as beginning to build a plausible methodology leading to replicability of findings in an inter-subjective way for this particular lexeme. Advanced experimentation may eventually prove the criteria inadequate; but for the present, I believe they provide an important move in the right direction. I hypothesise that some of these same criteria may also be useful for the analysis of other abstract and concrete nouns, and possibly for other lexical classes.

Following Evans and Tyler (2004a, b; Tyler & Evans 2001b, 2003) I suggest that there are two major types of evidence that can be used to narrow the arbitrariness of the selection of a Sanctioning Sense – linguistic and empirical. I suggest that no one piece of evidence is criterial but that when used together, a substantial body of evidence can be gathered. This CONVERGING EVIDENCE points to one lexical concept among the many distinct temporal lexical concepts constituting the Sanctioning Sense. I will here primarily focus on the linguistic evidence. Accordingly, I propose five criteria for establishing the Sanctioning Sense associated with *time*. The proposed criteria are as follows: (1) historically earliest attested meaning, (2) predominance in the semantic network, (3) predictability regarding other senses,[7] (4) a sense which has a plausible cognitive antecedent, and (5) a sense which relates to lived human experience, i.e., experience at the phenomenological level.

In terms of the first criterion, a likely candidate for the Sanctioning Sense constitutes the synchronic sense which most closely relates to the historically earliest attested sense. This follows as the first meaning to emerge is likely to have played some part in giving rise to the development of further meanings. Hence, the historically earliest sense has some claim to primariness.[8] In terms of the second criterion: predominance, I intend by this that the meaning component which is most predominant in the semantic network may assist in pinpointing which sense should be taken as the Sanctioning Sense.[9] The third criterion concerns the notion of predictability. Given my polysemy commitment (meaning extension is principled and motivated), and the assumption that language is a usage-based system (meaning-extensions derive from situated use as will be explicated, see Barlow & Kemmer 2000; Croft 2000; Traugott 1989; Hopper & Traugott 1993; Tomasello 2003; Tyler & Evans 2003), it follows that a likely candidate for the Sanctioning Sense will be one from which the other senses would most naturally be derived. That is, senses in the semantic network should, to varying degrees, be predictable based on the Sanctioning Sense. The fourth criterion concerns the notion of antecedent cognitive processing. As time relates to a subjective experience, and as work in cognitive and social psychology suggests that temporality relates to perceptual processing, a likely candidate for the Sanctioning Sense will be the meaning component which best matches a plausible antecedent temporal process/mechanism, e.g., the perceptual moment. Finally, the fifth criterion suggests that the synchronic lexical concept which best matches the lived experience of time will constitute the central lexical concept. In Chapter 7, I will argue that application of these criteria suggests that the Duration Sense constitutes the Sanctioning Sense.

In terms of empirical evidence, much more experimental testing along the lines of that done by Bietel, Gibbs, and Sanders (1997), Cuyckens, Sandra and Rice (1997), Gibbs and Matlock (1997), and Sandra and Rice (1995) should eventually provide evidence which would assist in assessing whether criteria of the kind adduced above provide an empirically accurate outcome.

6.3.4 The origination issue

Given that language change results in a proliferation of distinct senses, there must have been an ORIGINATION SENSE from which new or extended senses were first derived. A clear candidate for such a sense is the historically earliest sense (where such evidence exists).[10]

The Origination Issue is important if one is concerned with viewing polysemy as an outcome of motivated diachronic processes resulting in meaning-extension. Hence, the Origination Issue is primarily concerned with identifying which sense (or senses) may have motivated the development of the range of synchronic senses constituting a particular lexeme's semantic network.

However, as I have operationalised the notion of a semantic network primarily in synchronic terms, the Origination Sense associated with a particular lexical item may not necessarily coincide with the network's Sanctioning Sense. Accordingly, while the Origination Sense may provide important evidence for what might constitute the Sanctioning Sense, assuming that the Origination Sense has a synchronic equivalent, other criteria must also be employed (as suggested in the previous section).

6.3.5 The actuation issue

In Chapter 4 I suggested that ultimately meaning derives from our interaction with the environment. In order to be ecologically viable an organism (and indeed a species) must respond to its environment. Behavioural responses to regularities and patterns in the environment can become routinised, ultimately in terms of becoming biologically instantiated, as in the case of wake-sleep intervals for instance. This internalisation of responses to the environment affects how later responses to the environment proceed, in the sense that our interaction with the environment is hence forth embodied.

The fact that the nature of our experience is meaningful also represents an important impetus for the development of lexical concepts (i.e., word-meaning). The development of new meanings associated with words (the actuation issue), constitutes a complex interaction between the nature of experience and the way in which language is used, given that word-meaning is in large part determined by use. It has been previously recognised by language change theorists that lexical forms can develop new lexical concepts due to situated inferences or implicatures becoming conventionally associated with a particular lexical form (e.g., Bybee et al. 1994; Heine 1993, 1997; Hopper & Traugott 1993; Traugott 1989; Svorou 1994). These implicatures result from the nature of the world and the way in which we interact with it; in short, implicatures are contextually-derived meanings, which, through recurrence, can become conventionally associated with a particular lexical form associated with the context of use. Once an implicature has become conventionally associated with a particular form, this derived sense can be employed in contexts of use unrelated to the original context which gave rise to the implicature in the first place. Following Traugott (1989) and Hopper and Traugott (1993) I identify this process as PRAGMATIC STRENGTHENING.

In order to give an immediate concrete illustration of this process, consider the following examples:

(6.16)   a.   She is in the prison
          b.   She is a prisoner
          c.   She is in prison

The sentence in (6.16a) designates a scene in which the TR, *she*, is located in a particular bounded landmark, *the prison*. The express purpose of bounded landmarks of this kind is to restrict the freedom of the inmates. Hence, the state of being a prisoner, described in (6.16b) is tightly correlated in experience with being located within a particular kind of bounded landmark. Thus, it is the context itself (via inference and our knowledge of the real world), which provides the implicature of a particular state being associated with a particular bounded location. If an implicature is recurring, it can be reanalysed as distinct from the scene of which it is a part. Through continued use, this process may lead to the strengthening or conventionalisation of the implicature, resulting in its development as a distinct meaning component associated with the lexical form with which it is related, i.e., *in*.

As a consequence, *in* has, in addition to its 'containment' meaning in (6.16a), a conventional 'state' meaning associated with it. This is evidenced by (6.16c), where 'in prison', without the article, relates to a particular state, rather than a specific location. Indeed, *she* might be described as 'a prisoner' and as being 'in prison', even when working physically outside the confines of the prison on day-release, say.

Once instantiated in semantic memory this additional sense can be employed in new contexts of use unrelated to the context that originally gave rise to it. Thus, *in* has developed a conventionalised State Sense where the original spatial configuration which initially gave rise to the implicature is no longer required, as evidenced by examples of the following kind which employ an abstract landmark:

(6.17) a. We're in a state of war/emergency/holy matrimony/
            martial-law/anarchy
        b. She looked peaceful in death
        c. They're always getting in trouble

As the present study seeks to examine temporal lexical concepts, let's now consider an example relating to *time*. There is some evidence (discussed in Chapter 7) that the Duration Sense exemplified by the example in (6.18) may have been the historically earliest sense associated with *time*.

(6.18) My headache went after a short time

In order to illustrate the process of pragmatic strengthening we consider here how it might have given rise to further senses. The notion of pragmatic strengthening predicts that situated implicatures arising from experience can come to be conventionally associated with a particular lexeme as a new meaning component. This meaning component is then stored in semantic memory as a distinct sense. In order to illustrate this point, consider the following example in (6.19):

(6.19) Time is running out for those trapped beneath the earthquake rubble

In this sentence, given that a reading of a bounded interval is obtained in which survivors must be found, this usage of *time* prompts for the Duration Sense. Yet, in this particular context the Duration Sense gives rise to an implicature of finiteness. This is due to the fact that if a particular activity – the location and removal of the survivors – is not completed within a specified interval, then there will be non-trivial consequences, i.e., the death of any would-be survivors. While the implicature of finiteness is presumably a consequence of this specific context, the implicature may have given rise to the development of a new lexical concept, which in Chapter 14 I identify as the Commodity Sense.

An entity which is finite is accordingly valuable. Hence, in examples such as (6.19), as the amount of time – the interval – available for locating and retrieving survivors is finite, it is also extremely valuable, particularly as lives are at stake. Via pragmatic strengthening this implicature of value has, I suggest, been reanalysed as a distinct meaning component, which has come to be conventionally associated with the form *time*, and so instantiated in semantic memory. That a meaning of value is associated with *time*, independent of contexts of finite duration, is attested by the sentences such as in (6.20).

(6.20)   a.   My psychiatrist's time is so expensive!
         b.   Time is money. So start an Equitable 2000 Personal Pension Plan
              now   [The Sunday Times][11]

In these examples, *time* prompts for an entity which is inherently valuable. As such, *time* constitutes a commodity which can be bought and sold, as evidenced in sentences such as: *The advertisers bought more air time for their ads.* Clearly, this usage of *time*, and the attributes presupposed, provide meaning not apparent in the earlier example namely (6.19). After all, in (6.20), *time* prompts for an entity which is understood as inherently valuable (without requiring a context of finite duration in order to evoke such an understanding), and moreover, can be purchased, as is clear from the use of the term expensive in (6.20a). This suggests that the 'commodity' meaning does represent a sense distinct from the Duration Sense. Hence, a commodity interpretation, once instantiated in memory, is available to be used in contexts unrelated to the original situated use which gave rise to it. In this way, the Commodity Sense can be used absent a finite interval reading. This suggests that this may constitute a distinct lexical concept, instantiated in semantic memory.

   What is important to note from this discussion is that pragmatic strengthening serves to conventionalise implicatures which derive from salient aspects of contextualised experience. That is, recurring experiences form the basis of new senses becoming conventionally associated with a particular form. In the case of the Commodity Sense associated with *time*, the implicature of inherent value which becomes conventionalised arises from perceiving and experiencing some activities as correlating with a finite interval of duration, and moreover, successful completion is gauged by whether the activity is completed before the interval ends. In essence, experiential correlations often give rise to implicatures which are strengthened through use and ultimately conventionalised via pragmatic strengthening.[12]

   In arguing that pragmatic strengthening gives rise to 'new' lexical concepts, it is often the case there may be several plausible explanations for the derivation of new senses, which may reflect multiple paths of development. That is, the Commodity Sense may have derived from a number of different experiences, which reinforce the meaning component of value associated with *time*. For instance, since pre-industrial times the amount of payment in exchange for labour has been measured in terms of intervals such as the day, and later in terms of the hour with the advent of accurate mechanical clocks in the eighteenth century (Barnett 1998; Whitrow 1988). As amount of payment correlates with amount of time worked, this implicates that time is valuable. Accordingly, another way that the Commodity Sense may have arisen is due to the association of money on the one hand, with intervals of time spent at work on the other.

In addition, there may be a third possible explanation which may have given rise to, or reinforced, the development of the Commodity Sense. As the amount of time one has available correlates with achievement of one's goals, an implicature of value is associated with time. This follows as in order to achieve a particular goal, which is desirable, we require time in which to do so. Hence, a lack of time correlates with an inability to achieve objectives, while more time correlates with a greater opportunity for doing so.

As this discussion has illustrated, pragmatic strengthening serves to simultaneously associate new lexical concepts with lexical items (by extending the array of meanings instantiated in a particular semantic network), and enlarge the range of lexical concepts by adding, for instance, a concept of temporal value to the range of temporal concepts subsumed by the conceptual system. This illustrates that language represents a powerful means not only of prompting for meaning, but also of mediating the formation of new conventionalised meaning and hence conceptual structure.

Although the primary objective of Part II is to uncover the distinct lexical concepts for *time* in the synchronic system, by virtue of application of the various criteria adduced above, I will, in passing, consider plausible paths of derivation. However, such discussion is meant to be suggestive only, and would require serious historical research in order to be corroborated. Such a historical study is not my main concern in this book.

6.4 Principled polysemy

In terms of constructing a semantic network which accurately models synchronic lexical knowledge and organisation, the empirical work by Sandra and Rice (1995) suggests that it may not be the case that a particular lexical

form has a single Sanctioning Sense, by virtue of which language users categorise all other senses associated with a lexical item. Thus, their empirical work
raises questions concerning the view that we can define polysemy as a strictly
synchronic phenomenon in which there is a relationship, which speakers are
consciously aware of, holding between distinct senses of a particular lexical
form. This is an empirical question which we do not yet have sufficient evidence to address. If extensive experimental evidence shows that language users
systematically and consistently fail to perceive some senses as being related,
then we must call into question that what we are terming polysemy constitutes a phenomenon that is wholly synchronic in nature. While I believe all
the senses in a particular semantic network are diachronically related, in terms
of the adult lexicon there may be differences in the perceived relatedness between distinct sets of senses, due to routinisation and entrenchment obscuring
the original motivation for the derivation of senses from pre-existing senses
such as the Sanctioning Sense (see Rice et al. 1999, in particular). Hence, one
of the reasons I, and in previous work, Andrea Tyler and I, term our approach
'principled polysemy' is to reflect the view that, due to processes of language
change, not all senses associated with a particular phonological form may be
recognised by a language user as being synchronically related. That is, while
meaning extension is highly motivated, it may result in a semantic network,
which may appear, to the language user (and perhaps also the linguist), to be
only partially motivated.

Other reasons for using the term 'principled polysemy' include: (1) giving
an account of the relationship between diachrony and synchrony in a semantic network, i.e., the distinction between an origination sense vs. a sanctioning
sense, (2) accounting for semantic extension, the phenomenon of polysemy,
due to the interaction between lexical and semantic structure, contexts of use
and situated language use (pragmatic strengthening), (3) avoiding the polysemy fallacy by setting forth explicit criteria for determining distinct senses
versus contextual uses of a particular sense, and (4) providing explicit criteria
for determining the sanctioning sense, and elsewhere, (5) explicitly articulat-
ing the inferencing strategies and processes, etc., that give rise to the meaning
of novel uses of a lexeme in context (see Evans & Tyler 2004a, b; Tyler & Evans
2001b, 2003).

6.5 Conclusion

This chapter has proposed a theory of word-meaning termed principled poly-semy. The main tenets of this approach can be summarised as follows. A form such as *time* has, at the synchronic level, a number of distinct lexical concepts independently stored in semantic memory. These derive in a principled way from a historically earlier Origination Sense (or senses). At the synchronic level the distinct senses can be analysed as being related by virtue of a semantic network. The senses are organised with respect to a Sanctioning Sense, which typically (although not inevitably) has parallels with the diachronically earliest sense. The distinct senses are the result of a dynamic process of meaning-extension, which is a function of language-use, and the nature of socio-physical experience. Finally, language users do not inevitably recognise that all senses associated with a particular form are synchronically related. Hence, the more peripheral members in the semantic network may be stored as independent en-tries associated with a particular form. Relations between senses are modelled in terms of relative distance to the central Sanctioning Sense. This approach allows identification of degrees of relatedness, with more peripheral members being less-related to the Sanctioning Sense than more central senses.

A methodology is proposed for conducting a lexical-semantic analysis of *time*. This includes criteria for determining when a usage constitutes a dis-tinct sense and for establishing the Sanctioning Sense. Hence, the view which emerges is that a single lexical form such as *time* is associated with a large ar-ray or a semantic network of inter-related senses or lexical concepts – concepts stabilised in memory for the purposes of external representation via language. It is to the analysis of *time* that we now turn.

PART II

Concepts for time

CHAPTER 7

The Duration Sense

The purpose of this chapter is to present a lexical-semantic analysis of the lexical concept of Duration indexed by *time*. In particular, I claim that the Duration Sense constitutes the Sanctioning Sense for *time*. Accordingly, after presenting the Duration Sense in a little more detail than was possible earlier (§7.1), I present evidence for the Duration meaning as constituting a distinct sense (§7.2). I then apply the criteria for identifying the Sanctioning Sense (§7.3) developed in the previous chapter. Once I have established that the Duration Sense constitutes the central sense, I will adduce the conventional ways in which this lexical concept appears to be elaborated (§7.4 and §7.5). In addition, I will discuss some plausible experiential motivations for the pattern of elaboration uncovered. I then discuss two salient variants of this lexical concept, namely the 'protracted duration' and 'temporal compression' readings (§7.6). I consider how these variants are elaborated in terms of motion events in §7.7. Finally, as the Duration Sense is held to constitute the central sense in the semantic network, §7.8 briefly introduces the rest of network, by way of previewing the analysis to be presented in subsequent chapters.

More generally, if a plausible and internally coherent model of *time* can be adduced, based on the methodology in the previous chapter, the ensuing analysis will further validate the utility and insights regarding lexical and conceptual structure developed in Tyler and Evans (2001b, 2003, to appear; Evans & Tyler 2004a, b). As such, a consequence of the present analysis will be to further extend and support a more sophisticated understanding of the nature of conceptual structure and its relationship with word-meaning.

The findings presented in this and subsequent chapters are important in another respect. The main conclusion to emerge from this part of the book will be that a single lexical form such as the English *time*, and indeed other forms such as *present*, *past* and *future* (see Chapter 15), reference a range of identifiably distinct lexical concepts. The identification of these temporal concepts, including the distinctive ways in which they are elaborated, will form the basis, in Part III, for an understanding of more complex cognitive models of time, including how such cognitive models are constructed and integrated.

Figure 7.1. The Duration Sense for *time*: An interval relating two events, sequentially related to other intervals

7.1 Defining the Duration Sense

As I will define it, *time* in its Duration Sense prompts for a lexical concept which constitutes an interval bounded by two 'boundary' events, i.e., the beginning and ending of the interval. I will define duration as the INTERVAL holding or extending between the two boundary (beginning and ending) events. I will term the beginning event the ONSET, and the ending event the OFFSET. As an interval is defined in terms of an onset and an offset, it is entailed that an interval results from a before-after relation holding between two discrete events. Put another way, an interval of duration results from SUCCESSION. After all, if two events are not experienced as being successive we cannot experience duration (as will be explicated).

In order to make the foregoing more concrete consider Figure 7.1, which provides a diagrammatic representation of the Duration Sense. In Figure 7.1, the two boundary events are designated by the terms *onset* and *offset*. The onset refers to the beginning 'event', while the offset refers to the ending 'event'. An interval represents the relational component holding between the successive bounding events, which accordingly constitute a before-after ADJACENCY PAIR. As adjacency pairs (i.e., the temporally 'adjacent' constituents forming a before-after relation, such as an onset and offset, or two adjacent intervals) typically do not occur in isolation (each onset-offset pairing being adjacent to other such before-after pairs: an offset simultaneously constitutes the onset of the next interval), adjacency pairs can be construed as forming part of an EVENT SEQUENCE (i.e., a series of temporally contiguous adjacency pairs). Moreover, just as onsets and offsets constitute event sequences, so too do intervals, which are defined by such relations, constitute event-sequences. Hence, the notion of temporal succession can be analysed in terms of a two-way distinction between events corresponding with the boundary events which define intervals, and the successive intervals themselves. The dashed lines in Figure 7.1 represent other intervals in terms of which the highlighted interval (which is undashed) is profiled.

However, the notion of succession associated with the two levels of before-after adjacency pairs described above derives from the phenomenon of duration. That is, adjacency and thus succession results from a bounded interval (cf. the perceptual moment in the region of 3 seconds described in Chapter 2). As perception is a process which is on-going, so the adjacency pairs (bounding events and intervals) are related in terms of an on-going event-sequence.[1]

In order to give an immediate indication of in what way intervals (1) are co-extensive with particular states, activities or processes derived from external sensory experience, and (2) serve to unify this 'external' experience in terms of succession, i.e., an experiential event-sequence, let us consider our own basic unit of experience, the individual human lifespan.

The human lifespan represents an interval delimited by an onset, birth, and an offset, death. This interval can be construed as subsuming other intervals, for instance, as designated by beginning and completing primary or secondary school, matriculation at and graduation from university, and embarking on a career and retirement. These intervals can be further analysed as subsuming finer distinctions, in terms of the beginning and end of the year, or the academic term (or semester), or beginning work for a new employer and leaving for the next one. As events are perceived as being successive, they can be related in an almost infinite way and variety. At the level of a single 24 hour period, itself an interval designated by an onset of day and an offset of night and based upon a single revolution of the Earth upon its axis, we can construe events as being related at varying degrees of specificity. At one level, we might relate leaving for the office with returning home, and designate this interval 'the working day'. At another level we might relate the boarding and disembarking from the bus or train which takes us to work, and designate this interval 'the commute'. Even more fine-grained construals are possible, preparing and eating dinner, the start and end of a programme on television, listening to a piece of music, etc. Upon reflection it appears that many entities are in some sense temporal given that they profile certain kinds of intervals. Lexical items such as *concert*, *song*, *meeting*, *lunch*, etc., denote particular events or activities whose meaning is in part temporal, given that these events represent intervals. For instance, each of these experiences can be assigned a temporal value as in the sentence: *The meeting lasted for 2 hours.*

7.2 Evidence for the Duration Sense

Having considered how events are related by virtue of an interval holding between an onset and an offset, let us re-consider evidence for Duration Sense being prompted for linguistically by the form *time*. This usage of *time* is evidenced
in the following examples in which *time* prompts for intervals of certain kinds:

(7.1) a.   The relationship lasted a long/short time
        b.   It was some/a short/a long time ago that they met
        c.   [I]n the past, all that time that you were away from me, you really
             went on existing.   [Iris Murdoch][2]
        d.   During their ill-fated marriage they fought a lot/some/much of the
             time
        e.   The time of life is short; To spend that shortness basely were too
             long   [Shakespeare][3]
        f.   My face, during this time, can best be imagined as a study in strain
                                                                         [BNC][4]
        g.   He returned to Germany for good in 1857, moving for a time to
             Berlin   [BNC][5]

In each of these examples, *time* references an interval which is co-extensive
with a particular state or process. In (7.1a) the interval is co-extensive with, and
hence bounded by, a particular (romantic or marital) relationship. In (7.1b) the
interval is delimited by the period holding between the moment when friendship was first established and now. In (7.1c) the interval is delimited by the
period which two people spent apart from one another. In (7.1d) the interval
is co-extensive with, and thus bounded by, a failed marriage (i.e., the successive acts of getting married and subsequently divorced). In (7.1e) the interval
is co-extensive with a human life-span, and hence bounded by the successive
events of birth and death. In (7.1f) the interval is co-extensive with a particular event/experience which caused strain. In (7.1g) the interval corresponds
with the period in which the subject lived in Berlin. As *time,* in each of these
examples, prompts for a delimited interval (and given that an interval is constituted and thus defined in terms of the relation holding between two or more
successive events), these examples do correspond to the characterisation of the
Duration Sense given in Figure 7.1.

7.3 Duration as the Sanctioning Sense

I now consider Duration as the Sanctioning Sense associated with *time*. In Chapter 6 I provided five criteria comprising linguistic, cognitive and phenomenological tests for adducing the Sanctioning Sense for *time*. These included the criterion of earliest attested meaning, the criterion of predominance, the criterion of predictability, the criterion of cognitive antecedents, and the criterion of phenomenological experience. The reasons for thinking that the Duration Sense exemplified in (7.1) constitutes the Sanctioning Sense for *time* are compelling.

Let's first consider the criterion of earliest attested meaning. This states that the synchronic sense which most closely approximates the earliest attested meaning associated with *time* is likely to be the Sanctioning Sense. This follows as meaning-extension proceeds over time, deriving ultimately from what I have termed an Origination Sense. A clear candidate for such a sense is a lexeme's earliest attested sense. According to the OED a 'duration' sense represented the earliest attested meaning associated with *time*.[6] The form *time* is hypothesised to have derived from an earlier form *tî-mon*, comprised of a reconstructed verb root *tî*, 'to extend/stretch', and the suffix *mon*, denoting an abstract entity. Processes such as stretching or extending are temporally protracted and hence correlate with our experience of duration (in the sense defined). The fact that stretching or extending are necessarily bounded and thus delimit intervals follows from the fact that physical bodies can only stretch or extend so far. In this way, the processes of extending or stretching represent an interval between two events (the beginning and ending of the extending or stretching). The fact that the earliest attested meaning associated with the form *time* (the form *tide* was used in Old English)[7] is related to the notion of an interval, and that the etymology of *time* also relates to this notion, suggests, on the basis of the first criterion, that the synchronic Duration Sense, which roughly corresponds to the historically earliest attested sense associated with *time*, is a likely candidate for the Sanctioning Sense.

Turning now to the second criterion, this pertains to predominance. This suggests that the most likely candidate for the Sanctioning Sense is that meaning component which is most predominant in the semantic network. As the analysis proceeds it will become clear that the concept of Duration features in over half the distinct senses in the semantic network for *time*. This adds further weight to treating the sense exemplified in the examples in (7.1) as the Sanctioning Sense.

The third criterion suggests that the primary sense is likely to be that sense on the basis of which the other distinct senses can be most plausibly predicted. As I will argue during the course of subsequent chapters, the meaning associated with *time* pertaining to a Duration best meets this criterion.

The fourth criterion concerns cognitive antecedents. This criterion suggests that the temporal lexical concept most likely to constitute the Sanctioning Sense should have a plausible cognitive antecedent. In Chapter 2 I argued that perceptual processing may be underpinned by temporal processing, and specifically the phenomenon known as the perceptual moment. As was observed, perceptual moments exist at all levels of neurological activity with a durational span ranging from a fraction of a second to an outer limit of 2–3 seconds. Moreover, I argued that perceptual moments may serve an 'updating' function crucial to perceptual processing. As the sense lexicalised by *time* in the sentences in (7.1) designates an interval of duration, it therefore appears to be closely related to a cognitive antecedent of our experience of temporality. Accordingly, I suggest that the sense evident in (7.1) has a plausible cognitive temporal antecedent (to which we have conscious access, i.e., the awareness of a duration which corresponds to 'now'), and as such, on the basis of the fourth criterion constitutes a likely candidate for the Sanctioning Sense.

The fifth and final criterion suggests that the Sanctioning Sense is likely to be that sense which can be most closely related to our phenomenological experience of time. In terms of lived human experience it is our awareness of and ability to assess magnitude of duration which first and foremost allows us to distinguish past from present, and thus allows us to experience events as successive. Hence, succession is a consequence of our awareness of duration. Without such we would live within a straightjacket of an updated now continually replayed. As the Duration Sense relates most directly to this phenomenological experience, this is suggestive that it does indeed constitute a likely candidate for the Sanctioning Sense.

Before concluding this section it is important to note that the Sanctioning Sense relates to a specific lexical concept. In other words, the Sanctioning Sense does not relate to a more general concept of time (e.g., the common-place view discussed in Chapter 1). In Part III, I will argue that the common-place view of time, together with its variants such as Moving Time and Moving Ego (as opposed to particular lexical concepts, e.g., Duration which may give rise to it), constitutes a generalised cognitive model which is highly complex and elaborate. Hence, at this point, I am primarily concerned with identifying the distinct lexical concepts, of which the Sanctioning Sense is but one, that may contribute to this more complex cognitive model.

7.4 Elaboration in terms of physical length

One of the most salient ways in which the Duration Sense is elaborated concerns physical length, employing lexical concepts indexed by the forms *long* and *short*. Consider the following examples: as attested by examples such as the following:

(7.2) a. The relationship lasted a long time
       b. They had only been together a short time before he proposed

This leads to a consideration of why the Duration Sense should be elaborated in terms of physical length. As the unelaborated Duration Sense pertains to the phenomenological experience of time, derived ultimately from perceptual processing, we must reject any suggestion that the Duration Sense is elaborated in terms of length content *because* (in its unelaborated form) it is inherently linear in nature. After all, linearity is derived from external sensory experience and specifically, perceiving a relationship between contiguous spatial locations. That is, whatever it is that our experience of duration is, it cannot be spatial linearity. Hence, why should a language such as English elaborate the Sanctioning Sense for *time* in terms of horizontal extension?

I suggest that the elaboration of the Sanctioning Sense, the lexical concept of Duration, in terms of lexical concepts relating to length, e.g., *long*, *short*, etc., is motivated by a tight correlation in experience between the experience of duration, which constitutes an assessment of temporal quantity, and length. That is, the nature of the correlation provides a means of relating the notion Duration and lexical concepts pertaining to length at the conceptual level. However, while length can be horizontally, or vertically, extended, it is lexical concepts relating to horizontal, as opposed to vertical, extension which elaborate the Duration Sense. This follows as human interaction with the environment, particularly self-initiated locomotion, most saliently concerns the horizontal as opposed to the vertical spatial axis. After all, our self-locomotion is constrained by gravity such that we move across a landscape in a horizontally-extended way. This privileges horizontal, as opposed to vertical, extension. Hence, while there is tight correlation in experience between vertical elevation and quantity, which motivates expressions of the following kind: *The price of shares is currently high*, we do not employ forms such as *high* or *low*, *tall* or *small*, etc. in elaborating Duration. In the following, for instance, we do not conventionally employ the lexical concept *tall* and thereby understand that a particular journey lasted a significant period of time:

(7.3)   ?The journey lasted a tall time

The clearest examples of a tight correlation in experience between our experience of duration, and that of horizontal extension, come from the ubiquitous experience of the journeys we undertake on a daily basis. We describe journeys in terms of their *length*, which follows as a journey is measured in terms of distance. Distance constitutes an assessment of physical length and thus a quantification of length. A *long* journey constitutes a greater distance, while a *short* journey constitutes a journey of less distance to travel. Crucially, journey length correlates in an extremely tight way with our experience of duration. Longer journeys are typically experienced as lasting for a greater period of time, while shorter journeys are experienced as lasting for a lesser period of time. Correlations of this kind may give rise to an association at the conceptual level such that lexical concepts relating to Length come to be metaphorically mapped onto the lexical concept of Duration.

Evidence that this has occurred not only emerges from straightforward examples such as: *a long/short time*, but examples such as the following in which a journey can be construed either in terms of an assessment of distance, or in terms of an event which correlates with a particular interval of duration.

(7.4)   How long is the journey?

Hence, the question in (7.4) could either be a request for information about physical length, in which case the answer might be given in miles or kilometres, or the question might constitute a request for information about duration, in which case the answer might be specified in terms of hours. This ambiguity follows precisely because journeys do serve to correlate both distance and duration.

Before closing this discussion it is important to emphasise that it is the mechanism of experiential correlation, introduced in Chapter 4, which appears to facilitate the elaboration of the Duration Sense in terms of Length. However, we must be careful not to confuse this elaboration with what is inherent and literal about Duration. While Length comes to constitute (at least in part) the nature of this verbal concept, the inherent nature of Duration remains an assessment of temporal quantity.

7.5 Elaboration in terms of quality of experience

Another common way of elaborating the Duration Sense is in terms of the perceived quality of the experience. Consider some representative examples from
the British National Corpus in which the pre-modifiers *brilliant* and *mixed*
respectively elaborate the nominal *time*:

(7.5) a.   You'll have a brilliant time, it's such a laugh but you can't drink, that's
            the only thing, you can't drink inside   [BNC][8]
       b.   The rest of the Peachtree side have had a mixed time   [BNC][9]

In (7.5a) while *brilliant* relates to an interval which correlates with experiences
assessed as being of good quality, *mixed* relates to an interval which correlates
with experiences assessed as being of both good and bad quality. These elaborations, then, relate to assessments as to quality of the experience co-occurring
with a particular duration, rather than to the nature of the duration itself.

7.6 Temporal compression and protracted duration

In Chapter 2 I introduced the phenomena of 'temporal compression' and 'protracted duration'. Temporal compression is the phenomenon in which temporal experience is felt to be proceeding 'more quickly' than usual, while in
protracted duration it appears to be proceeding 'more slowly' than usual.[10] As
we have seen in Chapters 5 and 6, these phenomena are indexed by the lexeme
time, as evidenced by the following examples:

(7.6) Time flies (by) when you're having fun

(7.7) Time crawls (by) when you're bored

In addition to examples of this kind, in which they have non-specific reference, temporal compression and protracted duration can have specific reference, as evidenced by the acceptability of the definite article, in my dialect, in
contextualised uses of the following kind:

(7.8) Yesterday evening at the fair, the time seemed to fly by

(7.9) While I was waiting in the surgery for my doctor's appointment the time
       just seemed to crawl by

At this point it is worth briefly comparing and contrasting the formal behaviour of the 'temporal compression' and 'protracted duration' variants of

the Duration category with examples such as those given in (7.1). That is, the Duration category subsumes a distinction between a putatively normal versus abnormal experience of duration. Temporal compression and protracted duration relate to experiences of duration which are abnormal, in so far as they deviate from what Flaherty (1999) terms SYNCHRONICITY, the normal experience of duration (recall the discussion in Chapter 2). Moreover, while the use of *time* in examples such as: *The relationship lasted a long time,* relates to duration associated with a particular entity, namely the relationship which constitutes the 'subject' of the utterance, the 'temporal compression' and 'protracted duration' variants relate to a temporal entity in its own right, namely a kind of durational experience which is judged to be 'abnormal', or at least marked in some way.

On the face of it, formal criteria might suggest that examples such as *time* in: *The relationship lasted a long time,* constitutes a count noun. The rationale for this claim would be that it can be determined by an indefinite article: *a long time.* This would be at odds with the protracted duration and temporal compression variants which cannot be determined by an indefinite article, and hence, based on formal criteria, are mass nouns. However, another formal criterion for assessing whether a particular noun is mass or count relates to whether it can be pluralised. As the nominal *time,* in *The relationship lasted a long time,* cannot be pluralised, this suggests that it is in fact a mass noun. Indeed, I suggest that expressions such as *a long/short* serve as quantifying collocations. In other words, these expressions, like quantifiers such as *some,* serve to prompt for what Talmy (2000) terms a PORTION-EXCERPTING or BOUNDING operation.

I suggest a similar analysis for the example in (7.1g). Here the use of the indefinite article represents a quantifier, designating a relatively brief period, rather than referring to a unitary instantiation. Hence, on this account, the instances of *time* in (7.1), like those in (7.6) and (7.7) constitute mass nouns.

Interestingly however, the 'temporal compression' and 'protracted duration' variants do not appear to be capable of undergoing the portion-excerpting operation. That is, they cannot be preceded by quantifiers. Consider sentences such as the following:

(7.10)   a. *Some/a short time seems to have vanished

['temporal compression']

b. *Some/a short time seems to have whizzed by

(7.11)   a. *Some/a short time seems to have stood still

['protracted duration']

b. *Some/a short time seems to have dragged by

This may be the result of an incompatibility between the two distinct patterns of elaboration involved, namely between the elaboration of Duration in terms of length content on one hand, and lack of visibility, relative rapidity of motion, or stationariness, on the other. In other words, while the 'normal' experience of duration can be elaborated both in terms of length and motion, as attested by sentences of the following kind:

(7.12)   The relationship went on for a long time

the patterns of elaboration associated with the 'protracted duration' and 'temporal compression' variants preclude quantification, which would result in a portion-excerpting operation as they cannot be elaborated in terms of length.

7.7 Elaboration of temporal compression and protracted duration

Consider the examples in (7.13) and (7.14) which evidence the elaboration of the two variants of the Duration Sense:

'protracted duration'

(7.13)   a. Time stood still
          b. Time seemed to be passing/moving slowly
          c. The time dragged

'temporal compression'

(7.14)   a. Time whizzed/zoomed/flew/sailed/raced/dashed along
          b. Time sneaked/tiptoed by
          c. The time has vanished/disappeared

The conventional readings obtained from the sentences in (7.13) are of a duration which seems to be protracted. This reading of a 'protracted duration' is achieved by employing motion events in which motion is not apparent, as in (7.13a), or else motion is slow, as in the examples in (7.13b–c). The lexemes involved are *stand still, be moving slowly/move slowly, be passing/pass slowly* and *drag* respectively. In the examples in (7.13) on the other hand, the duration is compressed, such that time has 'gone by quickly', resulting in a reading of 'temporal compression'. The temporal compression reading is achieved by employing motion events which pertain to motion which is rapid, as in (7.14a), which involve barely-perceived motion as in (7.14b), or constitute the end-result of motion, resulting in the entity no longer being visible, as in the examples in (7.14c). The lexemes involved include the following: *whizz along, zoom along, fly along, sail along, race along, dash along, sneak, tiptoe, vanish, disappear.*

The question then is, why should these durational experiences be elaborated in terms of the range of motion events illustrated in (7.13) and (7.14)? The answer seems to bear on the observation that the density of conscious information processing correlates with the degree to which the stimulus array is being attended. For instance, in a near-death experience (a 'full' interval), or while waiting for an appointment with nothing to do (an 'empty' interval), more of the stimulus array is being consciously attended to, hence there is a greater awareness of situation and self. This, accordingly, gives rise to the experience of a protracted duration. Equally, in activities characterised by routine complexity, such as an uneventful and routine drive to work, we might arrive at the office and marvel that the journey seems to have 'gone by' in 'a flash'.

Similarly, this notion of the degree to which an entity is, or can be, attended to correlates with the nature and manner of motion. For instance, in a situation in which an entity moves very slowly past us, there is a correlation between lack of speed and an increased ability on the part of the experiencer to observe and hence attend to the details of the entity. Conversely, if the entity proceeds rapidly, or if the entity proceeds past the experiencer in a stealthy manner, there is a correlation between the nature or manner of the motion and the relative inability on the part of the experiencer to observe and hence attend to the entity. In other words, manner of motion correlates, in experiential terms, with our ability to attend to the details of the entity, or with our ability to perceive an entity's passage.

This suggests that the motivation for elaborating 'protracted duration' and 'temporal compression', in terms of the manner of motion phenomena in (7.13) and (7.14) respectively, is the experiential correlation between our relative ability to attend to details of objects depending on the nature or manner of the motion they are undergoing. For instance, the experience of protracted duration results from a greater attention to the perceptual stimulus array. This variant of the Duration Sense is elaborated in terms of motion which is slow or stationary, exactly the kind of motion which facilitates greater attention to the details of an object. Equally, the experience of temporal compression results from less attention to the perceptual stimulus array. This is elaborated in

terms of motion which is rapid, or else motion which is stealthy in nature, so
that it is scarcely perceptible, exactly the kind of motion which fails to facilitate
attention to the details of a particular object.

Hence, from this we can predict that not just any kind of motion event
can serve to elaborate specific temporal concepts, such as these two variants.
While the range of motion events provided in (7.13) and (7.14) are scarcely
comprehensive, there are clear constraints on what kind of motion event can
serve to elaborate these readings. The nature of the motion must relate to the
level of detail which can be observed in a passing object. For instance, consider
the following:

(7.15) a. ?The time appears to be flowing by
                         [Intended reading: protracted duration]
         b. ?The time feels as if its going/passing by
                         [Intended reading: protracted duration]
         c. ?The time has arrived   [Intended reading: protracted duration]

(7.16) a. ?The time has flowed by
                         [Intended reading: temporal compression]
         b. ?The time has gone/passed by
                         [Intended reading: temporal compression]
         c. ?The time has arrived   [Intended reading: temporal compression]

It is clear from the oddness of the examples in (7.15) that we cannot employ just
any kind of motion event in order to conventionally derive a 'protracted duration' reading, which is to say a durational interpretation. We need to employ
content which pertains to very slow or laboured motion, or else a lack of motion, e.g., *Time stood still.* The present analysis provides a level of detail which
complements conceptual metaphor style analyses (recall Chapter 5). After all, a
putative mapping such as TIME IS OBJECTS IN MOTION fails to predict that some
motion events can serve to provide 'protracted duration' readings, and others
cannot. By treating the 'protracted duration' reading as due to a specific lexical
concept, the Duration Sense, rather than a more generalised mapping, and by
positing that there is a more specific correlation than: time correlates with motion, but rather: speed of an object's motion past an experiencer correlates with
ability to observe details of the moving object, the present approach is able to
offer a revealing analysis of why the examples in (7.15) are anomalous in terms
of a 'protracted duration' reading.

Similarly, this perspective provides an elegant account of why the examples
in (7.16) are anomalous with respect to a 'temporal compression' reading. By
virtue of 'temporal compression' relating to a lack of attention to the percep-

tual stimulus array, and the correlation between rapid motion and the inability to attend to details of a particular object, we would expect that only motion events relating to rapid motion (as opposed to other kinds of motion) can be employed in order to elaborate this variant of the Duration Sense.

7.8 An overview of the semantic network

A number of distinct senses appear to be derived from the Sanctioning Sense. Accordingly, by way of previewing subsequent chapters I present in Figure 7.2 a diagrammatic overview of the semantic network for *time*. This illustrates that based on application of the criteria outlined in Chapter 6 there are 8 distinct senses prompted for by the form *time*. A sense is represented by a node. The putative degree of relatedness between distinct senses is represented by arrows relating particular senses. It is also intriguing to speculate that degree of relatedness may reflect diachronic path of derivation. Indeed, I will speculate on possible paths of derivation for each sense, based on both (albeit partial) historical evidence and plausibility, given the nature of the lexical concepts in question, and the historical context in which they may have emerged. However, verifying the nature of the relationships holding between various senses, and indeed verifying the proposed network, is ultimately both a historical and an empirical question which lies beyond the scope of the present work. Moreover,

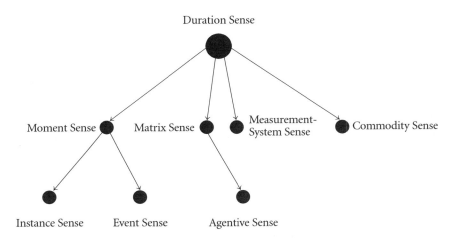

Figure 7.2. The semantic network for *time*

it is important to note that there may be more than one possible derivation for each distinct sense.

It is evident from Figure 7.2 that my claim is that not all the senses are directly related to the Sanctioning Sense. It may be possible, therefore, to provide a variety of plausible accounts for how a particular sense was derived given the nature of experience and historical evidence. Such multiplicity of explanations, (reflecting multiple paths of development), would not however undermine the basic approach nor the underlying assumptions of the present analysis. Rather, I suggest that it appropriately reflects the flexibility and utility of language as a symbolic instrument in assisting in the externalisation of thought and thus facilitating communication.

7.9 Conclusion

In this chapter I have argued that the Duration Sense constitutes the Sanctioning Sense for the semantic network of *time*. This assumes that a lexical item such as *time* constitutes a category of distinct but related lexical concepts, which native speakers can, and do, categorise with respect to a Sanctioning Sense. The Sanctioning Sense is held to constitute the lexical concept which language users take to be the core or primary meaning associated with the lexeme *time*. Five criteria were employed for determining that the Duration Sense constitutes the Sanctioning Sense. These were (i) the criterion of earliest attested meaning; (ii) the criterion of predominance; (iii) the criterion of predictability; (iv) the criterion of cognitive antecedents; and v) the criterion of phenomenological experience. I also considered conventional patterns in the elaboration of this distinct lexical concept including the way in which the two variants of the Duration Sense ('protracted duration' and 'temporal compression') are elaborated. I observed that patterns of concept elaboration, for the Duration Sense, appear to be motivated by experiential correlation.

CHAPTER 8

The Moment Sense

In this chapter I consider the Moment Sense and, present evidence that it constitutes a distinct lexical concept from the Duration Sense.

8.1 Evidence for the Moment Sense

The Moment Sense is evidenced by the examples in (8.1). Here *time* prompts for a conceptualisation of a discrete or punctual point or moment without reference to its duration:

(8.1) a. The time for a decision has arrived/come
       b. Doctors had warned that Daniel, five, of Sinfin, Derby, could die at any time   [BNC][1]
       c. His ambition, which was to drive him so hard in later life, resulted in his being made choirmaster by the time he was fourteen [BNC][2]
       d. What size was she at the time of change?   [BNC][3]
       e. What time is it?
       f. The UN has recently endorsed the principle that an international peace conference on Palestine might be useful at an appropriate time   [BNC][4]

Given my methodology, in order to be able to claim that the examples in (8.1) index a sense distinct from the Sanctioning Sense I have to be able to demonstrate at least two things: first, that these examples provide additional meaning not apparent in the Duration Sense (the Meaning Criterion), and second that the putative Moment Sense either has distinct patterns of concept elaboration with respect to the Duration Sense (the Concept Elaboration Criterion), or that it appears in distinct grammatical constructions (the Grammatical Criterion).

8.1.1 The Meaning Criterion

In the examples in (8.1), and unlike the Duration Sense, *time* does not prompt for a reading relating to an interval, but rather to a discrete point; in fact, a Duration reading is completely absent. Accordingly, in view of the Meaning Criterion, these instances of *time* would appear to bring additional meaning, suggesting that we are dealing with a lexical concept distinct from the Duration Sense.

8.1.2 The Concept Elaboration Criterion

In terms of the second criterion, which relates to concept elaboration, a Moment reading appears to be elaborated solely in terms of deictic motion: that is, motion which presupposes a particular deictic centre with respect to which the motion takes place. Moreover, the deictic centre often appears to coincide with the starting or ending point of the motion. The following example is both illustrative and typical:

(8.2) The time for a decision has come/arrived/gone/passed

In (8.2), unlike the motion associated with the Duration Sense (recall the elaboration of the 'temporal compression' and 'protracted duration' readings in Chapter 7), what is important is that motion occurs with respect to a salient deictic centre rather than the relative rapidity (or otherwise) of the motion event. For instance, it is with respect to a specific deictic centre that a temporal Moment can *come*, or *arrive*, or *pass*. That is, the deictic centre constitutes the locus of experience. Hence, by virtue of a temporal moment's fleeting co-location with this locus of experience (the 'experiencer'), the particular temporal moment is conceptualised as having occurred.

   The question which arises concerns why it appears so natural to elaborate this lexical concept in terms of deictic motion of the kind described above. As observed, a temporal moment is temporally discontinuous. As such, by virtue of being discrete, in the sense that it is punctual, it can be said to occur. For something to occur, it is often the case that motion is involved. For instance, in everyday experience, to reach a particular destination we must undergo motion in order to get there. Hence, the anticipated occurrence of arrival correlates with motion. Similarly, the anticipation of the arrival of an object correlates with its motion towards us. As we can only experience something occurring if we are coincident with the occurrence, then the motion which often corre-

The Moment Sense 125

lates with occurrences such as arrivals or departures is deictic in nature (see Moore 2000).

A whole range of occurrences are correlated with deictic motion in our everyday experience. For instance, we experience rain by virtue of clouds moving in the sky towards us. If objects hurtle towards us, e.g., stones, cars, etc., we know from experience that unless we move aside we will experience severe discomfort. This suggests that a new experience often results from the motion of objects towards us, and indeed our own motion towards particular objects and locations. In this way, occurrences are often the result of ego-directed motion, or self- or other-propelled motion towards a particular location/object. In either case, the motion is anchored to a particular ego, and hence deictic in nature. It may be due to this tight correlation in experience, in which deictic motion often results in new experiences, that occurrences such as temporally discontinuous moments are elaborated in terms of deictic motion, as evidenced by the examples in (8.1).

The view that it is the correlation between deictic motion and the occurrence of a new event which motivates the elaboration of the Moment Sense in terms of deictic motion, e.g., *arrive*, appears to be on the right track for the following reason. Sentences involving the Moment Sense appear to be semantically anomalous when elaborated in terms of motion concepts which are not deictic in nature. For instance, the intended readings are not appropriately conveyed in the following examples where the lack of deictic motion verbs and/or spatial particles fail to evoke a deictic centre towards which motion is directed:

(8.3) ?The time for a decision flies/stands still

[Intended reading: Moment Sense]

Based on the foregoing, as the Moment Sense appears to be elaborated in terms of motion events which are of a distinct kind, vis-à-vis the Duration Sense, then in view of the Concept Elaboration Criterion, this suggests that the Moment Sense does indeed constitute a distinct sense.

8.1.3 The Grammatical Criterion

Now let's consider the third criterion which relates to grammatical distinctiveness.

In grammatical terms, the elaboration of the Moment Sense in terms of motion is clearly distinct from the elaboration of the Duration Sense. While the latter is formally a mass noun, the Moment Sense constitutes a count noun, as evidenced by its ability to be determined by the indefinite article:

(8.4) Due to the volatile nature of the market, we left instructions to sell at an appropriate time

Hence, the three criteria considered strongly suggest that the Moment reading constitutes a distinct lexical concept.

8.2 The Moment Sense versus the Duration Sense

The distinction between the Duration and Moment Senses can be illustrated by considering some contextual variants of the Duration Sense. There is significant historical evidence that salient intervals were lexicalised by the forms *tide* or *time*. As observed in the previous chapter, *tide* was the Old English form of *time* and is now archaic. However, *tide* is still used in modern English with a meaning pertaining to the interval separating high and low water. *Tide* is also apparent in literature and poetry in particular, where it is used in conjunction with other expressions to refer to an interval of a particular kind, particularly religious festivals or periods in the year, e.g., *Christmas-tide, Easter-tide, June-tide, New-Year's tide, summer's tide*, etc. These have modern equivalents employing the form *time*, which include the following: *Christmas-time, term-time, spring-time, summer-time, night-time, morning-time, evening-time*, etc. Other intervals lexicalised by both *tide*, and later *time*, included an hour, and for *time*, a year, as attested by (8.5) and (8.6) respectively:

(8.5) a.   be foure & twenty tydes in day & in ðe nyɛt   [OED][5]
       b.   To knowe... euery tyme of the nyt by the sterres fixe   [OED][6]

(8.6) Of such numbers, the three times and a half, the 42 months, and the 1260 days, are mutually equivalent   [OED][7]

In modern English the lexical form *time* no longer has a conventional reading of an hour or a year. Yet, in the highly conventional expression: *What time is it?* we can still see the original motivation for using *time* (due to the earlier meaning of hour associated with *time*), which replaced the now archaic expressions: *What hour is it?* and: *What's o'clock?* It is interesting to observe that in other European languages the lexeme referencing 'hour' is still employed in parallel expressions, as in French: *Quelle heure* [=*hour*] *est-il?*; and German: *Um wieviel Uhr* [=*hour*] *ist es?*, rather than the forms: *le temps*, and *die Zeit*, respectively.

The foregoing notwithstanding, at the synchronic level *time* still does contextually prompt for a salient interval, namely 'an age', as is attested by the examples in (8.7):

(8.7) a.   It is one of the hallmarks of our time   [BNC][8]
       b.   Anne Frank lived in a time when the world was a dangerous place

The point then is that as the Duration Sense associated with *time* prompts for a Duration reading, salient intervals such as an hour, a year, and an age, have conventionally been or can be contextually lexicalised by the form *time*. The reason for this stems from the fact that as *time* lexicalises an interval co-extensive with a state or process, or holding between boundary events, other salient intervals have during the course of the development of the English language come to be lexicalised by the form *time*. The current practice of combining *time* with other salient intervals such as *dinner*, in *dinner-time*, and *Christmas*, as in *Christmas-time*, and indeed intervals characterised by a prevailing condition, e.g., *fun-time, down-time*,[9] etc., can be seen as being motivated by the same principle. In contrast, the Moment Sense relates to a discrete temporally discontinuous moment, without explicit reference to a particular interval of duration.

8.3 Deriving the Moment Sense

Let us now consider the specific issue of how the Moment Sense may have been derived from the historical antecedent of the Sanctioning Sense. The Moment Sense was lexicalised by both *tide* and *time* at a very early stage in the development of English, appearing well before many of the other senses evident in the semantic network (recall Figure 7.2). There are two plausible motivations for the development of this sense. The first relates to the phenomenon of TIME EMBEDDEDNESS.

Within social psychology time embeddedness describes "the fact that all social acts are temporally fitted inside of larger social acts" (Lewis & Weigert; cited in Flaherty 1999:86). Time embeddedness is a consequence of our social experience (in the sense of our interpersonal coordination and interaction) being temporally constructed. According to Flaherty, "Lewis and Weigert conclude that "modern industrialized and rationalized society can function only if most of its members follow a highly patterned and dependable daily round." There is, then, regimentation of temporal experience in accordance with the time of clocks and calendars" (Ibid.:98–99). As certain events are embedded within other events, intervals can be analysed as participating in other intervals. For instance, salient intervals such as hours are subsumed by another interval, namely the day.

In mediaeval Europe life was highly influenced and regulated by religion and religious practice and convention. Christianity was deeply entrenched in everyday life. In monasteries, the mediaeval seats of learning and education, the day was divided into seven hours, termed the CANONICAL HOURS. A bell would ring announcing the new hour – it is from the Latin word for bell, *cloca*, that the modern English term for a time-reckoning device, *clock*, has derived. Each canonical hour corresponded with a different activity, and began with prayer, each hour having its own particular prayer (Barnett 1998).[10] This division of the day represented a highly regulated and conventionalised means of stipulating the nature of the activity to be engaged in, and an instance of time embeddedness.

It is highly plausible that due to time embeddedness of this kind, in which certain intervals were embedded within others, the embedded intervals came to be reanalysed as subsumed by the greater interval, in this case the day, without reference to their duration. Such a reanalysis, as in the case of the canonical hours, would have been strengthened by a discrete signal such as a bell chiming. As an hour was already lexicalised by the term *tide/time* in English, then a reanalysis of hours as discrete 'points' within an interval, i.e., a day, would have facilitated the use of the lexeme *time* to implicate a point without reference to its duration.

Indeed, there is some evidence that the Moment Sense associated with *time* derived from time-embeddedness within a religious context. From an early stage in the development of the language it is clear that the now archaic *tide* was used to denote religious festivals and services (e.g., *Allhallowtide, Christtide, Eastertide, Lammas-tide, Shrovetide, Whitsuntide*, etc.), and even for those occasions which were short in duration, (e.g., saints' days, festivals which lasted for one day a year: *St. Andrew's tide, St. Botulf's tide*, etc.). There is evidence that in Old English *tide* also came to be used to denote discrete 'points' in the day such as *noon-tide*. Clearly, the use of *tide* to lexicalise noon, which cannot be construed as an interval, suggests that the reanalysis of *tide* from prompting for a Duration reading, to that of the Moment Sense, must have taken place. It is only once *tide/time* had developed a conventional Moment meaning that other non-durational divisions (e.g., noon) of a particular interval such as a day could be lexicalised by *tide* and *time*.

The process whereby a contextually-situated implicature becomes conventionally associated with a particular lexical form, in this case *time*, I referred to in Chapter 6 as pragmatic strengthening. Due to the use of *time*, in these contexts, to reference embedded intervals within a larger interval, *time* may have come to implicate points within a larger interval without reference to their inherent duration. Due to continued use of first *tide* and later *time* in this way, I suggest that this implicature came to be strengthened, i.e., conventionally in-stantiated in memory, such that the Moment Sense became a distinct lexical concept associated with the form *time*.

I noted above that there may be two motivations for the derivation of the Moment Sense. Having dealt with the first, time embeddedness, I will now examine the second. This concerns the notion of temporal compression. Al-though temporal compression can occur when a particular stimulus array is not being attended to (recall Chapter 2), Flaherty (1999) observes that tem-poral compression most often emerges in retrospect, where past intervals ap-pear to be relatively devoid of activity, in retrospect, and thus to be contracted (Flaherty 1999; cf. Pöppel 1994). Temporal compression of this kind is attested by examples such as (8.8), which evidence the temporal compression of past experience:

(8.8) a.   Looking back, my youth seems to have whizzed by
        b.   Where did all that time[=past] go?
        c.   The term/semester has sped by

Flaherty suggests that one explanation for temporal compression is due to the erosion of episodic memory. Unlike semantic memory (knowledge) or proce-dural memory (motor-sensory patterns), episodic memory (the recollection of events) is particularly prone to deterioration. Accordingly, as the experience of duration correlates with the quantity of memory taken up (Ornstein [1969] 1997), the deterioration of episodic memory results in the contraction of past temporal experience, and hence the sensation of temporal compression. Ac-cording to Flaherty this is the reason that the past appears to have gone by ever more quickly the older we get.

From the perspective of the Moment Sense, past intervals held in mem-ory may, due to the erosion of episodic memory, lose their durational signif-icance, and accordingly become 'point-like'. Hence, the use of *time* to refer to past intervals may implicate a Moment Reading. This is illustrated in (8.9):

(8.9) I wasn't a particularly happy person at the time; lonely, in a rather dead-end job and with few personal relationships   [BNC][11]

In this example *time* prompts for an interval. While it was presumably full of activity, in retrospect it implicates a particular point in the speaker's life. In such examples, through pragmatic strengthening the implicature may have become conventionally associated with the form *time*, giving rise to the Moment Sense.

While both time embeddedness and temporal compression are likely to have played some role in the conventionalisation of the Moment Sense, it is worth reiterating that it is only by virtue of the Moment Sense being instantiated in memory that the examples in (8.1) occur. In each of these examples *time* prompts for a reading of a discrete moment without reference to its duration. That is, once the Moment Sense had been conventionalised, it could be applied to contexts of use independent of an interval of duration.

8.4 Conclusion

In this chapter I have presented evidence for a Moment reading associated with *time* constituting a distinct lexical concept. In so doing, I applied three criteria introduced in Chapter 6. These constitute the Meaning Criterion, the Concept Elaboration Criterion and the Grammatical Criterion. In terms of concept elaboration, it was found that the Moment Sense is elaborated in terms of motion events oriented with respect to a deictic centre. Moreover, the deictic centre often appears to constitute the terminal point in the motion trajectory. In grammatical terms, the Moment Sense is a count noun. This presumably reflects the fact that temporal moments can be enumerated.

Chapter 9

The Instance Sense

This chapter considers evidence for a distinct Instance Sense. In this lexical concept, *time* prompts for a reading in which an instance of a particular event, activity, process or state is being referenced, rather than an interval as in the Duration Sense, or a discrete temporal point (embedded within an interval), as in the Moment Sense. Moreover, as it is an instance which is being referenced, it can be enumerated.

9.1 Evidence for the Instance Sense

Consider the following examples which evidence an 'instance' usage.

(9.1) a. Devine improved for the fourth time this winter when he reached 64.40 metres at a meeting in Melbourne   [BNC][1]
     b. This time, it was a bit more serious because I got a registered letter [BNC][2]
     c. He did it 50 times in a row
     d. Once it was clear that the room could not be held, he would order its evacuation, men leaving two at a time by the far window [BNC][3]
     e. They bought the Cashmere scarves at £50 a time

Lines of evidence for these examples constituting a distinct Instance Sense are considered below.

9.1.1 The Meaning Criterion

In each of the sentences in (9.1) *time* references a particular instance (i.e., occurrence) of an event or activity, rather than an interval or a moment. For example, in (9.1a), if we attempt to construct a Moment reading for *time*, we find that *time* does not mean, for instance, that Devine improved for a fourth consecutive moment, or that he improved on the fourth moment of trying. In terms of a possible Duration reading, *time* does not mean that the improvement lasted for a period of four moments. Rather, it means that there were four distinct instances of improvement, each instance representing an improvement on a previous improvement. Clearly, this adds meaning not apparent in the two senses thus far considered. So, in view of the first criterion for identifying distinct senses, the Meaning Criterion, the Instance reading would appear to relate to a distinct lexical concept.

9.1.2 The Concept Elaboration Criterion

However, for a particular reading to count as a distinct lexical concept it must also satisfy either the Concept Elaboration Criterion or the Grammatical Criterion. Due to the semantics associated with this lexical concept: it relates to an entity which constitutes an instance of something else, the 'instance' reading has little in the way of distinctive content ascribed to it. Hence, there are no salient or striking patterns of concept elaboration specifically associated with this lexical concept. Consequently, in so far as it appears that this lexical concept cannot be elaborated in terms of some of the more striking content ascribed to previously considered lexical concepts, the Instance reading appears, based on the second criterion, to relate to a distinct lexical concept. After all, the Instance Sense cannot be elaborated in terms of Length, or in terms of various kinds of motion events, unlike, for instance, the Duration Sense and the Moment Sense.

9.1.3 The Grammatical Criterion

In terms of the third criterion, which relates to grammatical patterning, the Instance Sense is highly distinctive. Like the Moment Sense, the Instance Sense is formalised as a count noun. However, unlike the Moment Sense (and the Duration Sense), the Instance Sense can be pre-modified by both ordinal numbers (9.1a) and cardinal numbers (9.1c). This follows as the Instance Sense relates to distinct occurrences of the same or similar kind of event or activity, and hence is iterative. This contrasts with temporal 'moments' and 'intervals' which are unique instances of temporal substrate, and hence are unlikely to be modified in this way. Thus, the Grammatical Criterion provides further evidence that the Instance reading does constitute a distinct lexical concept.

9.2 Derivation of the Instance Sense

It is likely that the Instance Sense derived from an antecedent of the Moment Sense. Indeed, the Moment and Instance Senses are hypothesised to be closely related synchronically (recall Figure 7.2). The Instance Sense appears early in the historical development of the language, and, along with the Duration Sense, the Moment Sense and the Event Sense (to be discussed in the next chapter), is, according to the historical evidence, one of the few senses in the synchronic network for *time* to have been lexicalised by the archaic *tide*.

A plausible motivation for the derivation of the Instance Sense relates to the fact that the various intervals embedded within larger intervals such as a day and a year were enumerable. For instance, in the previous chapter I observed that in the middle ages a day was divided into the seven canonical hours. Given that each of these divisions came to be analysed as a distinct point embedded within an interval, these divisions are themselves instances of the division of the day. That is, they constitute particular instances, which can be enumerated, by virtue of not being unique. Similarly, as months of the year are particular instances of divisions in the year, then the practice of suffixing the name of the month with *tide* in Old English, may have given rise to the implicature that each month was a particular instance of a certain kind of activity, namely dividing up the year. Hence, each month constitutes a particular instance of a division. This implicature, through pragmatic strengthening may have become reanalysed as distinct from the particular contexts in which it occurred, and thus has become conventionally associated with *time* in semantic memory.

The following example illustrates this point:

(9.2)   Now above all times, she felt, was not the time to push her luck [BNC][4]

In the sentence in (9.2) both instances of *time* prompt for the Moment Sense. This is clear as the sentence begins with the lexeme *now*, which references a particular temporal moment, rather than an instance of a particular activity or event as in the Instance Sense. However, the Instance Sense is implicated through enumeration. That is, as a number of different moments are referenced, as attested by the pluralisation of the first instance of *time*, each temporal point is construed as being an instance of a similar event, namely a temporal moment. Once pragmatic strengthening has conventionalised this notion of an instance associated with *time*, it can be applied to any kind of event or activity, not simply the enumeration of temporal moments. This is evidenced in the examples in (9.1) in which a diverse range of activities can be enumerated by virtue of the Instance Sense being instantiated in semantic memory. These

range from the instance or occurrence of an improved sporting performance in
(9.1a), to the occurrence of a business transaction involving cashmere scarves
in (9.1e).

9.3 Conclusion

This chapter has considered evidence for a distinct Instance Sense associated
with the lexeme *time*. A particularly noteworthy finding is that this particular
lexical concept appears not to have conventional patterns of conceptual imagery (concept elaboration) associated with it. I suggested that this may follow as an instance is precisely that, an instance (of something else). Hence,
instances only have structure in so far as they are tokens of other types of
experience, and have no inherent structure beyond the experiences they are
instances of. However, this feature serves to distinguish the Instance Sense
from other lexical concepts associated with *time*, and presumably reflects a
fundamental cognitive ability to distinguish distinct instances of particular
occurrences.

CHAPTER 10

The Event Sense

In this chapter I consider evidence for a distinct Event Sense associated with *time*. In this reading, *time* prompts for a conceptualisation in which a specific event is referenced. An event constitutes an occurrence of some type, characterised by certain features or characteristics which mark the occurrence as distinct from background experience. One way in which this can be achieved is by being temporally discrete. Hence, while the Moment Sense references a temporal point (within a particular temporal event-sequence), the Event Sense references an experiential point in an event-sequence. That is, an event is embedded in ongoing experience/event-sequences, just as temporal moments are embedded in larger temporal intervals.

10.1 Evidence for the Event Sense

In terms of the representation of the Duration Sense (recall Figure 7.1), those aspects of the representation of temporal structure which are point-like constitute the boundary events, namely the onset and offset which define the notion of an interval. Interestingly, the linguistic evidence for an Event Sense relates to boundary events, which is to say events which constitute beginnings or endings. Consider some examples:

(10.1) a. The young woman's time [=labour] approached
  b. Arsenal saved face with an Ian Wright leveller five minutes from time after having a jaded, end-of-season look   [BNC][1]
  c. The man had every caution given him not a minute before to be careful with the gun, but his time was come as his poor shipmates say and with that they console themselves   [BNC][2]
  d. The barman called time

10.1.1 The Meaning Criterion

In (10.1a) *time* prompts for a particular boundary event, namely the beginning of child-birth. In (10.1b) *time* prompts for the end of a soccer match in which the London team, Arsenal, equalised five minutes from the close of play. In (10.1c) *time* prompts for the event of death, which constitutes life's outer boundary, while in (10.1d) the barman signals the end of licensing hours (the period during which patrons may consume alcohol in a particular establishment) by calling 'time'. The event in each example is apparent by virtue of the transition made salient by the boundary. The boundary constitutes the beginning or ending of an interval of duration, which is to say the onset or the offset. For instance, in (10.1a) it is actually the onset of labour which is being signalled by *time*. In (10.1b) *time* references the offset of a football match. In (10.1c) the offset of life is signalled, while in (10.1d) the offset of licensing hours is prompted for. In this sense then, and in view of the Meaning Criterion, *time* signals a particular boundary event, namely the event which delimits a particular interval.

In order to further highlight the distinctiveness of the Event Sense with respect to the Meaning Criterion, I briefly contrast this sense with the previous three lexical concepts considered: Instance, Moment and Duration. The reason for doing this is that the semantics of the Event Sense do share certain similarities with the other lexical concepts, and as such it is worth clarifying in what way this lexical concept is distinct.

Let us start by briefly considering in what way the Event Sense is distinct from the Instance Sense, for example. In a sentence such as the following:

(10.2)   He did it 5 times in a row

time indexes the Instance Sense (and not the Event Sense). The reason for this is as follows. In the Event Sense, *time* indexes a specific event, i.e., an occurrence of some kind. In the example in (10.2) however, *times* refers to the doing, prompted for by the lexeme *did*. The event in this example is prompted for by the lexeme *it*. As *time* references the doing (by an agent) and not the event, i.e., the thing done, we must conclude that these two meanings, Instance and Event, are distinct, and that *time* is prompting for a different reading in (10.2) vis-à-vis the use of *time* in (10.1) which indexes the Event Sense.

Now let's consider the Event Sense in contrast to the Duration Sense. In the Duration Sense *time* relates to the durative aspect associated with an interval, rather than one aspect of the interval, namely the onset or offset. The Event Sense, however, designates a particular event without regard for its durative

aspect. This is not to say that events themselves cannot be construed as constituting intervals. However, in the Event Sense as lexicalised by *time*, the Event is
construed as punctual, a boundary which marks a transition, and hence signals
an occurrence (as evidenced by the examples in (10.1)).

Finally, let's consider how the Event Sense is distinct from the Moment
Sense. Clearly there are similarities between these two senses, not least the fact
that both are punctual in nature. However, the distinction is that while the
Event Sense (as evidenced by the examples in (10.1)) relates to a particular external occurrence, which is to say, something that happens, the Moment Sense
relates to a purely temporal event, i.e., an event defined purely in terms of its
relation to a temporal event-sequence.

10.1.2 The Concept Elaboration Criterion

Now let's consider the remaining two criteria for establishing whether the Event
reading constitutes a distinct lexical concept. I begin with the second criterion:
Concept Elaboration.

A consequence of the similarity of the Event Sense to the Moment Sense is
that the Event Sense is elaborated in a similar way to the Moment Sense. That
is, temporal Events are elaborated in terms of deictic motion. The following
example is indicative:

> (10.3)   a.   His time [=death] has come/arrived
> b.   His time is approaching/getting closer

Moreover, like the Moment Sense, the Event Sense cannot be elaborated in
terms of just any kind of motion event:

> (10.4)   ?His time [=death] has flown/moved/crept/sailed/stood still
> [Intended reading: Event Sense]

Just as with temporal moments, an event such as death constitutes an occurrence, and thus can be contrasted with its non-occurrence, i.e., life, which precedes death, and the period following death, when the body decays. As observed in Chapter 8, for something to occur it is often the case that motion is
involved; hence, the anticipated occurrence of arrival correlates with motion.
Similarly, the anticipation of the arrival of an object correlates with its motion
towards us. As we can only experience something occurring if we are coincident
with the occurrence, then the motion which often correlates with occurrences
such as arrivals or departures is deictic in nature. As I observed in Chapter 8,
if objects hurtle towards us, e.g., stones, cars, etc., we know from experience

that unless we move aside we will experience severe discomfort. This suggests that a new experience often results from the motion of objects towards us, and indeed our own motion to particular objects and locations. In this way, occurrences are often the result of ego-directed motion, or self- or other-propelled motion towards a particular location/object. In either case, the motion is anchored to a particular ego and hence is deictic in nature. It may be due to this tight correlation in experience, in which deictic motion often results in new experiences, that occurrences such as temporally discontinuous moments and events are elaborated in terms of deictic motion.

Indeed, the parallels between the Moment and Event Senses run deeper than just the nature of their elaboration in terms of motion. There is a conventional conceptual metonymy in which events stand for the times at which they are due to occur. In a sentence such as: *The start of the performance is five minutes away*, the event lexicalised as *the start of the performance* is standing for the time at which the performance will begin. That is, events and moments correlate in experience with one another in an extremely tight way. Particular events occur at particular moments. Hence, the nature of the motion content which serves to elaborate the Event Sense is probably not distinct from the motion events which elaborate the Moment Sense. On this basis, the second criterion cannot be employed to establish the Event reading as a sense distinct from the Moment Sense. For this we must rely on the Meaning Criterion, discussed above, and the third criterion which relates to grammatical evidence. It is to this that we now turn.

10.1.3 The Grammatical Criterion

Unlike previous senses considered, including the Moment Sense, the Event Sense does not undergo determination by the definite or indefinite articles. This is evidenced by (10.1b, d), in which no articles are present. In this the Event Sense appears to be behaving akin to a proper noun (recall Table 6.1). However, unlike proper nouns, or the Matrix Sense (see Chapter 11) or the Agentive Sense (see Chapter 12), the latter which, as we will see, does appear to closely resemble a proper noun, the Event Sense is unable to constitute a bare noun in subject position (in active sentences). In such positions it is premodified by a noun phrase (NP), such as an attribute possessive pronoun in (10.1c), or a genitive NP with possessive enclitic -'s, as in (10.1a). Moreover, there is evidence that the Event Sense is countable, as we will see in the next section. In so far as the Event Sense manifests distinct grammatical behaviour, this constitutes evidence that we should consider it to be an independent lexical concept associated with *time*.

10.2 Further examples

Other examples of the Event Sense include the following:

(10.5)   a.   Because there wasn't a welfare state, life was hard for the poor in Victorian times
         b.   His dress-sense is a little behind the times

In these examples *time* references a particular set of events which are indicative of a particular event-sequence in history which shares a particular characteristic or characteristics. In (10.5a) the events prompted for by *times* are those which took place during the reign of Queen Victoria. In (10.5b) the events prompted for are those pertaining to the latest developments in fashion. As particular event-sequences are conceptualised as having internal structure, with a number of occurrences constituting the sequence, this sequence can be conceptualised in terms of its boundary conditions, and hence the Event Sense is licensed.

For instance, as a unity Queen Victoria's reign was bounded by two events: her accession to the throne in 1837 (the onset), and her own death in 1901 (the offset). However, within this span of 64 years a number of other intervals can be picked out with their own transitions, and thus salient events which are identified as 'Victorian' by virtue of being subsumed by Victoria's reign. For example, Victoria's betrothal to Albert in 1840 marked a salient occurrence which resulted in a change of state, being unmarried to being married. The Great Exhibition of 1851 organised by Victoria and Albert constituted the self-conscious Victorian monument to the cultural and technological achievements of Britain as the first industrialised nation, and by virtue it constituted an act of recognition of what had come before. This event marked a salient point in the transition from pre-industrialised nation to industrialised nation. The death of Albert in 1861 constituted a salient event by virtue of representing another transition, the ending of a marriage, the loss of the royal consort, the loss of youth, etc. Victoria's Golden Jubilee celebrations in 1887 marked her first fifty years on the throne and hence represented a further transition, and so on. Because events are salient due to the transitions they signal (an event after all is an event by virtue of being differentiated from surrounding or background experience, e.g., the event of marriage), and as such, events can be subsumed by a larger event, e.g., The Victorian age (which in turn is differentiated from the ages which preceded and followed), the application of *times* in (10.5) references the Event Sense.

It is for similar reasons that a common name for newspapers employs the phrase *times*, e.g., *The New York Times*, *The Times* (of London), etc., which references the Event Sense, i.e., a series of salient events which are unified by virtue of relating to the present.

10.3 Derivation of the Event Sense

The Event Sense, like the previous senses considered, was also lexicalised by the form *tide*, and thus has been apparent in the language for a relatively long time. A plausible motivation for this sense may have been the correlation between a particular moment (the onset or offset of a temporal interval) and the event which takes place at that moment. Put another way, as events happen at specific moments, then a particular moment implicates a particular event with which it is correlated. As the Event Sense appears to relate to interval boundaries, and as an interval boundary correlates with the occurrence of a new event, prominent onsets or offsets (i.e., specific temporal moments) could, through pragmatic strengthening, have come to prompt for the event which correlates with the interval boundary (the temporal moment), especially as the lexeme *time* already referenced the concept of a temporal Moment.

For instance, with respect to the example of the canonical hours, a bell signalled that it was time for prayer, and moreover, a different prayer was required for each canonical hour. The bell therefore signalled the onset of a new interval (the time, i.e., moment, for prayer), which correlated with and hence implicated the event of praying. As such, the Moment Sense is likely to have given rise to the Event Sense. In this way, we have a means of relating temporal event-sequences (internal time structure) with experiential event-sequences (external event structure).

10.4 Conclusion

This chapter has presented evidence for treating examples such as those in (10.1) as constituting a distinct Event Sense. In so far as this lexical concept is associated with *time*, it seems to relate to discrete boundary events. A notable feature of this lexical concept is that it appears to be grammatically unusual in that it does not undergo determination by the definite or indefinite articles, although it can be pre-modified by other nominal constructions.

CHAPTER 11

The Matrix Sense

In the previous four chapters I have dealt with lexical concepts which appear to relate to fundamental aspects of our cognitive character. That is, the ability to experience duration, and a temporal moment, the ability to perceive and apprehend events, and the ability to categorise particular temporal moments and events as constituting instances of event-types, would seem to constitute basic cognitive abilities which enter into almost every aspect of perceptual processing and cognitive evaluation. In short, the processes and mechanisms that such lexical concepts relate to suggest themselves, with good reason, as being among the foundational mechanisms of our cognitive architecture.

In this, and subsequent chapters, we consider lexical concepts associated with *time* which have less claim to being foundational, in this sense. In order to distinguish phenomenologically foundational temporal lexical concepts closely associated with perceptual and cognitive abilities, from those which appear to be derived more from socio-cultural imperatives such as the Matrix Sense, to be considered in this chapter, I will refer to the former as PRIMARY temporal concepts, and to the latter as SECONDARY.[1] This distinction will be important in Part III when we consider how both primary and secondary concepts contribute to complex cognitive models for time. A consequence of the socio-cultural importance ascribed to secondary temporal concepts, of the kind to be considered in this and subsequent chapters, is that these lexical concepts have rich patterns of concept elaboration, as will be seen.

We first encountered the Matrix Sense in Chapter 5. In that chapter I suggested that in the Matrix Sense, *time* prompts for an entity which is unbounded. In present terms we can say that in this sense *time* relates to an entity that it is not constrained by the interval holding between individual events, i.e., by an onset and offset (recall Figure 7.1 of the Duration Sense). As such, it indexes an entity which has an infinite elapse, and thus is conceived as subsuming all other events, the Matrix in terms of which experience is possible. Accordingly, I will argue that the Matrix Sense prompts for an entity which rather than being an attribute of other events and entities, is itself (conceived as) an independent entity.

11.1 Evidence for the Matrix Sense

Evidence for the Matrix Sense constituting a distinct lexical concept comes from the Meaning Criterion, and the Concept Elaboration Criterion. Moreover, supporting evidence is suggested by the Grammatical Criterion. In this section I will address the Meaning and Grammatical Criteria. As the Matrix Sense constitutes a lexical concept which has an important and salient position in English-speaking culture, it is consequently elaborated in quite diverse and complex ways. For this reason I will reserve a discussion of patterns of concept elaboration for later sections.

Examples of the Matrix Sense are provided below:

(11.1)   a.   [T]ime, of itself, and from its own nature, flows equably without relation to anything external   [Newton][2]
         b.   I hold fate/ Clasped in my fist, and could command the course/ Of time's eternal motion   [John Ford][3]
         c.   Time flows/runs/goes on forever
         d.   Time has no end
         e.   The unending elapse of time
         f.   Those mountains have stood for all time
         g.   Nothing can outlast time
         h.   We live in time

11.1.1 The Meaning Criterion

The examples in (11.1) reveal that *time* indexes a temporal Matrix, which appears to be conceptualised as the 'backdrop' against which other events occur. That is, these examples fail to prompt for a conceptualisation involving a relation between salient events and hence the notion of an interval. Accordingly, the sentences in (11.1) relate to an entity which is unbounded.

This is particularly clear with the example in (11.1a). This example is drawn from Newton's *Principia Mathematica*,[4] in which the notion of 'absolute time' was famously propounded. According to Newton, 'absolute time' constitutes an entity possessing ontology independent of external events; that is 'absolute time' constitutes a real entity against which the rate of change of events can be measured. Hence, on this view, time is a manifold which 'contains' events, and is thus independent of events. As this manifold is simply in the world 'out there', the 'passage' of time represents *the* event which subsumes all other events. For Newton this view of time represented a theoretical primitive, constituting an entity which guaranteed that events experienced at a distance from one another (i.e., events which are not coincident) could be taken as being simultaneous.[5]

This view of the entity prompted for by *time,* as being something infinite, eternal and independent of all other events, is apparent in the other examples in (11.1). In each, *time* prompts for an entity whose passage is unaffected by external events and indeed within whose frame events unfold and states persist. That is, in this sense *time* no longer prompts for a relation (by virtue of its own succession), but rather it serves to manifest the succession of other events. In the sentences in (11.1b) through (11.1e) *time* prompts for an entity which is infinite. In (11.1f–g) a reading is prompted for in which *time* is permanent, and in (11.1h) the entity prompted for 'contains' existence.

Given that these examples no longer provide a reading of an interval holding between salient events, as in the Duration Sense, but rather an entity which is independent of external events, unbounded and infinite, and given that this lexical concept does not appear to be like any of the others so far encountered, then on the basis of the Meaning Criterion for determining distinct senses, the examples in (11.1) appear to constitute a distinct lexical concept. As has been previously observed, as the entity prompted for constitutes a temporal 'manifold' which is conceived as extending infinitely, and thus subsuming all other events, this sense is termed the Matrix Sense.

11.1.2 The Grammatical Criterion

Now let's consider the Grammatical Criterion. As was first noted in Chapter 5, the Matrix Sense is formally a mass noun. The reason for thinking this is that it cannot be determined by the indefinite article. In this it follows the pattern associated with the Duration Sense. In addition, we also observed that the Matrix Sense cannot be determined by the definite article. I suggested that this may be because the Matrix Sense already has unique reference. Part of the meaning associated with this lexical concept is that it is unique.

As the Matrix Sense constitutes a single entity which is unbounded in nature, it is very difficult to find examples of the operation which I identified in Chapter 7, following Talmy (2000), as portion-excerpting or bounding. Examples of such an operation are evidenced by the use of quantifiers such as *some.* While such an operation applies to the Duration Sense, as we saw in Chapter 7 and as attested by examples such as the following: *They lived together for (quite) some time,* it is less clear that this operation can apply to the Matrix Sense. The use of *time* in the sentence just given relates to the Duration Sense, and not the

Matrix Sense, as it concerns duration, rather than an entity which is identified as an unbounded and infinite elapse, the event subsuming all others. However, this is not to say that quantifiers are incompatible with the Matrix Sense, as evidenced by the example in (11.2):

(11.2)   The cycle of species evolving and becoming extinct has persisted for all time

The lexical item *all* is compatible with the Matrix Sense as it is consistent with what this lexical concept expresses. In other words, *all* does not serve to bound an entity which by definition cannot be bounded.

11.2 Concept elaboration employing motion content

A consequence of viewing the temporal Matrix as constituting an entity independent of the events subsumed by it is that is conceptualised as existing *independently* of other events, objects and entities, constituting an infinite elapse. John Langone (2000), in his popular treatment of time, appears to have the temporal Matrix in mind when he writes, "Without it we could barely measure change, for most things that change on this Earth and in the universe happen in time and are governed by it" (Ibid.:7). From this it is clear that Langone is assuming that it is by virtue of what I am terming the Matrix Sense that we are able to 'measure' change, due to events unfolding within it. Indeed, the book-jacket confirms as much suggesting that, "We all know that time is the template with which we define our lives". Accordingly, the temporal Matrix is being conceived as a template, an instrument which serves as a reference for measurement.

An extremely common way for the Matrix Sense to be elaborated is in terms of motion. As we saw in the previous section, Newton in his exposition of 'absolute time' seems to have shared this view of time as a template, which he suggested "flows equably without relation to anything external". It serves to reveal change, and hence manifest events, by virtue of its "equable" motion, which forms the backdrop, or reference frame against which all else can be measured. Accordingly, by conceptualising the Matrix Sense as an entity undergoing constant and uniform motion, it can be construed as acting as a "template", measuring and revealing change.

On this view, the temporal Matrix manifests events. The fact that it has motion ascribed to it allows us to conceptualise the temporal Matrix as 'carrying' new events along with it into being and view. On this conceptualisation time "flows equably without relation to anything external" precisely because in this sense, it is conceptualised as being independent of anything else, and thus is the 'regulator' of events. Events occur 'in time', and can thus be sequenced with respect to one another, by virtue of the temporal Matrix which manifests them, and thus organises and structures their occurrence. It is interesting to observe then that while Duration is in principle distinct from the concept of change, change is very much part of our conception of the Matrix Sense.

The Matrix Sense is commonly elaborated in terms of the motion event described by the lexeme *flow*, as evidenced by the ubiquity with which it is likened to bodies of water such as streams or rivers which prototypically 'flow'. Consider the following examples which evidence this elaboration; the sentence due to Marcus Aurelius, in (11.3d), reveals the antiquity of this imagery:

(11.3) a. Time like an ever-rolling stream
            Bears all its sons away   [Isaac Watts][6]
        b. A wanderer is man from his birth,
            He was born in a ship
            On the breast of the river of Time   [Matthew Arnold][7]
        c. Time is like a river made up of the events which happen
                                                       [Marcus Aurelius][8]
        d. Time is but the stream I go fishing in   [H. D. Thoreau][9]

In the light of examples such as these, we might well wonder why the Matrix Sense should be elaborated in terms of the manner of motion ascribed to bodies of water associated with rivers and streams. A number of reasons suggest themselves. While in the Matrix Sense time is the event in which other events occur, so are rivers and streams the entities in which other events take place, such as fishing, the sailing of boats, the activities of fish, water fowl, swimmers, etc. Similarly, while the Matrix Sense manifests events, so rivers and streams manifest objects, such as flotsam, boats and the passage of water. Given that streams and rivers have a current, as water moves under the force of gravity, so objects are borne along. The appearance of a new object on the river correlates with the occurrence of a new event. Just as the Matrix Sense is on-going, it continues and so it is infinite, so too from the perspective of a localised experiencer on a river bank, the flowing water constituting rivers and streams appears to stretch into the distance and beyond, being seemingly infinite, as attested by the following aphorism attributed to Heraclitus: *One cannot step into the same river twice.* Moreover, the ascription of *flowing* to *time* is a feature of diverse and unrelated languages, as is attested, for instance, in Japanese (Shinohara 1999) and in Chinese (Yu 1998). This suggests that what is strikingly similar about both rivers and the temporal Matrix may well be a good candidate for a cross-linguistic universal, in those languages which have similar versions of the temporal Matrix.

The foregoing is suggestive that the behaviour of rivers and streams is perceived as being related to the Matrix Sense in some way. It seems unlikely that the relatedness can be due to experiential correlation. Two reasons suggest themselves.

First, we cannot be said to 'experience' the Matrix Sense, as it represents a conceptualisation of an eternal entity. As our experience is not eternal (our lives are finite), the Matrix Sense is clearly not as closely related to the phenomenological experience of time as previous lexical concepts considered, as suggested by its designation as a secondary temporal concept. Hence, the temporal Matrix, not being a directly perceived experience, cannot correlate with other aspects of experience.

Second, in the temporal Matrix conception, it is not just the motion associated with bodies of water which is ascribed to the Matrix. The temporal Matrix can be conceptualised *as* a river, licensing expressions such as: *Time is a river*; *We're sailing down the river of time*, etc. Hence, as the Matrix Sense does not relate to a phenomenological experience which correlates with flowing motion, and as it is the whole notion of a river which can serve to elaborate this lexical concept, it appears unlikely that it is experiential correlation which motivates the appropriation of flowing motion content by the Matrix Sense.

I suggest that the mechanism which serves to elaborate the Matrix Sense in terms of the behaviour of rivers and streams is that of perceptual resemblance, introduced in Chapter 4. Given that bodies of water are continuous and dynamic, in that at any point water is continually being replaced by new water, then bodies of water, such as rivers, manifest exactly the same kind of characteristics as are ascribed to the Matrix Sense. Due to this resemblance, other expressions which connote rivers can be employed in order to describe the Matrix Sense, as in the following:

(11.4)   Time slithers/meanders along/on forever

As the flowing of rivers is often likened to the motion of animals such as snakes (given that there is a perceived resemblance between the physiology and manner of motion of reptiles such as snakes, and that of rivers, e.g., they are long and thin, and move in a meandering fashion), the Matrix Sense can be elaborated in terms of this more figurative description of bodies of water.

However, as we have seen previously with other lexical concepts, while certain kinds of motion content can serve to elaborate particular lexical concepts such as the Matrix Sense, e.g., *flow, slither, meander,* etc., or, *river, stream,* etc. not just any motion event, or entity prototypically associated with a particular kind of motion, will do.

Motion events which do not relate to salient characteristics of the Matrix Sense fail to appropriately elaborate it. For instance consider the following:

(11.5) a. ?Time creeps past   [Intended reading: Matrix Sense]
       b. ?Time stood still   [Intended reading: Matrix Sense]
       c. ?Time whizzed by   [Intended reading: Matrix Sense]
       d. ?Time has arrived   [Intended reading: Matrix Sense]

As none of the kinds of motion concepts employed in (11.5) relate to the ongoing and infinite nature of the Matrix Sense, but rather, imperceptible motion in (11.5a), stationariness in (11.5b), rapid motion in (11.5c) and deictic motion in (11.5d), these lexemes produce semantically anomalous sentences if a Matrix Sense reading is intended.

Having characterised the Matrix Sense as distinct from the previous lexical concepts considered, we see that the Matrix Sense is not concerned with the phenomenologically most fundamental aspect of temporality, namely duration, but rather can be characterised by its eternal nature (it continues indefinitely), and its ability to manifest events (i.e., to 'bring' new events to light), by serving as a 'template' against which other events can be experienced, and with respect to which (and hence each other), events can be related. It is this characterisation which makes rivers and streams such apt images for the purposes of elaborating the Matrix Sense. Thus, by careful application of the three criteria for distinguishing lexical concepts associated with *time*, we are able to view the way in which the Matrix Sense is elaborated as a consequence of the expressive needs of this particular lexical concept, as distinct from the requirements associated with the other temporal lexical concepts considered.

Now let's consider other ways in which the Matrix Sense can also be elaborated in terms of motion. A particularly salient way of elaborating the Matrix Sense is in terms of passage or passing:

(11.6) a. Time passes
       b. The passage of time

While the ascription of 'passes' and 'passage' to the temporal Matrix may be also due to the river/stream analogy, after all, rivers can be conceptualised as 'passing', expressions such as these often implicate a change in the world state, as suggested by the following attested example:

(11.7)   Time passed. A million other things happened, most of them forgot-
ten. I broke up with my girlfriend and, after a while, met, fell in love
with and married someone else.   [The Observer][10]

In this example, the narrator appears to be equating the 'passage' of time with
change. There is a tight correlation in experience between motion and change
which may also motivate such elaborations. In psychology for instance, motion is often treated as a subset of change, for instance motion correlates with
change of place (e.g., Miller & Johnson-Laird 1976). As the Matrix Sense is
conceptualised as relating to an entity which manifests change, it may be that
due to the correlation between motion past an experiencer and the conse-
quent change in the world-state, the Matrix sense can be elaborated in terms of
examples such as those in (11.7).

Lexical concepts associated with the lexeme *time* are additionally elaborated in terms of content pertaining to marching:

(11.8)   Time marches on

In this example the lexical concept being prompted for appears to be more
agentive in character. As the Agentive Sense, to be presented in the next chapter, is closely related to the Matrix Sense, and indeed, may be derived from it (as
we will see), it may be that in examples such as this, our experience of change
is being conceptualised as an effect of time. That is, by serving as the backdrop,
the template against which we are able to establish and measure change, time
'causes' change and hence the experience of new events. The use of *march* connotes irrevocable, uniform and unbounded motion, and so fits the pattern of
motion which elaborates the Matrix Sense (irrevocable and uniform motion
serves to manifest i.e., 'bring' new events into existence or view). However, the
association of marching with people, and especially soldiers, brings with it an
agentive nuance, reflecting perhaps, the conceptualisation that by manifesting events, time is, in essence, agentive. The connotation of soldiers and force
further enriches the agentive nuance. This illustrates the close relationship between the Matrix and Agentive senses. Another common way of elaborating
the Matrix Sense in terms of motion is illustrated by the following example:

(11.9)   Time runs/goes on forever

In the sentence in (11.9), the infinite nature of the entity prompted for by *time*
is being emphasised, as attested by the approximate paraphrase employing the
lexeme *continue*:

(11.10)   Time continues forever

If the infinite aspect of the Matrix Sense is being emphasised by the elaborations in (11.9), we must then consider why the lexical items *run* and *go* can be
conventionally employed in order to denote continuity in this way.

In experiential terms there is a tight correlation in experience between
motion and continued functioning. The continued participation of people in
many different kinds of activity is often correlated with their continued motion. For instance, the continued participation of competitors in a foot race
such as a marathon correlates with their continued motion. If a competitor
stops running for instance, it is likely that he or she has dropped out of the race
and is no longer a functional participant. This salient experiential correlation
between motion and continued functional participation plausibly motivates a
conventional association between certain kinds of motion, as lexicalised by *go*
or *run*, and continued functioning, evidenced in the examples below:

(11.11)   a.   My 1968 VW Beetle is still going/running
          b.   That old car is still an excellent runner!
          c.   The machine isn't running properly
          d.   I can't get it going

In each of these examples, *going* or *running* refers not to motion, but rather
to continuance and functioning. It does so due to pragmatic strengthening,
such that the implicature of 'continued functioning' has become a conventional
sense associated with *go* and *run*. A car can be *a good runner*, even when it is
parked with its engine switched off. If a car is still *running* or *going*, it still has
the potential to be operational, and hence continues to function properly. The
experiential correlation between *going* and continuance constitutes a plausible
motivation for elaborating the Matrix Sense in terms of something which *goes*.
This sense can be conceptualised as *going on* forever because it continues or
functions in a continuous and unbounded way. Hence, this is suggestive that
experiential correlation (as opposed to perceptual resemblance) gives rise to
the elaboration of the Matrix Sense in terms of motion phenomena as in the
examples in (11.11).

In sum, this discussion of the Matrix Sense illustrates that the elaboration
of this sense in terms of motion content is potentially motivated in a number of
different ways, which reflects the particular aspect of the sense which is being
emphasised. As the Matrix Sense is relatively complex, denoting an entity conceived as independent of all others, unbounded, infinite, and an entity which
manifests other events, these different aspects lead to slightly different ways in
which the sense can be elaborated. This results in the Matrix Sense being elaborated in terms of motion concepts which on first inspection might appear to

be very close in meaning, but on further analysis reveal that different nuances are being conveyed. This analysis also provides evidence for viewing the Matrix Sense as being elaborated by virtue of a number of different sets of experiential correlations and perceptual resemblances.

11.3 Elaboration employing non-motion content

I now turn to a consideration of the way in which the Matrix Sense is elaborated in terms of non-motion content. It appears that the entity prompted for by *time* in the Matrix Sense can be elaborated in terms of conceptual content pertaining to bounded (three-dimensional) locations, as well as planar (two-dimensional) locations. In order to illustrate this point, consider the examples below:

'Three-dimensional' bounded locations

(11.12)   a.   H. G. Wells wrote about travelling **through** time
          c.   We live **in** time

'Two-dimensional' planar locations

(11.13)   a.   In the movie the protagonist travels back **across** time to save the world
          b.   We'll only know how successful the treatment has been by assessing improvement **over** time

It seems that the entity prompted for by *time* in each of these examples is indeed the Matrix Sense. The reason for thinking this is that, in each sentence, *time* prompts for an entity or Matrix which subsumes other events, and is thus independent of the events themselves. As such, the occurrence of events can only happen by virtue of occurring (i.e., being 'located') within the Matrix of time. That is, *time*, in this sense, prompts for a background event, against which the activities and processes in the examples above can be conceptualised as occurring, and states as persisting

In order to see why the Matrix Sense should be elaborated in terms of such conceptual content, let us first consider the elaboration of the Matrix Sense in terms of 'three dimensional' bounded locations. The spatial particles *through* and *in* apparent in the sentences in (11.12) are conventionally associated with 'three-dimensional' bounded locations as shown by the examples in (11.14):

(11.14) a.   The Eurostar travels **through** a tunnel beneath the English Channel
         b.   We live **in** a house with green gables

In these examples the spatial particles *through* and *in* relate a trajector (TR) –
the motile entity or the entity potentially capable of motility, e.g., *the Eurostar*,
a fast passenger train which travels between London, Paris, and Brussels, and
we, which references people – and a landmark (LM) – the frame of reference
which is typically larger than the TR and immobile, *the tunnel*, and *the house*
respectively. In the examples in (11.14), the TR constitutes the located entity,
while the LM constitutes the locating entity. In both cases, by being contained
by a bounded location, as designated by the relations *through* and *in*, the location and/or (potential) motion of the referent is identified. After all, without a
frame of reference there would be no means available for distinguishing motion
from lack of motion (stasis), nor of locating TRs.

As three-dimensional bounded locations constitute a salient and effective
frame of reference, in so far as they determine the perceptual boundaries to
which a TR has access, they constitute more than just a frame of reference for
location, but delimit the nature and extent of what can be experienced. For
instance, containers such as prison cells constitute an ultimate limit on one's
freedom, and other bounded locations such as houses and tunnels both delimit
the perceptual field we have access to, but also determine and constrain the
nature of the motion that a particular TR can engage in. For instance, a tunnel
by virtue of its physical dimensions while enabling motion along a front/back
axis precludes motion along any other axis such as the vertical or lateral axes
(see Tyler & Evans 2003: Ch. 7).

In view of the foregoing, I suggest that as bounded locations are perceived
as constraining and delimiting, in the sense that they serve to bound the nature
and extent of one's experience in a number of ways, and as the Matrix Sense is
conceived as denoting an entity which bounds the nature of experience, in the
sense that events and processes can only occur within the Matrix of time, and
states can only persist by virtue of doing so against the backdrop of the temporal Matrix, through perceptual resemblance the Matrix Sense is elaborated in
terms of content pertaining to bounded locations.

Now let us turn to a consideration of the elaboration of the Matrix Sense
in the examples in (11.13). In those examples the Matrix Sense is elaborated in
terms of a 'two dimensional' planar location, as suggested by the use of *across*
and *over*. There is some evidence which is suggestive that the use of *across* and
over to elaborate the Matrix Sense may be related to what has often been referred to as the TIME-LINE. This model originally derived from mathematics

(Sklar 1974), and is evident in examples such as the following, in which the Matrix Sense is being elaborated in terms of a linear trajectory:

(11.15) a. Let's track the effects of this procedure longitudinally **over** time
         b. We will study evolutionary pressures **across** time

As previously, the evidence that the referent of *time* in these examples is the Matrix Sense is that the referent of *time* encompasses the events in question, namely *the effects of the procedure* and *evolutionary pressures* respectively.

The use of the spatial particles *over* and *across* can conventionally refer to a physically extended entity, as evidenced by the following:

(11.16) a. London bridge stretches **over** the river Thames from St. Paul's to Southwark
         b. The washing line extends **across** the yard

While the Matrix Sense is not a physically extended entity such as London bridge or a washing line, the fact that the examples in (11.16) can employ *over* and *across* suggests that in (11.13) the Matrix Sense is being conceptualised in terms of a physically extended entity. The Matrix Sense is often modelled in terms of a time-line, particularly when seeking to document gradual and extended historical change within the limits of a diagrammatic representation, e.g., in paleontology, archeology, genealogy (see Turner 1987),[11] in logic (see Reichenbach's 1947 formulation of time and tense), and even in linguistics (see Comrie's 1985 account of tense in which he proposes a theory of time-reference with the aid of a diagrammatic time-line).

This being so, we must consider why linear models should seem to be so natural for temporal representation, and thus are employed to elaborate the Matrix Sense, as attested by the use of *across* and *over* in (11.13) and (11.15). It was Galileo (1564–1642) who first symbolised time geometrically, partitioning a line into equal divisions by points along the line (Sklar 1974). Descartes made geometrical principles central to his method for a rigorous epistemological foundation. Accordingly, just as space could be understood employing Cartesian co-ordinates, so too any arena of knowledge, including time, could be analysed employing such reasoning. This represented the advent of the so-called time-line. In this way, a line, which is extended, subsumes further divisions and points. Similarly, in the Matrix Sense, the entity prompted for by *time* is conceptualised as subsuming both events which happen and states which persist. As a line's extension is (in principle) unbounded, and as it subsumes further divisions, it represents an analogue of the Matrix Sense, which is also unbounded. Hence, due to perceptual resemblance, the Matrix Sense can be elaborated in terms of a linear representation, as attested by the use of *over* and *across* in the examples in (11.13).

11.4 Derivation of the Matrix Sense

The next issue to consider is how the Matrix Sense may have been derived. I suggest that a Matrix conception could only have become associated with *time* if temporality is in some way reified. That is, it must be generalised away from the individual intervals from which it derives, and thus divorced conceptually from its bounded durational character, anchored to the subjective (and hence egocentric) awareness of the human experiencer. In the process, temporality may become conceptualised as an independent entity in terms of which on-going temporal experience is defined and situated. This process may have occurred due to our awareness of on-going temporal experience being correlated with our conscious experience of events, which are conceptualised as being external to us and so attributed to an objective world. That is, temporal experience correlates with putatively external experience. Due to this extremely tight correlation it is plausible that temporality came to be associated with 'external' events, processes, states and even objects. As such, temporality has come to be attributed to the external world which thus came to be conceptualised as possessing its own temporality independent of the subjective experience of time with which the external world is correlated.

Once temporality has become attributed to the external world, the notion of permanence, a pre-requisite for the concept of eternity becomes possible. After all, if an entity such as a tree for instance, does not have ascribed to it its own temporality (e.g., the view that it persists independently of an observer), then it cannot endure without being correlated with an experiencer's on-going perception (and hence temporal awareness). Once this conceptual pre-requisite has been invoked, a tree can be conceptualised as being a permanent feature of the world (and thus existing independently of a human experiencer), as its own intrinsic temporality is attributed to it. Clearly, most people do not doubt that trees continue to exist when the curtains are drawn occluding such objects from view. It may be then that the notion of object permanence, which develops early in infancy, is related to the correlated relationship between ongoing perceptual awareness and the world at large, which facilitates a conceptualisation of the world as partaking of temporality independent of the human experiencer (see Bergson [1922] 1999:Ch. 3).

I suggest that by ascribing temporality to the external world (due to the correlation between internal temporality and a putatively external on-going world-state), this world-state, which is conceptualised as anteceding and continuing beyond the finite egocentric experience, may have given rise to an implicature of extendedness, in the sense of infinite duration, associated with the lexeme *time*. In order to trace the rise of this implicature in detail, consider the following example:

(11.17) He lived before my time

In our everyday experience there is ubiquitous evidence that our own individual lifespan is not co-extensive with the existence of our environment. Through both individual memory and collective memory (history), we learn that some things antedate us. The clearest examples are the people around us, our parents, who are older than us. In this way, we understand that someone else's time is not 'my' time, and that this 'other' time can antedate our own. Time then, can both precede and presumably follow our own experience of it, as attested by the example in (11.17). Accordingly, it is conceptualised as not being contingent upon our own experience of it. Yet, the sense prompted for in (11.17) is the Duration Sense, referencing an interval of duration rather than invoking the notion of eternity associated with the Matrix Sense.

In terms of our conceptualisation of the objects around us and the events which we experience both through our own observation and through cultural transmission (e.g., news, history, story, etc.), we have access to temporal intervals which are far greater than our own. This being so, such temporal intervals may be so great that they implicate infinite duration as in (11.18):

(11.18) a.   The joiner squirrel or old grub, Time out o' mind the fairies' coach-
              makers   [Shakespeare][12]
         b.   The ancient hills have been around for a longer time than human
              history records

In (11.18a) the implicature of unboundedness is due to a duration which is so long that it is beyond recollection. The joiner squirrel and old grub have served as coachmakers to the fairies longer than collective memory (fairy history) can recall. In (11.18b) there is also an implicature of unbounded duration also due to a lack of collective recollection. This implicature is strengthened by the fact that the duration associated with salient features of the landscape may correlate with a number of temporal intervals of lesser duration. Hence, for each entity whether animate of inanimate, there will always be a range of temporal intervals which overlap and subsume others (recall the discussion of time embeddedness in Chapter 8). While a range of hills may have a longer duration than human history, which has a longer duration than a particular human civilisation, which in turn has a longer duration than an individual human lifespan, which has a longer duration than the individual events and circumstances making up a lifespan, ultimately the universe itself (in modern physics), or God in monotheistic religious traditions, can be viewed as possessing or defining the ultimate durational interval (recall Newton's view of 'absolute time').

Due to the ascription of temporality to the world at large, the use of the form *time* in ways which implicate a duration of unbounded length, due to the conceptualisation of intervals which for all practical purposes are immeasurable (not least because of the finite human lifespan), may have been responsible for giving rise to the association of this lexical form with a conception of eternity. In the Matrix Sense, *time* does not refer to distinct durational intervals, but rather to an ongoing and inherently unbounded durational elapse, subsuming all other temporal divisions. That is, distinct intervals of duration result from events happening and states persisting in time. Accordingly, *time* prompts for an unbounded entity (the view that time flows "without relation to anything external" of Newton), which can only be divided by virtue of arbitrarily selecting delimiting events, or natural periodicities. Through the use of the form *time* in contexts where the Duration Sense gives rise to an implicature of unboundedness, pragmatic strengthening has served to conventionally associate a Matrix Sense with the form *time*, in which an entity is referenced which constitutes a Matrix within which existence unfolds, and, due to its ongoing nature, it serves to manifest events (bring them into being), as suggested by the ascription of motion events described by terms such as *flow*. This sense is evidenced in the following attested examples:

(11.19) a.   Eons before there were people to be curious about it, time was here, hidden in the rhythms of nature   [John Langone][13]

b.   Time is embroidered in our consciousness and culture and in our very beings. It touches everything that surrounds us, everything that exists, from living organisms to layers of rock   [Ibid.]

In the example in (11.19a) we see quite clearly that *time* prompts for an entity independent of the entities, events and states to which it gives temporal definition, an entity which has an unbounded duration. In the example in (11.19b) the notion expressed by this sense of an 'all-enveloping' Matrix is even clearer. Here we see that the entity being prompted for is being conceptualised as inhering in all aspects of nature, licensing existence itself. In this way, the Matrix Sense denotes an entity of infinite duration, and in so doing is conceptualised as the event subsuming all other events. As Langone (2000) puts it, in this conceptualisation time is "a reality apart from the events that fill it" (Ibid.: 10).

The equating of eternity with the entity prompted for by *time* can be traced back to at least classical Greek thought, which in turn influenced how the Romans conceptualised the concept associated with the Latin form *tempus,* cognate of the English form *time.* In the Platonic dialogue *Timaeus,* Plato provides a speculative cosmology (although largely based on earlier myths and religious beliefs). Following his theory of forms, Plato describes time as reflecting eternity. As he puts it,

> The nature of the Living Being was eternal, and it was not possible to bestow this attribute fully on the created universe; but he determined to make a moving image of eternity, and so when he ordered the heavens he made in that which we call time an eternal moving image of the eternity which remains for ever at one.   (Ibid.: 51; translated by Sir Desmond Lee)

Plato thus treats time as a moving image of eternity, manifested in the cyclical motion of the celestial bodies. It is interesting to note in passing, that the Platonic (and indeed Greek) view of time was of a cyclical (as opposed to a linear) entity. Further evidence of the eternal nature of the Matrix Sense, abundant in literature, is attested by the following example:

(11.20) Before the hills in order stood,
         Or earth received her frame,
         From everlasting Thou art God,
         To endless years the same.
         A thousand ages in Thy sight
         Are like an evening gone;
         Short as the watch that ends the night
         Before the rising sun.
         Time like an ever-rolling stream
         Bears all its sons away;
         They fly forgotten as a dream
         Dies at the opening day.   [Isaac Watts][14]

According to the OED, the use of the form *time* to prompt for what I terming the Matrix Sense occurred much later than the earliest attested usage of *time* to prompt for the Duration Sense, and it appears that the Matrix Sense was not lexicalised by the earlier form *tide.*[15] From this it does not follow that the concept of eternity, for instance, which forms part of the meaning of the Matrix Sense, did not exist prior to this date. What this does suggest is that in diachronic terms, the conception of an infinitely unbounded temporal Matrix which manifests all other events, only became associated with the lexeme *time* once *time* had first developed a meaning of Duration, the Sanctioning Sense. Moreover, the exposure to Latin, and classical thought in mediaeval England, and during the Renaissance (Hughes 2000), in which the form *tempus* already had a matrix-like sense associated with it, may have played a part in the development of such a sense being linked with the English form *time*.

11.5 Conclusion

In this chapter we have considered evidence which supports a distinct Matrix Sense associated with *time*. This sense constitutes what I have termed a secondary temporal concept, in so far as it is not directly grounded in our phenomenological experience of time. Rather, the Matrix Sense appears to constitute a socio-cultural construct, which has rich patterns of concept elaboration associated with it, both in terms of motion and non-motion content. Moreover, the patterns of concept elaboration associated with the Matrix Sense appear to involve both perceptual resemblance and experiential correlation.

In so far as the Matrix Sense is a secondary temporal concept, this constitutes a lexical concept which is largely 'created' by virtue of the patterns of concept elaboration which constitute it. In this, it is distinct from the primary lexical concepts considered earlier, which being grounded in phenomenological experience, necessarily antecede the elaborations which serve to enrich them. In the next three chapters we will consider further secondary temporal concepts conventionally associated with *time*.

CHAPTER 12

The Agentive Sense

In this chapter we consider the second of the secondary temporal concepts associated with *time* to be examined. This constitutes the Agentive Sense. While the Matrix Sense relates to an entity conceived as the template by virtue of which events can be judged to have occurred, further reification results in the Agentive Sense. This relates to an entity which is conceived not just as serving to manifest change, but in addition, as one which actually brings about and hence causes change. Accordingly, I will argue below that the Agentive Sense represents a development of and extension from the Matrix Sense.

12.1 Evidence for the Agentive Sense

In order to give an immediate sense of the Agentive meaning associated with *time*, consider the following examples:

(12.1)   a.   Time is the great physician   [Benjamin Disraeli][1]
           b.   Time is the greatest innovator   [Francis Bacon][2]
           c.   Time, the avenger!   [Lord Byron][3]
           d.   Time, the subtle thief of youth   [Milton][4]
           e.   Time has aged me
           f.   Tempus edax rerum
               'Time the devourer'   [Ovid][5]
           g.   Time has left its scars
           h.   Time has yellowed the pages
           i.   Time transformed her
           j.   Only time will tell
           k.   Time reveals all

In order to be able to claim that in these examples *time* is prompting for a lexical concept distinct from others considered so far, as previously, I need to be able to demonstrate two things. First, these instances associated with *time* must add new meaning not apparent in the other senses. This of course relates to the

Meaning Criterion for determining distinct senses. Second, additional evidence must come from either the Concept Elaboration Criterion, or the Grammatical Criterion. Indeed, as we shall see, both these criteria support the view that the Agentive reading apparent in the examples in (12.1) constitutes a distinct Agentive Sense.

12.1.1 The Meaning Criterion

In the sentences in (12.1), *time* prompts for an entity which has the ability to affect us and our environment. It can variously heal, as in (12.1a), innovate (12.1b), steal our youth (12.1c), and age us (12.1e). It can devour (12.1f), inflict scars (12.1g), yellow pages (12.1h), and transform people (12.1i). In addition, *time* can show and reveal as in (12.1j–k) respectively. In as far as *time* prompts for an entity which can affect us, then this constitutes the Agentive Sense.

Based on the sentences in (12.1), it seems fairly clear that there is additional meaning. Unlike the Duration Sense, for instance, the lexical concept indexed in these examples is capable of bringing about some effect. This contrasts with the Duration Sense in which an interval of duration is being prompted for. Similarly, the meaning prompted for by *time* in (12.1) adds meaning not apparent in the Matrix Sense. While in the Matrix conception *time* prompts for an unbounded durational elapse which consequently serves as a background 'template' against which change can be measured, in the Agentive Sense *time* appears to be actively involved in the occurrence of specific events. This follows as the Agentive Sense is being elaborated in terms of the agency associated with humans and animals, as will be discussed below. For instance, time can be a physician who heals (12.1a), or a thief who steals (12.1d), or even an innovator (12.1b) Equally time can become a very human agent, manifesting volition and thus avenging as in (12.1c). Similarly, time can be modelled on animal agency and devour as in (12.1f). Indeed, the personification of the agentive sense reaches its apotheosis in the cultural model of Father Time, as exemplified in the iconic representations of a balding man carrying a scythe and an hourglass in Western art since mediaeval times (Lippincott et al. 1999), and in examples such as the following:

(12.2) a. The plaine bald pate of Father Time himself   [Shakespeare][6]
        b. Time, you old gipsy man,
            Will you not stay,
            Put up your caravan
            Just for one day?   [Ralph Hodgson][7]

The Agentive Sense is particularly prevalent in literature where time is often viewed as an unseen 'power' which brings about change. In the following example drawn from J.R.R. Tolkien's *The Hobbit*, Gollum asks Bilbo Baggins to solve a riddle by identifying the entity he describes:

(12.3)   This thing all things devours:
        Birds, beasts, trees flowers,
        Gnaws iron, bites steel;
        Grinds hard stones to meal;
        Slays king, ruins town,
        And beats high mountain down.[8]

The answer, of course, is time.

12.1.2 The Concept Elaboration Criterion

It has already become apparent from the discussion so far that the Agentive Sense is elaborated in terms of acts which bring about a change of state. To make this explicit, consider the following examples based on those presented in (12.4):

(12.4)   a.   Time devours all
       b.   Time reveals all
       c.   Time heals all wounds
       d.   Time has transformed him into an old man

The result of being devoured is that the entity being acted upon is no longer a discrete entity and hence no longer exists; the result of being revealed is to be exposed or rendered visible; being healed results in becoming better or well; and being transformed results in a markedly different form and state. It appears that the elaboration of the Agentive Sense in such terms is due to experiential correlation. After all, the change of state in each of the examples above is unlikely to occur unless there is an agent which performs the devouring, revealing, healing and transforming. Thus, such acts correlate with agents. Moreover, these kinds of acts typically require agents with a particular skill or facility. That is, the acts are not accidental or random, but are contingent in some way. For instance, *devour* conjures up images of a ferocious beast, *reveal* and *transform* evoke the image of a magician or sorcerer, while *heal* connotes some kind of healer such as a medic. In short, each of the agents evoked by these terms possesses special features or abilities which enable them to bring about a relatively rapid and marked change in state.

Conversely, the Agentive Sense seems unlikely to be elaborated in terms of acts or processes which do not result in a change of state or indeed which produce only a gradual change of state. For instance, while the Agentive Sense is elaborated in terms of *devour*, as attested by (12.4a), and as emphasised in (12.5) below, this lexical concept is less likely to be elaborated in terms of the examples in (12.6):

(12.5)   Time has devoured my youth

(12.6)   a.   ?Time has slowly nibbled away at my youth
          b.   ?Time has corroded my youth
          c.   ?Time has eroded my youth

While the examples in (12.6) are by no means uninterpretable, they are not particularly striking nor effective ways of elaborating the Agentive Sense. This may be because gradual change is less likely to be evident, and may not even correlate with a specific agent. For instance, erosion could be the result of multiple factors, including general weathering, without a single agent being necessarily more or less important and/or salient. Hence, as the expressions *nibbled away slowly*, *corroded* and *eroded* describe processes which are gradual, they fail to appropriately correlate with a specific agent, namely an entity upon which the change is contingent and dependent. Consequently, it appears that the Agentive Sense requires elaboration in terms of the specialised ability or facility associated with particular kinds of agent. In this, the Agentive Sense is distinct from the other lexical concepts so far considered.

In addition to being elaborated in terms of acts which result in a marked change of state, the Agentive Sense can also be elaborated in terms of the effects such acts have as in the sentences in (12.7) through (12.10). As in the previous examples, these effects are normally contingent upon, and hence correlate with a specific agent:

(12.7)   a.   Time stole/took my best years
          b.   The burglar stole/took my best watch

(12.8)   a.   Time has yellowed the pages
          b.   The clown has whitened his face/The artist has painted her canvas yellow

(12.9)   a.   Time has left its scars
          b.   The soldier's sword left a scar

(12.10)   a.   Time has furrowed his brow
          b.   The farmer with his plough has furrowed the field

Thus, I suggest that as change is correlated with a specific and identifiable agent, that is, as change is contingent upon specific agents, as illustrated in the b. sentences in (12.7) through (12.10), such contingent effects can serve to elaborate the Agentive Sense associated with *time*. It is presumably because specific and contingent agents are typically (although not inevitably) human in our experience that the Agentive Sense so often appears to evidence person-ification. This is clear from the following selection drawn from Shakespeare, in which the acts ascribed to the Agentive Sense are so human-like:

(12.11) a. But wherefore do not you a mightier way
            Make war upon this bloody tyrant, Time?   [Shakespeare][9]

        b. Time is like a fashionable host
            That slightly shakes his parting guest by the hand,
            And with his arms outstretched, as he would fly,
            Grasps in the comer: welcome ever smiles
            And farewell goes out sighing   [Shakespeare][10]

        c. Love's not Time's fool, though rosy lips and cheeks
            Within his bending sickle's compass come   [Shakespeare][11]

        d. Time travels in divers paces with divers persons. I'll tell you who
            Time ambles withal, who Time trots withal, who Time gallops
            withal, and who he stands still withal   [Shakespeare][12]

12.1.3 The Grammatical Criterion

The Agentive Sense is unique in that it appears to behave akin to a proper as opposed to a common noun (although see the discussion of the Measurement-system Sense in Chapter 13). For instance, while the Agentive Sense appears to share some grammatical characteristics with mass nouns – for example the 'protracted duration' and 'temporal compression' readings – neither the Agentive Sense nor the 'protracted duration'/'temporal compression' readings can be pluralised, the latter have an article contrast between 'the' and zero, as illustrated for 'temporal compression' in (12.12):

(12.12) a. Time flies when you're having fun

        b. Looking back, the time we shared together on that dinner date
            seemed to have flown

As the Agentive Sense has no such contrast, we can say that the Agentive Sense does not take an article, and as such cannot undergo determination by an article. In this it behaves like a proper noun (recall Table 6.1).[13]

One salient diagnostic of a mass noun is that it cannot be determined by the indefinite article, as illustrated for the Matrix Sense in (12.13):

(12.13) *A time flows on forever

The Matrix Sense is interesting as unlike the 'protracted duration'/'temporal compression' readings, it does not appear to show an article contrast. That is, it does not appear possible for the Matrix Sense to undergo determination employing the definite article either, as was observed in the previous chapter:

(12.14) *The time flows on forever

In this regard it behaves like the Agentive Sense. On the other hand, the Matrix Sense does show some characteristics normally associated with mass nouns. After all, as we saw in Chapter 11, it can be quantified by *all*. However, the Agentive Sense appears not to be capable of determination in this way either:

(12.15) *Some/all time will tell

This failure to undergo determination by a lexeme such as *some* or *all*, combined with an inability to undergo determination by an article in subject position suggests that the Agentive Sense behaves grammatically like a proper noun:

(12.16)   Time is a great healer
          cf. Sid is a great healer

Hence, the Agentive Sense, from the perspective of its grammatical properties, does indeed appear to be distinctive. Indeed, given that this lexical concept relates to an entity which is agentive, and given that humans are agents par excellence, and further, often appear to constitute the basis for the elaboration of this sense, it appears natural, therefore, that the Agentive Sense would be formalised as a proper noun.

12.2 Comparison with Lakoff and Turner (1989)

In their treatment of time metaphors in literature, Lakoff and Turner (1989) proposed a whole catalogue of what they suggested were distinct metaphors licensing the ascription of various kinds of agency to Time. Some examples included the following: TIME IS A CHANGER, TIME IS A DESTROYER, TIME IS A DEVOURER, TIME IS A HEALER, TIME IS AN EVALUATOR, TIME IS A PURSUER, TIME IS A RUNNER, TIME IS A THIEF, etc. On their view, Time can be elaborated in diverse ways by virtue of the metaphoric mappings posited.

However, the present perspective offers a slightly different way of viewing the situation. By positing an Agentive Sense associated with *time*, it is by virtue of a single distinct lexical concept that personification imagery is licensed. In other words, personification is due to an Agentive lexical concept being instantiated in semantic memory, rather than by virtue of antecedent metaphoric mappings which 'create' these particular conceptualisations.

From the present perspective, a particular temporal lexical concept, here the Agentive Sense, in part constrains the nature of the content in terms of which it can be elaborated. That is, not just any kind of agentive imagery can be employed to elaborate this sense. Rather, the Agentive Sense requires specific kinds of content, as seen in the previous section.

In terms of the plethora of conventional images associated with the Agentive Sense, e.g., Time as a devourer, Time as a thief, etc., it is likely that the association of these images is due to conventional association of these particular images with this lexical concept, due to their strong evocation of agency. By virtue of the process of conventionalisation, the patterns of elaboration come to constitute, in part, the lexical concept itself. However, from this it does not follow that there is no Agentive lexical concept absent the patterns of concept elaboration, although such elaborations do serve to enrich the concept, and how we conceptualise it. Hence, particular ways of elaborating the Agentive Sense, if seen as apt or striking, can through repetition and routine use, come to be appropriated by the temporal lexical concept as part of its conventional representation.

An example will serve to illustrate this point. To my knowledge, the first attested reference to time as a devourer was due to the Roman author Ovid (43 BC – 17 or 18 AD), who in his Metamorpheses (xxv. 234) described time as follows:

(12.17) Tempus edax rerum
          'Time the devourer of things'

When first coined, this description would have been novel. But being apt, given our particular conceptualisation of the Agentive Sense, this way of elaborating this notion of time has been appropriated by the English literary tradition. Through continued use, the particular symbolisation, *time as a devourer*, has come to constitute a highly conventionalised way of referencing the Agentive Sense.

12.3 Derivation of the Agentive Sense

Now let's consider how the Agentive Sense may have come to be convention-alised as a distinct lexical concept. A plausible path of derivation may view the Agentive Sense as deriving from an antecedent Matrix Sense. For instance, the Matrix Sense by manifesting new events implicates agentivity. The temporal Matrix 'brings' with it new events and thus in this way our conception of a Matrix correlates with an awareness of change in the world-state. It may be this correlation between a matrix conception, and an awareness of change, that has led to time as being reanalysed as causing change.

In order to support this thesis, we must find an example of the Matrix Sense in which an agentive meaning is implicated. Once implicated such situated im-plicatures can be reanalysed as distinct meaning components and become con-ventionally associated with particular lexical forms, in this case *time*. One such example is the following due to Marcus Aurelius, part of which was presented in the previous chapter:

> (12.18) Time is like a river made up of the events which happen, and its current is strong; no sooner does anything appear than it is swept away, and another comes in its place, and will be swept away too.
>
> [Marcus Aurelius][14]

In this example the referent of *time* is being likened to a river. As was observed in Chapter 11, the lexical concept being prompted for by *time* in this example is the Matrix Sense. That is, time (the river) is conceptualised as the manifold or event subsuming all other events. However, a consequence is that the time-river event is conceptualised as facilitating our experience of new events in an on-going way. This is suggested by the comparison of time's effect with a river's strong current. While the Matrix Sense associated with *time* serves to manifest the experience of new events, so a river's current serves to replace old water with new in a relentless fashion. This imagery implicates an agentive mean-ing (i.e., an implicature that it is time which manifests a new event, and cru-cially, thereby changes the world-state, and *causes* us to have a new experience). Hence, examples such as this implicate that the Matrix Sense can affect us.

Through continued use of the form *time* to denote the Matrix Sense in con-texts in which an Agentive meaning is implicated, I suggest that the Agentive meaning became strengthened. The process of pragmatic strengthening con-cerns the reanalysis of a situated meaning so that it becomes conventionally associated with the lexeme in question.

Once the Agentive Sense has become instantiated in the semantic network associated with *time*, it can be used in ways unrelated to the original context of use which gave rise to it. That is, once in memory, we can employ the new sense in new contexts not dependent upon the originating context. After all, we can refer to *time* as yellowing pages, as in (12.1h) above. Yet, it is chemical changes in paper which account for its yellowing, and not an objectively 'real' temporal agent. However, as some changes, such as the yellowing of paper, are both gradual and do not have an overt agent, the Agentive Sense conceived as bringing about change is conceptualised as being responsible for causing other kinds of changes such as the yellowing, and indeed ageing more generally, as in (12.1e).

12.4 Conclusion

In this chapter we considered evidence for positing a distinct Agentive Sense conventionally associated with *time*. It was argued that the Agentive Sense relates to an entity which has the ability to affect us and our environment. It was further suggested that this secondary temporal lexical concept is likely to have derived from the Matrix Sense. The imagery which serves to conventionally elaborate the Agentive Sense relates to human agency. In this lexical concept *time* is highly personified, a feature reflected in its grammatical behaviour, which resembles that of a proper noun.

CHAPTER 13

The Measurement-system Sense

In this chapter we consider what I will term the Measurement-system Sense. In this sense *time* prompts for a lexical concept which represents a measurement system. Temporal measurement arises due to the correlation between periodic behaviour in the external world and our experience of duration. As periodic behaviour correlates with internal temporal experience, it can be employed to represent temporality. Bergson ([1922] 1999) makes this point with the following example:

> If I draw my finger across a sheet of paper without looking at it, the motion I perform is, perceived from within, a continuity of consciousness... [which is to say]...duration. If I now open my eyes, I see that my finger is tracing on a sheet of paper a line that is preserved...Now, this line is divisible, measurable. In dividing and measuring it, I can then say, if is suits me, that I am dividing and measuring the duration of the motion that is tracing it out.   (Ibid.:34)

The point here is that physical (i.e., visual and aural) symbols can be employed to represent (i.e., measure) the duration with which they are correlated.

An example of this is periodicity. As some physical entities and events exhibit PERIODICITY – a predictable cycle or rhythm of behaviour – such entities and events are highly useful for 'measuring' the duration with which they are correlated. It is this principle which underpins the concept of a clock, for instance. Clocks serve to divide the day into equal parts, originally into hours signalled by bells (as in the canonical hours), and later into minutes and seconds with the advent of accurate pendulum clocks from 1656, and accurate spring-powered clocks from 1700 onwards (Barnett 1998; Whitrow 1988).

13.1 Evidence for the Measurement-system Sense

In the Measurement-system Sense, *time* prompts for an entity which constitutes a system for measuring duration. A temporal measurement-system is defined primarily in terms of its rate of periodicity and in some time-measurement systems by its place of occurrence (as in time-reckoning, i.e., time as measured by clocks). Some examples of the Measurement-system Sense are provided below. In the examples in (13.1), *time* prompts for measurement systems for marching and dancing, in (13.2) for music, in (13.3) for metre, in (13.4) for time-reckoning (i.e., division of the day based on a 24 hour day-night cycle), and in (13.5) for the payment of labour:

Marching and dancing

(13.1) a. In quick time, 108 paces, or 270 feet, are taken in a minute; and in slow time, seventy-five paces, or 187 feet. In double time, 150 paces of thirty-six inches, making 450 [feet] in a minute. [OED][1]

   b. The time having been given on a drum, on the word March, the squad will move off.   [OED][2]

   c. They performed the dance to waltz-time

Music

(13.2) a. In modern Music, the word Time is applied to rhythmic combinations of all kinds, mostly indicated by fractions, (3/8 etc.) referring to the aliquot parts of a Semibreve – the norm by which the duration of all other is notes is and always has been regulated.

                                                               [OED][3]

   b. To play out of Time   [OED][4]

   c. To beat time   [OED][5]

Metre

(13.3) a. The short syllable… is considered as the original unit for the measure of time in the rhythm, and is called a time or mora. [OED][6]

   b. The Measure of single Time is the Space in which we commonly pronounce any of the Liquids or Consonants, preceded by a Vowel

                                                               [OED][7]

   c. [A] double or compound time is composed of two or more single times   [OED][8]

Time reckoning

(13.4) a. In the 1850s Railway Time was introduced as standard

b. Don't forget to move the clocks forward with the start of Summer
    Time[9]
c. Eastern Standard Time is five hours behind Greenwich Mean
    Time

Payment for labour

(13.5) a. We get paid double time on public holidays
        b. Doctors get paid time and a half once they've worked over 40
            hours

13.1.1 The Meaning Criterion

In each of the examples above, *time* prompts for a system of measurement
which serves to regulate and co-ordinate a particular kind of interpersonal activity. In (13.1) the activity being regulated is marching and dancing, in (13.2)
the activity is music, in (13.3) the activity is the oral performance of verse,
which involves metre, in (13.4) the activity is time-reckoning, and in (13.5)
the activity is the calculation of payment for labour. The Measurement-system
Sense adds meaning not apparent in any of the other senses. Hence, on the basis of the Meaning Criterion for determining distinct lexical concepts, it would
appear that the Time-measurement reading does indeed relate to a distinct
lexical concept.

13.1.2 The Concept Elaboration Criterion

In addition to satisfying the Meaning Criterion, further evidence for the
distinctiveness of the Measurement-system Sense comes from the nature of
the conceptual content which serves to elaborate this lexical concept. As the
Measurement-system Sense is most saliently evidenced when dealing with
time-reckoning, the ensuing discussion of elaboration patterns will concern
itself with this usage.

Time-reckoning constitutes the practice of measuring physical periodic behaviour which happens to correlate with our phenomenological experience of
time. That is, it is the periodic behaviour of a physical entity (substance or device) which is being measured rather than the phenomenological experience
itself. A typical idiomatic usage evidencing this sense constitutes the following
example, in which a child might be being addressed by an adult:

(13.6)   Have you learnt to tell the time yet?

In (13.6), the lexeme *time* refers to a system of measuring daily intervals. Evidence that this is so comes from the use of *tell*, which elaborates the process of 'reading' a time-reckoning device. For the uninitiated or the young, learning how to 'interpret' such devices is an important part of becoming acculturated. The periodic behaviour of 'clocks', i.e., time-reckoning devices, is presented to the time-reckoner via an interface such as a clock 'face' or a digital reading. A time-reckoning device serves to subdivide the interval of a day, based upon a localised time-measurement system such as Greenwich Mean Time, into two sets of 12 hours, or 24 hours, each further subdivided into 60 minutes, and each minute subdivided into 60 seconds. A time-reckoner must acquire the skill of being able to interpret the information provide by the time-reckoning device, as elaborated by the lexical concepts referenced by *tell*, hence, *tell the time* in (13.6).

Another way in which time-reckoning can be elaborated is in terms of motion content, as evidenced by (13.7):

(13.7)   The time is approaching noon

There is a long tradition of time-reckoning in which clocks have manifested motion. One of the most salient forms of motion manifested is due to the motion of the clock 'hands' across a circular analogue clock or watch 'face'. As the literal motion of the hour hand towards the numeral 12, symbolising noon, correlates with the on-going function of the measurement process, this may have motivated the elaboration of the Measurement-system Sense in terms of motion. Hence, on the present account, the example in (13.7) references 'clock time', which constitutes the measurement of periodic behaviour associated with the uncoiling of a spring, or the oscillation of quartz crystals, etc., as opposed to, for instance, the phenomenological experience of time. Hence, the ascription of motion to *the time* in this example is due to a tight correlation between the motion of a clock hand, and the on-going process of measurement.

Given the correlation between the actual motion associated with clocks and the phenomenological experience of time, and the kind of motion clocks most saliently manifest in order to represent their periodic behaviour (e.g., the motion of 'hands' clockwise around a 'face' towards (and past) particular calibrations), it is this which determines the nature of the motion concepts which can serve to elaborate the Measurement-system Sense. For instance, the Measurement-system Sense is typically elaborated in terms of deictic motion, as exemplified by lexemes such as *approach, moving towards*, etc., and as implied by the prepositions which identify the location of clock hands against a conceptual frame of 'clockwise' (as opposed to 'anticlockwise') motion:

(13.8)   a.   We're moving towards bed-time
         b.   The time is approaching 11pm

(13.9)   a.   The time is (a) quarter to eight
         b.   The time is (a) quarter past eight

Other kinds of motion concepts cannot productively be employed as they do not match-up with the behaviour associated with the motion of hands around a clock-face.

Finally, it is important to observe that the nature of the motion content which serves to elaborate the Measurement-system Sense, while oriented with respect to the deictic centre, is distinct from the motion which elaborates the Moment and Event Senses considered in earlier chapters. In those earlier lexical concepts, the motion which serves to elaborate, is oriented, at least implicitly, with respect to an animate deictic centre, e.g., *The time for a decision is moving closer (to us); His time [=death] is approaching (him)*. In the Measurement-system Sense, the deictic centre with respect to which motion is oriented, constitutes an inanimate landmark, typically a particular calibration on the clock 'face', as in (13.10) below, or a particular temporal moment which metonymically represents a particular calibration with which it correlates, as in the use of *noon* in (13.7) which stands for the numeral 12.

(13.10)   The time is approaching 12 (o'clock)

Hence, the nature of the deictic motion which elaborates the Measurement-system Sense is distinct from the motion content which elaborates the Moment and Event Senses.

13.1.3 The Grammatical Criterion

Grammatically the Measurement-system Sense is distinct in that it can take the form of a count noun, a mass noun or a proper noun. No other sense associated with *time* appears to have such flexibility. To illustrate this, re-consider some examples presented earlier, reproduced below. The examples in (13.1b) and (13.2c) illustrate the Measurement-system Sense as a mass noun. Formally, the hallmark of a mass noun is that it is determined by a zero article rather than the indefinite article, as in (13.2b). This sentence would be ungrammatical with the indefinite article.

Mass Noun

(13.1)   b.   The time having been given on a drum, on the word March, the squad will move off.

(13.2)   c.   To beat time

The examples (13.3a, c) illustrate the Measurement-system Sense as a count noun, in which *time* is determined by the indefinite article.

(13.3)   a.   The short syllable... is considered as the original unit for the measure of time in the rhythm, and is called a time or mora.

          c.   [A] double or compound time is composed of two or more single times

Finally, the example in (13.4c) illustrates this sense as a proper noun. *Eastern Standard Time* and *Greenwich Mean Time* relate to specific time-reckoning systems, and do not show an article contrast, unlike mass or count nouns. Moreover, Greenwich Mean Time is conventionally spelt with initial capital letters, like names, and cannot undergo determination by an article.

(13.4)   c.   Eastern Standard Time is five hours behind Greenwich Mean Time

This behaviour suggests that given that the lexical concept indexed by *time* in these examples, which can refer to kinds of measurement systems, e.g., *He worked overtime* (mass noun), or units of measurement-systems, e.g., *A time is a short syllable* (count noun), or to a specific measurement system, such as Greenwich Mean Time (proper noun), it follows that it can be profiled, grammatically, in the three ways described.

      Accordingly, the Grammatical Criterion provides further evidence that the Measurement-system Sense constitutes a distinct lexical concept.

13.2 Periodicity and the co-ordination of activity

Now let's briefly consider the nature of the periodicities which serve to co-ordinate the kind of activities and processes discussed earlier: Marching, dancing, music, metre, time-reckoning and the payment of labour.

      The type of march is defined in terms of the number of steps of a certain distance per minute. In music (and by extension dancing which is often accompanied by music), the periodic behaviour employed to measure duration is the operation of a metronome, which emits clicks with varying degrees of frequency. This symbolisation is commonly replicated by beats on a drum or other instrument, or by the hand gestures of a conductor. In terms of time-reckoning, the basic period is the 24 hour day. Since at least circa 3,500 BC, when records detail the first sundials being built in Egypt, a number of natural periodic behaviours have been harnessed for the purposes of time-reckoning. These include the apparent motion of the sun across the sky, the flow of water or sand, the burning of graduated wax-candles or sticks of incense, the swing of a pendulum, the uncoiling of a spring, the oscillation of quartz crystals, and the decay of caesium atoms used in modern atomic clocks (Barnett 1998; Coveney & Highfield 1990; Lipincott 1999; Whitrow 1988). In addition to periodic behaviour, measurement systems for time-reckoning must also standardise the place or region which will be taken as the starting point for the 24 hour interval. This reflects the fact that as the Earth revolves upon its axis, and around the Sun, some parts of the Earth will be in darkness while others are in light. Hence, it is not practicable that the whole planet should operate to the time based on a single place. The basic interval for the calculation of payment for labour was traditionally the day. However, since the advent of accurate clocks and industrialisation, it has become the hour.

13.3 Derivation of the Measurement-system Sense

It is likely that the Measurement-system Sense developed from the Duration Sense by employing periodic behaviour to measure duration. As there is a tight correlation in experience between periodic behaviour and a temporal interval, as noted above, and as periodic behaviour is iterative in a predictable way, the iterations can be counted, constituting a physical symbolisation of duration. In this way, periodicity can be employed to measure duration. Temporal measurement is particularly useful for the kinds of activities described above (i.e., marching, dancing, music etc.), which require co-ordination among individuals. As the particular measurement-system correlates with the particular durations which comprise the particular activity, the form *time* which denotes Duration (in the Sanctioning Sense), implicates the Measurement-system employed to measure the intervals of duration in question. Hence, through pragmatic strengthening, it is perhaps natural that *time* should have developed a Measurement-system Sense.

13.4 Conclusion

This chapter has been concerned with the Measurement-system Sense for *time*. This constitutes a distinct lexical concept conventionally associated with *time*, which indexes a system for measuring duration. As Measurement-systems have a number of component parts, and can be construed in a number of ways, e.g., the component units ('times') which make up the measurement-system, the entity designated or measured ('to beat time'), by virtue of the measurement-system, and the (unique) measurement-system itself (GMT vs. EST), this lexical concept can be formalised as a count, mass or proper noun.

CHAPTER 14

The Commodity Sense

We now turn to the final sense associated with *time* to be discussed. Like the three previous senses considered, the Commodity Sense is also a secondary temporal concept, a lexical concept which can be viewed as primarily a socio-cultural product, rather than relating to phenomenologically basic or universal aspects of human cognition. In this chapter I will present evidence for the Commodity Sense as indexing a distinct lexical concept associated with the English lexeme *time*. I will argue that the Commodity Sense refers to an entity which is conceived as being valuable and hence can be exchanged, traded, acquired, possessed, etc.

14.1 Evidence for the Commodity Sense

In order to provide an immediate exemplification of the Commodity Sense, consider the following illustrative examples:

(14.1) a. Remember that time is money   [Benjamin Franklin][1]
      b. Time has become a scarce commodity. Everyone wants more of it
                                                        [The Observer][2]
      c. Self-assessment tax and finding a stakeholder pension are both examples of the state taxing our time
                                                    [The Observer][3]
      d. They sold/bought more advertising time
      e. They are selling time-shares on the Costa Blanca
      f. The psychiatrist charges a lot for her time
      g. A few techniques to create more time in your day
      h. She's invested a lot of time in that relationship
      i. We're not getting enough back for the time we're putting in

14.1.1 The Meaning Criterion

In the Commodity Sense, *time* prompts for an entity which is inherently valuable, as attested by its being equated with money in (14.1a), or a scarce commodity in (14.1b). As such *time* constitutes a commodity which can be bought and sold, for instance (14.1d–f), or which constitutes an investment which yields returns, as (14.1h–i). Clearly, this lexical concept provides meaning not apparent in the other senses considered. On the basis of the Meaning Criterion then, this Commodity reading evidenced in (14.1) would appear to constitute a distinct lexical concept.

14.1.2 The Concept Elaboration Criterion

As the central characteristic of this sense is of an entity which is valuable, content pertaining to entities conceived as valuable, such as commodities, can serve to elaborate the Commodity Sense. In this it is distinctive from any other lexical concept lexicalised by *time*.

A salient example of a valuable commodity is money, and just as we can *spend, invest, borrow*, and *budget* money, so too we can *spend, invest, borrow*, and *budget* time. Other entities which are valuable, including resources, can also serve to elaborate the Commodity Sense. For instance, content relating to valuable resources such as personnel, natural resources such as forests, water, minerals, etc., and manufactured products, can all serve to elaborate the Commodity Sense. For instance, we *manage* people, and other resources and commodities, and so too can *manage* time. Prospectors *find* oil, gold, silver, etc., and so too we can *find* the time to do something. Manufactured products are *made*, and so too we can *make* time for tasks, others and ourselves. Consider some examples based on the perceived resemblance between the Commodity Sense and money:

(14.2) We need to **spend** more time together
   Cf. They **spend** too much money on clothes

(14.3) We need to **invest** our time more wisely
   Cf. We need to **invest** our money more wisely

(14.4) We can make a killing by **selling** air-time to advertisers
   Cf. Prospectors made a killing by **selling** euros on the major exchanges

(14.5) I need **a better return** for the time I'm putting in
   Cf. I'd like **a better return** for the money I'm putting in

(14.6)   We should try and make **more efficient use** of our time
Cf. We should try and make **more efficient use** of our savings

In the foregoing, due to the resemblance between the perceived value of money and the sense being referenced by *time*, the Commodity Sense is elaborated in terms of conceptual content pertaining to Money. In the following examples, we see that any valuable entity that provides a return, and hence can be construed as a commodity and so valuable, can serve to elaborate the Commodity Sense:

(14.7)   We must **manage** our time more effectively
Cf. We must **manage** the personnel more effectively

(14.8)   We're **wasting** time discussing this
Cf. We're **wasting** valuable resources doing this

(14.9)   I've **lost** a lot of time today in ridiculous meetings
Cf. The museum has somehow **lost** one of its priceless artefacts

'How much time can you spare?'
Another salient way in which the Commodity Sense is elaborated is in terms of expressions relating to quantity. Consider some examples:

(14.10) a.   How much time can you spare?
         b.   I can spare 10 minutes of my time
         c.   Can you give me some time to think about it?

In these examples, the entity referenced by *time* is being elaborated in terms of a physical entity which can hence be quantified. The quantification, while relating to an assessment of temporal magnitude, like the Duration Sense employs quite different patterns of elaboration. Rather than being elaborated in terms of Length, e.g., *a long time*, the Commodity Sense is elaborated in terms of an entity which can be *given*. Accordingly, questions that employ expressions such as *how much?* relate to the Commodity Sense. In this, the Commodity Sense again resembles commodities such as money, which historically were assessed by weight, and to which expressions such as *how much?* applied. Indeed, the examples in (14.10a) is paralleled by the example in (14.11):

(14.11) How much money can you spare?

'The sands of time'
Finally, another way in which the Commodity Sense is conventionally elaborated is in terms of motion. This relates to the idiomatic expression in (14.12):

(14.12)   Time is running out

In this example, *time* references an interval, which is almost complete, and hence is 'running out'. The question arises as to why this particular collocation *running out* should prompt for the reading that a particular interval is almost over.

Historically intervals of short duration were measured by the action of hourglasses. Hourglasses were invented in Europe in the middle ages prior to the advent of mechanical clocks, and were used in colder North European climates where water clocks could not be used the entire year (Whitrow 1988). Hourglasses typically consisted of two glass chambers. Sand would run from one chamber into the other, and the time taken for the sand to run into the bottom chamber correlated with a particular delimited period of time, e.g., an hour, although other calibrations were possible. Although they were conceived as time-reckoning devices, by virtue of only being able to measure short periods of time they were often used in classrooms, or in courts of law, for instance, where advocates were allotted a certain amount of time for speaking. As the running of the sand out of the upper glass chamber indicated only a short and finite period of time, the running sand correlated with this finite interval being measured. As the expression: *the sands (of time) are running out,* would have correlated with the interval being measured almost being finished, *running out* gave rise to the inference that an allotted interval was almost over. The expression *the sands* represented the interval being measured, i.e. time. In later usages *time* came to be substituted for *the sands*, although in current usage it is still possible to employ *the sands* in conjunction with *time*, as the following attested example demonstrates:

(14.13)   Sands of time run out for strife-torn factory   [BNC][4]

Due to pragmatic strengthening, the implicature of finiteness and a period of time being close to its completion has been strengthened such that *running out* comes to have a conventional meaning akin to 'a particular commodity is almost gone'. This can be employed in a diverse range of contexts in which the supply of a particular commodity is almost exhausted, as evidenced in the examples below.

(14.14)   We're running out of milk/money/resources/supplies/patience/
          generosity/people

That is, due to pragmatic strengthening, the collocation *running out* became
associated with a meaning of 'almost finished/complete'. Given this sense, the
elaboration of the Commodity Sense in terms of *running out* is well-motivated
and predictable. As intervals of duration are bounded, they are finite in extent,
and thus can be experienced as almost complete. Given the meaning associated
with *running out* it is also now evident why this particular elaboration implicates a Resource or Commodity meaning. As a fixed interval of duration imposes constraints on what can be achieved by virtue of being bounded, then if
an interval is 'running out' there is less opportunity to accomplish a particular
task. This implicates that the duration is valuable.

Taken together the patterns of elaboration considered above suggest that,
in view of the second criterion, the examples in (14.1) do count as a distinct
lexical concept.

14.1.3 The Grammatical Criterion

In terms of the third criterion, the Commodity Sense, like the Matrix and Duration Senses, is a mass noun. Evidence for this comes from the fact that the
Commodity Sense undergoes the operation of portion-excerpting, in which a
mass noun can be bounded. For instance, in sentences such as: *Can you spare
me some time?* the Commodity Sense is determined by the quantifier *some*. It
will be recalled from Table 6.1 (Chapter 6) that quantification of this kind is
one of the formal indices of a mass noun.

To see how the Commodity Sense is formally distinct from the Matrix and
Duration Senses, consider the following examples:

(14.15) a.   Can you spare me some of your time?
         b.   How much time do you have/can you spare?

In (14.15a) the Commodity Sense is being pre-modified by the attributive possessive pronoun *your*. This serves to distinguish this sense from the Matrix
Sense. The Commodity Sense is distinct from the Duration Sense in that it
can appear in interrogative constructions employing the phrase *how much?* as
in (14.15b). This sentence relates to time as a commodity or resource which
can be quantified as it is conceived, in this sense, as having physical extent.
This contrasts with the Duration Sense, which, in its canonical usage, relates to
the duration associated with events and entities, recall the examples provided

in (7.1) in Chapter 7. That is, the Duration Sense serves as an assessment of the temporal magnitude of events, rather than temporality in its own right, i.e., as having substance, as here. Consequently, it would be ungrammatical to ask: *How much time did the relationship last?* (cf. *How long did the relationship last?*).

14.2 Derivation of the Commodity Sense

There are three plausible motivations for the derivation of the Commodity Sense from the Duration Sense. First, as intervals of time are finite, in certain contexts this may implicate value:

(14.16) The trapped submariners have only a short time before their air runs out

In this example *time* prompts for the Duration Sense, given that a reading of a bounded interval, in which submariners must be rescued, is obtained. Yet, the Duration Sense in this particular context gives rise to an implicature of value. This is due to the fact that if a particular activity – the location and removal of the submariners – is not completed within the specified interval, then there will be non-trivial consequences, i.e., the death of any potential survivors. An entity which is finite is accordingly valuable. Hence, in examples such as (14.16), as the amount of time available for locating and retrieving survivors is finite, it is also extremely valuable, particularly as lives are at stake.

A second motivation for the derivation of the Commodity Sense relates to the payment of labour. In the modern industrialised world, as we are paid in terms of conventionally fixed temporal intervals, typically the hour, then this reinforces the implicature that time is valuable.

A third motivation for the Commodity Sense, and one related to the preceding two, is the correlation between amount of time available and achievement of one's goals. As having more time entails greater opportunity to realise goals and objectives, this also implicates that time is valuable. Via pragmatic strengthening, the implicature of value has been, I suggest, reanalysed as a distinct meaning component which has come to be conventionally associated with the form *time*, and so instantiated in semantic memory.

Once *time* has developed a Commodity Sense, which treats Time as inherently valuable, then it becomes natural to attempt to *maximise* time's *value*, by *managing, saving,* and *budgeting* time, while avoiding *wasting* or *losing* time. Moreover, it has become possible for employers to be concerned that employees are *stealing* company time through feigned sickness. As the British Sunday newspaper, *The Observer*, has put it, "Like any commodity that is scarce, time has become a battleground. Workers and bosses battle over time: witness the hostility of executives to the Working Time Directive and parental leave" (Ibid.: The Mad Rush to Save Time, 3rd October, 1999).

14.3 Conclusion

This chapter has been concerned with the Commodity Sense, the final sense associated with *time* to be considered. While I have been conducting an analysis of the lexical concepts associated with the English form *time*, it is to be expected that different cultures and languages may have a different array of such lexical concepts. This will be particularly the case for secondary temporal concepts, such as the Commodity Sense, which has derived due to cultural imperatives and social practices. However, how other less well-studied cultures conceptualise time is a vast uncharted area, and given the current rate of language death, one which requires the urgent attention of linguists.

CHAPTER 15

The Present, Past and Future

Hitherto I have considered lexical concepts associated with the form *time*. In order to develop a fuller understanding of the complexity associated with the conceptual structure of temporality, we need to consider how these lexical concepts, and their elaborations, are integrated into three highly sophisticated cognitive models of time, Moving Time and Moving Ego, and the Temporal Sequence Model, to be explored in Part III. However, we must first consider other temporal concepts which contribute to this complexity. Hence, in this chapter we consider the lexical concepts symbolised by the forms *present*, *past* and *future*. Once we have considered these we will then be in a position to examine, in further detail, the two complex models to which these lexical concepts apply, namely the Moving Time and Moving Ego models of temporality.

There are two lines of evidence which suggest that the lexical concepts referenced by the forms *present*, *past* and *future* are distinct from the lexical concepts indexed by *time*. First, like the lexical concepts or senses prompted for by *time*, they are identified by distinct lexical forms. Given my assumption that language reflects conceptual structure, then by virtue of being symbolised by distinct forms, the lexical concepts referenced by *present*, *past* and *future* would appear to relate to concepts distinct from those lexicalised by *time*.

The second line of evidence which supports this view is that there is evidence of antecedent cognitive mechanisms and processes to which the lexical concepts referenced by *present*, *past* and *future* can be traced. As with the Duration Sense, for instance, I am suggesting that these lexical concepts may ultimately be derived from cognitive processes and hence constitute primary temporal concepts in the sense defined earlier.

As the lexical concepts Present, Past and Future may derive from antecedent cognitive functioning they are necessarily subjective in origin, as opposed to concepts based on external sensory experience. For subjective concepts such as these to be accessible to the conceptual system, and hence linguistic encoding, they are likely to be elaborated in terms of conceptual content derived from sensory experience (recall the discussion in Chapter 3). Thus, this chapter will also attempt to illustrate the way in which these lexical con-

cepts are elaborated. Such considerations will also have cross-linguistic consequences, as potential differences in how the lexical concepts of Past and Future, for instance, are elaborated in different cultures may provide important
insights into the different ways in which various cultural groups have privileged different aspects of conceptual structure, as revealed by different choices
in terms of concept elaboration and the sensory experience selected. In particular, we will briefly consider evidence that Aymara, a language spoken in
Bolivia, Peru and northern Chile, elaborates Future and Past in a markedly
different way from English (Lakoff & Johnson 1999; Miracle, Yapita, & Moya
1981; Núñez & Sweetser in preparation).

15.1 Present, Past and Future

In Chapter 2 I argued that temporal awareness is co-extensive with perceptual processing. The reason, I suggested, that this is the case, is that temporal
mechanisms may underlie perceptual processing. That is, perception, which
correlates with the dynamic "flow" of conscious experience, may be fundamentally temporal in nature. I argued that due to the existence of a cognitively
instantiated mechanism, the perceptual moment, perceptual processing is enabled. This line of reasoning leads to the conclusion that as perception may,
in essence, be enabled by cognitively instantiated temporal mechanisms, temporality is not, at base, a feature of an external physical world, but rather derives from perceptual processes which can ultimately be traced to neurological
antecedents.

      This situation is an outcome of one salient design feature associated with
the brain. Damasio (2000) notes that if we take the notion of a hammer, there is
not a single place in the brain where knowledge relating to hammers are stored.
That is, word-meanings (lexical concepts) are not discrete bundles of mental
structure neatly filed and stored in a putative mental 'lexicon'. Rather, different aspects of knowledge relating to hammers, e.g., what they look like, what
they feel like, the actions associated with hammers, etc. are based in different
areas of the brain in separate cortices. As Damasio observes, "The separation
[of knowledge] is imposed by the design of the brain and by the physical nature
of our environment. Appreciating the shape of a hammer visually is different
from appreciating its shape by touch; the pattern we use to move the hammer
cannot be stored in the same cortex that stores the pattern of its movement
as we see it; the phonemes with which we make the word hammer cannot be
stored in the same place, either" (Ibid.: 220). The integration of the various as-

pects of our knowledge about hammer is integrated seamlessly by virtue of the neurologically instantiated timing mechanisms discussed in Chapter 2. This results in being able to call to mind, in an apparently seamless way, an image of a hammer which includes information from a range of modalities.

A consequence of this timing mechanism, the perceptual moment, is that just as objects are 'constructed' by integrating stimuli from across different modalities, so too events are constructed. Pöppel (1994) argues that the event which correlates with the notion of the Present, the experience of 'now', can be traced to the perceptual moment with an outer range of 2–3 seconds (see also Chafe 1994; recall the discussion in Chapter 2). The perceptual moment in this range provides, he suggests, an experience which is constantly reconstituted, and thus is a likely precursor of our experience of 'now'.

Our next step is to suggest some cognitive antecedents of the lexical concepts Past and Future. A tradition dating back to Saint Augustine (354–430 AD) relates these concepts to that of the Present. Saint Augustine, in book XI of his *Confessions*, relates the Past and Future to Present as follows:

> What is now clear and plain is, that neither things to come nor past are. Nor is it properly said, "there be three times, past, present and to come:" yet perchance it might be properly said, "there be three times; a present of things past, a present of things present, and a present of things future."
>
> (Ibid.: XX, 26: 266)

In the Latin, Saint Augustine identifies the present of things past as *memoria*, 'memory'; the present of things present as *contuitus*, 'on-going perception'; and the present of the future as *expectatio*, 'expectation'. This tri-fold distinction in perceptual processing is reflected in cognitive psychology (e.g., Gell 1992; Miller & Johnson-Laird 1976; Neisser 1976), in which on-going perception (the Present) is viewed as modifying schemata held in memory (the Past). In turn, such schemata are employed in order to anticipate and interpret new input (the Future). That is, Past and Future may be related to perceptual sub-systems (i.e., memory, and anticipation/interpretation) necessary for the processing of on-going perception. Indeed, Chafe (1973) has suggested that there a number of ways in which anticipation mirrors memory.[1]

Within the sub-field of motivational psychology, there is a literature which deals with TIME PERSEPCTIVE, and particularly FUTURE TIME PERSPECTIVE. According to Lens and Moreas (1994), "Time perspective refers to past, present and future time that is part of an individual psychological life space" (Ibid.: 24). The important conclusion to emerge from such studies is that future time perspective is related to the "present anticipation of future goals" (Ibid.: 25). That is, future time perspective derives from anticipation in the present, based on outcomes in the past, rather than on future goals. Hence, such studies which relate the psychological future to motivation, treat the future as being embedded in the psychological present, a function of present anticipation. As such, "present anticipation rather than the future goal motivates behavior" (Ibid.:25).

Following Pöppel (1994) and others in the Augustinian tradition, I suggest that the concept associated with the form *present* may be traceable to the perceptual moment in the range of approximately 2–3 seconds. The concept of the Past relates ultimately, I suggest, to the memory system, which serves as a mechanism for retaining and integrating previous perceptual moments. Anticipation, which is a function of the present, may be a learning-effect of memory and hence may give rise to the concept of Future. Consequently, the lexical concepts associated with the forms *past* and *future* may ultimately be associated with internal functions, such as memory, and interpretative/anticipatory functions, which are related to, and necessary for, the processing of on-going experience, namely the present.

15.2 The Present and concept elaboration

Having identified cognitive mechanisms which plausibly antecede the primary temporal concepts Present, Past and Future, I turn now to a consideration of the nature of concept elaboration, and particularly the nature of the conceptual content which serves to elaborate them.

There is good evidence that the lexical concept lexicalised by the English form *present* is elaborated in terms of conceptual structure pertaining to the spatio-physical environment proximal to the deictic centre. Put another way, the Present is elaborated in terms of a physical location co-locational with the experiencer. For instance, in sentences such as: *Located here in present-day England, the Victorian era seems like a bleak place,* the temporal present is associated with the spatial deictic centre.[2] Moreover, the English lexeme *present* is derived from a diachronically earlier spatial sense denoting co-location or physical proximity, and is synchronically related to the lexeme *presence,* which has a spatial meaning of co-location. According to the OED, the form *present* derives from the past-participle of the Latin *præasse,* which meant 'to be before' or 'to be at hand', i.e., 'to be in the close vicinity of'. The form came into English via Old French, and retains its spatial sense of co-location in uses such as *to be present,* e.g., *All the students were present for the exam;* and in usages in which the verb designates introducing someone to someone else, as in the following example: *Allow me to present Mr. Smith to you*. In such sentences, the introduction can only typically be effected if the person being introduced is co-locational with the person to whom they are to be introduced (or at least visible, as in, for instance, tele-conferences). That is, there is a tight correlation in experience between being present and being introduced. Hence, the semantic development of the verb *to present* in its current sense meaning 'to effect an introduction' represents a natural development from the earlier meaning of physical co-location, and is plausibly motivated by experiential correlation and pragmatic strengthening.

The observation that conceptual content pertaining to the physical location which we occupy, that is the notion lexicalised by *here*, elaborates the subjective concept of Present, has been made by other scholars. For instance, Grady (1997a) notes that, "[I]t is reasonable to speculate that we associate the temporal present with the physical situation in which we find ourselves" due to experiential correlation (Ibid.: 122). As the temporal present inevitably correlates with the particular location we happen to occupy at any given time, then there is a tight and ubiquitous correlation in experience between the temporal present and our experience of our physical vicinity.

If then the experience of the present correlates with our physical location, and immediate vicinity, glossed by the term *here*, we might well wonder what kind of experience gives rise to the appropriate conceptual content. That is, what is the nature of the experience which gives rise to the concept here? This represents an important and intriguing question as it is presumably the same (or at least similar) conceptual content which serves to elaborate the lexical concept of the Present. I will refer to conceptual material which pertains to physical location as LOCATIONAL CONTENT – which is to say conceptual material redescribed from sensorimotor experience.

One plausible hypothesis is that the locational content is related to PRO-PRIOCEPTION – the perception of the experiencer's body as being distinct from the environment.[3] The sense-perceptory organs as well as the ability to self-locomote necessarily establish a distinction between a stable environment and the perceiving entity. For instance, there are a number of perceptual regions and boundaries which naturally emerge, resulting from such sensory and motor faculties. Below I will outline some possibly relevant distinctions in the locational ecology of the human environment, although plausible alternative distinctions could be made. Hence, the ensuing is meant to be suggestive only.

In the first instance, skin separates the experiencer from his or her environment, and represents what we might term our BODY-SPACE. The area termed body-space can be defined in terms of sensory information derived from physical contact, against, for instance, the skin, which forms a natural boundary. Thus, it is in the perceptual field of body-space where touch and taste provide sensory information. We might term the next perceptual field PERSONAL-SPACE, defined in terms of the extent to which we can reach or stretch, and within which, for humans, the sense-perception of smell is most acute. The next perceptual field might be termed PROXIMAL-SPACE, pertaining to the area beyond the personal-space boundary and up to a few metres around the experiencer, in which his or her visual, and auditory, sense-perceptions are undiminished. Beyond this we have what I will term MEDIAL-SPACE, where visual stimuli are relatively undiminished. A natural boundary which we could include in our definition of medial-space is that of natural enclosures such as copses, dells, caves, woods, forests, valleys, etc., and man-made enclosures such as vehicles, rooms, buildings, etc. Beyond this perceptual boundary we have what I will term DISTAL-SPACE, a region in which visual information is relatively diminished, being bounded by the horizon. From a perceptual-ecological perspective, i.e., from the point-of-view of an experiencer, there is no space beyond this boundary, in the sense that the horizon acts as a natural boundary on our perceptual recruitment of information. Figure 15.1 depicts the relationship holding between the various perceptual fields identified.

Clearly these perceptual fields constitute a cline rather than being discrete. However, due to the discontinuous nature of our bodies (we are not co-extensive with our environment), and hence the fact that our sensorimotor faculties provide information constrained by our location, these perceptual fields are salient to varying degrees.

The concept of Present while including body-space and personal-space information, might also, in certain situations, overlap with what I am terming proximal-space. In essence, due to an extremely tight correlation in experience between the temporal present (the current perceptual moment), and the location of the experiencer, the concept of Present is elaborated in terms of locational content pertaining to the experiencer's immediate vicinity. Hence, if we imagine that in Figure 15.1 an experiencer is standing at the inner-most concentric circle, which corresponds to the perceptual field of body-space, the locational content which serves to elaborate the lexical concept of Present plausibly includes body-space, personal-space, and depending upon the context, possibly proximal-space, and even medial- and distal-space.

For instance, if I talk on the telephone to someone in another city, country or even continent, I might refer to my city (e.g., Brighton) or country (the United Kingdom) as *here*; e.g., *What time does your flight from Washington DC*

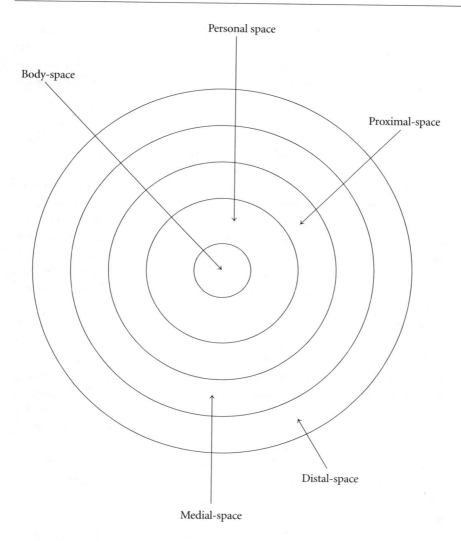

Figure 15.1. Perceptual fields

get here? even though in terms of my perceptual field, the physical extent of the city or country I am located in must be in the distal range.

Nonetheless, in terms of the elaboration of the Present in terms of locational content, as the perceptual fields must correlate with the experiencer's immediate physical vicinity, given that temporal experience is ultimately a subjective state and so is highly specific to the experiencer, the locational content which serves to elaborate the Present will be localised and so constitute content pertaining to the perceptual fields of body-space, personal-space and possibly proximal-space. Hence, similar sensory information which elaborates the lexical concept of Here also serves to elaborate the concept lexicalised by *present*.

15.3 The Past and Future, and concept elaboration

We now turn to a consideration of the way in which the Past and Future are elaborated. One of the most salient aspects of the human body is that the orientation of the sense-organs dictates the canonical direction of locomotion. That is, the front/back axis is asymmetrical. In terms of ecological viability it makes sense that direction of locomotion should correlate with the orientation of the sense organs, particularly the visual organs – humans like other primates have a highly developed visual modality relative to other modalities such as smell and hearing.

I suggested above that the concept of Future derives from the present anticipation of an objective or goal. Given human physiology and so the asymmetry of the front/back axis, goals are necessarily located in front of the experiencer, as this is the direction of orientation (and hence locomotion). Given that the lexical concept Future is embedded in present anticipation of objectives or goals, and that the experiencer self-orients with respect to his or her physical goal, then entities and locations which count as (physical) goals will necessarily be located in front of the experiencer. Put another way, there is a tight correlation between the present anticipation of realising a goal, and the goal being located in front of the experiencer. This follows as, in physical terms, the experiencer can only anticipate realising the goal if the goal is located in front of him or her.

For instance, if the experiencer seeks to repair a broken object (e.g., a teacup in which the handle has come away and requires being glued back into place), and hence anticipates a state of repair, he or she would typically effect the repair by placing the object in foveal vision, i.e., locating the object in front. Hence, in such examples, there is a tight correlation between anticipating the object's repair (the future goal), and the object's location in front of the experiencer.

What is interesting is that this correlation between anticipation and being located in front does not require self-locomotion.[4] However, the correlation is also apparent in such situations which do require locomotion, for the reasons given above. For example, in ball games such as cricket, if the experiencer is serving as a fielder, in order to retrieve a loose ball there is a tight correlation between anticipation of reaching the ball's location and hence it's retrieval (the goal), and the location of the ball being in front with respect to the fielder. Such examples additionally involve motion which mediates the realisation of the goal (arrival at the ball's location and hence its retrieval).

Based on the foregoing, we would expect that due to this tight experiential correlation, the lexical concept Future is elaborated in terms of content pertaining to being located in front of the experiencer, which is what we find, as attested by complex prepositions such as *in front of*:

(15.1) a. The future lies in front of us
        b. She has a bright future ahead/in front of her

Moreover, as evidenced in (15.2), other temporal concepts which are held to be future in nature relative to a particular experiencer (and hence the experience of the present), are elaborated in terms of being located in front of the experiencer:

(15.2) a. Old age lies way ahead of me
        b. Having children is in front of us
        c. The years ahead of us will be difficult

The point this illustrates is that the lexical concept Future appears to be elaborated primarily in terms of locational content (rather than in terms of motion content).

In contrast to the foregoing, we would expect the Past to be elaborated in terms of conceptual content pertaining to being located behind the experiencer. This follows as the Past, I have suggested, is ultimately derived from perceptual moments held in memory. Given that human sensory organs such as eyes are located on the front part of the body, there is less direct means of obtaining visual-sensory information about the environment located behind the experiencer. Accordingly, the experiencer must rely on visual information previously obtained, and stored in memory, regarding the environment located behind. When one task is finished we turn to the next task, often turning our back on that which is now complete.

As with the Future, this correlation is independent of motion; we tend to face away from objects when we have completed working on them, such that they are located behind us, or at least are no longer in foveal vision. Notwithstanding this, the same experiential correlation is apparent in motile situations. For instance, when undergoing motion the region located behind the experiencer was once seen and experienced (and so is past), but now information regarding this region is stored in memory. Based on the tight correlation between being held in memory and the lack of current visual information about the region located behind the experiencer, we would expect that the lexical concept Past is elaborated in terms of locational content pertaining to the region located behind the experiencer as lexicalised, for instance by *behind*. This is exactly what we find in sentences such as (15.3), which represent a conventional way of situating the Past:

(15.3)   The past is behind me

Similarly, concepts which pertain to the past (relative to an experiencer), are elaborated in terms of conceptual content derived from the region behind the experiencer:

(15.4)   a.   My childhood is behind me
         b.   Once divorced, she was finally able to put an unhappy marriage behind her

Finally, it is worth observing that the pattern in which the lexical concepts Past and Future are elaborated in terms of content pertaining to behind and in front of the experiencer respectively is cross-linguistically robust, occurring in languages as diverse from English as the Niger-Congo language Wolof (Moore 2000), Japanese (Shinohara 1999), and Chinese (Yu 1998). However, there are languages which present possible counter-evidence to this pattern, an issue we will explore in the next section.

15.4 Cross-cultural differences: Aymara

Some scholars have suggested that certain languages elaborate the concepts of Past and Future in terms of locational content at odds with the pattern found in languages such as English. In such languages, it has been claimed that the Past is conceptualised as being in front of the experiencer and the Future as being behind. The most robust evidence to have emerged to support this claim relates to Aymara, spoken in the Andean region of Peru, Chile and Bolivia (Lakoff & Johnson 1999; Miracle & Yapita Moya 1981; Núñez & Sweetser in preparation).

A range of linguistic and gestural evidence has emerged which strongly suggests that Aymara speakers elaborate their concept of Future in terms of being behind and the Past as in front. For instance, in Aymara the expression employed to denote the 'past' derives from the lexeme relating to the eye, or being located in front, as in (15.5), while the linguistic expression to denote the 'future' relates to be located behind, as in (15.6). This is suggestive that terms which may have originally related to a spatial location have derived a temporal meaning which appears to be at odds with the pattern found in a language such as English.

(15.5)   mayra   pacha
         front/eye/sight time
         'past time'

(15.6)   q'ipa   pacha
         back/behind   time
         'future time'

Núñez and Sweetser (in preparation) report on a study which provides gestural evidence supporting the view that Aymara speakers conceptualise the Past as being located in front and the Future as behind. A number of scholars (e.g., McNeil 1992) have observed that gesture is minutely co-timed to fit in with linguistic patterns, and may be less consciously attended to by the speaker. Hence, gesturing may provide further evidence for the nature of the conceptual structure underlying language. Reporting on a study conducted by Núñez et al. (1997), Núñez and Sweetser argue that while Aymara speakers appear to conceptualise the present as being co-located with the front of their bodies, as do English speakers, when referring to the past they gesture to a space just in front of them, and when referring to the future they gesture over their shoulder, i.e., behind them. Interestingly, when referring to events in the near past, Aymara speakers gesture to locations closer in front, while the space further in front is pointed to when more remote past times are referenced. Evidence of this kind correlates with the range of linguistic data provided by Miracle and Yapita Moya (1981) and Núñez and Sweetser to support the position that Aymara speakers elaborate the past as located in front and the future as behind.

In their paper on Aymara, Miracle and Yapita Moya (1981) observe that Aymara has a rich evidential system in which the speaker must mark the data source for a particular proposition, i.e., whether the data source is personal or non-personal knowledge. Indeed, they observe that Aymara culture privileges information which is attested, for instance, information which has been seen with one's own eyes. They further suggest that the reason that the future is conceptualised as being located behind, while the past is conceptualised as located in front, may be because we have not yet experienced, and so have not 'seen' the future, while we have experienced and so 'seen' the past. As that which is behind cannot be readily seen, given human physiology, and that which is located in front is readily visible, it may be for this reason that the future is conceptualised as located behind, and the past in front.

As Grady (1997a) has observed, there is a tight correlation in experience between seeing that something is the case and knowing that it is the case. For this reason he proposed KNOWING IS SEEING as a primary metaphor. Given that there is a tight correlation in experience between knowing and seeing, and given, as already intimated, that an important aspect of both the Past and Future, pertains to knowing – the Past is known as it has been experienced, while the Future is unknown as it is anticipated, and hence has not been ex-perienced – in a culture such as Aymara, where first-hand knowledge is valued over hear-say and reported knowledge, then there may be a strong motiva-tion for elaborating the concepts of Present, Past and Future in terms of vision. Moreover, a consequence of the elaboration of these concepts in terms of visual content may be that the Past is conceptualised as being located in front of the experiencer, due to the asymmetry of the front/back axis (i.e., our eyes being located in that part of our head which we label 'front', this contributes to the front/back asymmetry).

Hence, it may be that it is the elaboration of the concepts Future and Past – which relate to (not) knowing – in terms of visual content, and the functional consequences of this (that what is seen is necessarily located in front of the human experiencer, and what is located behind cannot be seen), which is what gives rise to the distinctive elaboration of Past and Future associated with Aymara. As English elaborates these concepts directly in terms of locational content, based on the body's front/back directional asymmetry, as discussed earlier, it for this reason that English elaborates the Future in terms of being located ahead, and the Past behind.

Before concluding this section, it is important to make the point that psy-chological studies have provided extensive experimental evidence that TIME PERSPECTIVE – the extent to which the Present, Past and Future are integrated in a continuous fashion as part of an individual's 'life-space' – is both an in-dividual and societal trait. That is, time perspective can vary from individ-ual to individual and across cultures (see Lens & Moreas 1994, and refer-ences therein). Hence, although the concepts of Present, Past and Future may have cognitive antecedents and are thus primary temporal concepts, the ways in which they are elaborated is a function of cultural-historical factors. Ac-cordingly, although the cognitive antecedents of Present, Past and Future may, given shared physiology and neurological architecture, be universal, different cultures may, in principle, conventionalise different elaborations and hence conceptions.

The way in which English speakers and Aymara speakers may elaborate their concepts of Past and Future could be one example of this, resulting in distinct concepts which are not synonymous and hence not completely trans-latable (in the sense of Lakoff 1987: Ch. 18).[5] While the concepts of English speakers are elaborated in terms of locational concepts, Aymara speakers ap-pear to elaborate their partially equivalent concepts in terms of visual content. A consequence of this is that the concepts for Past and Future in Aymara ap-pear to be elaborated in terms of locational content at odds with their closest English counterparts.

15.5 Mandarin and the Temporal Sequence Model

While Aymara appears to elaborate its concepts for Past and Future in terms of visual content, resulting in a conceptualisation in which the Past is located in front of the experiencer and the Future behind, we need to exercise caution regarding similar claims for other languages. Moore (2000) argues that previ-ous scholars have sometimes conflated what he terms 'Ego-based' models of time (e.g., the Moving Time and Moving Ego patterns described in Chapter 5; see also Chapter 17), with a distinct Front/Back Moving Time pattern (which I will term the COMPLEX TEMPORAL SEQUENCE MODEL, e.g., *Monday precedes Tuesday*; *Saturday follows Friday*), in which temporally-framed events are se-quenced with respect to one another, rather than with respect to the concept of Present (see Chapter 18 for a discussion of this model of temporality).[6] This has resulted in erroneous claims being made for the language in question.

A case in point are the claims made by Alverson (1994) for Mandarin. Based on relatively limited data Alverson suggests that in Mandarin the Fu-ture is conceptualised as being located behind the experiencer and the Past in front. However, Yu (1998) argues that in fact Mandarin speakers elaborate the Future in terms of locational content concerned with being in front of the experiencer, while the Past is elaborated in terms of locational content to do with being behind, the same pattern as in English. Yu (Ibid.: 109) holds that Alverson's erroneous claim is due to confusion over the correct reference point with the following terms: *yi-qian*, 'before, formerly, previously', and *yi-hou*, 'after, afterwards, later, hereafter'. Alverson argues that, "Events that have al-ready happened are those that are before (*yiqian*)...the experiencer... [e]vents that will come or are yet to come are all later or after/behind (*yihou*) the expe-riencer" (1994: 75). However, Yu observes that the reference point used with these terms is not the experiencer, but rather constitutes another temporal event. This situation is analogous to English sentences exhibiting the Complex Temporal Sequence model, such as those below:

(15.7)   a.   Tuesday comes after Monday
         b.   The forecasters predict that this year after a wet June there will be a hot July

(15.8)   a.   Monday comes before Tuesday
         b.   A wet June will come before a hot July

In these sentences the reference point is a temporally-framed event, *Monday* and *June*, in (15.7a, b) respectively, and *Tuesday* and *July* in (15.8a, b). Hence in (15.7a) *Tuesday* and (15.7b) *July* are located with respect to *Monday* and *June* respectively, while in (15.8a) *Monday* and (15.8b) *June* are located with respect to (15.8a) *Tuesday* and (15.8b) *July* respectively.

15.6 Conclusion

In this chapter I have argued that the concepts lexicalised by the forms *present, past and future* may be ultimately traceable to antecedent cognitive processes. Hence, these concepts, like the primary lexical concepts associated with the lexeme *time* relate to experiences which are at base subjective in nature. In a language such as English the conceptual content which serves to elaborate these concepts derives from locational content, due to the functional front/back asymmetry, a consequence of human physiology. In other languages, such as Aymara, there is now good evidence that it may be due to conceptualising Past and Future in terms of visual content, and the functional consequences of such an understanding in terms of relative location, that the pattern of concept elaboration is as it is. If this is so, it would account for the apparent consequence that the concepts of Past and Future in such a language are elaborated in a strikingly different way, vis-à-vis English.

PART III

Models for time

CHAPTER 16

Time, motion and agency

In Part II we explored the range of lexical concepts associated with the lexeme *time*. We further considered lexical concepts associated with lexemes such as *present*, *past* and *future*. However, how we conceptualise temporality does not solely involve manipulating discrete temporal lexical concepts. In addition, lexical concepts appear to participate in larger-scale cognitive models in which a number of discrete temporal lexical concepts are integrated. Before considering such models for time in Chapters 17 and 18, we must first consider the relation between motion and time.

As we have seen, motion content appears to be one of the most salient ways in which time is elaborated. Hence, it is important to explore the nature of this relationship. Moreover, this will lead to a consideration of the relationship between motion and agency, which will be important for the discussion in the next chapter.

16.1 Time and motion

Motion concepts appear to be among the most frequent to be employed in order to elaborate temporal concepts. Grady (1997a) points out that there is a tight correlation in our experience between motion and time – whenever an object undergoes motion, the motion event correlates with the passage of time. According to Grady, it is this tight correlation which motivates the elaboration of time in terms of motion.

Yet, while our experience of motion correlates with our experience of time, is it necessarily the case that time correlates with motion? After all, time is on-going in the sense that we experience time whether or not we experience motion (e.g., as when sitting in my chair without moving, with my eyes closed). Hence, why should motion serve to structure temporal lexical concepts rather than experiences which correlate with temporal experience in a more ubiquitous way?

For instance, breathing, which is ongoing, irrespective of whether we are stationary or in motion, presumably has a stronger claim as being more ubiquitously correlated with temporal experience than motion. However, while we often notice our own (and indeed other's) breathing, particularly for instance when we swim or duck our heads underwater, and are temporarily unable to breathe, or indeed during or after physical exercise when our breathing is laboured, breathing is not normally salient, a consequence of its not being under voluntary control.

Motion, however, is, in perceptual terms highly salient (Miller & Johnson-Laird 1976). After all, survival depends on our ability to detect motion. Indeed, such is the efficacy of our motion-detectors that certain responses which depend upon them, such as the impulse to duck when a hurtling object looms into view, are 'hard-wired' relieving conscious-processing of the fraction of second delay that might result with potentially fatal consequences (Dennett 1991). While motion is highly salient, there is also reason to believe that it might be nearly as ubiquitous as ever-present processes such as breathing. Research on the psychology of vision (e.g., Gibson 1986) suggests that almost from birth infants are subjected to the visual flow of experience (the optic array) which 'moves' past us well before we have the ability to self-locomote. Our visual apparatus perceives the world around as 'flowing past', as we are carried in our care-givers' arms. This phenomenon, in which the environment appears to be in a continual state of motion, suggests that motion is perceptually both ubiquitous and salient, and thus forms a tight and ubiquitous correlation with on-going temporal experience.

Based on the kind of conceptual metaphors which have been proposed in the literature (recall Chapter 5), it appears that it is often assumed that temporal concepts are elaborated in terms of motion trajectories which are horizontally extended (i.e., 'straight lines'). This follows as the Moving Ego mapping, for instance, is modelled on the nature of motion undergone by human agents, e.g., TIME IS (MOTION ALONG) A PATH, (Grady 1997a), or TIME IS A LINE (Shinohara 1999). While in principle paths (and even lines), and the motion which correlates with them, need not be straight (as acknowledged by Shinohara), the kinds of examples employed often appear to presuppose straight paths as a model for the elaboration of temporal concepts. Accordingly, it is worth reminding ourselves that the association of time with conceptual structure pertaining to motion trajectories which are horizontally extended (as in motion along straight paths), is arguably a cultural construct.

In classical Greece the motion associated with time was conceptualised as cyclical (connecting point A with point A as in Figure 16.1), rather than hori-

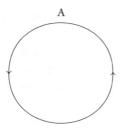

Figure 16.1. A cyclically extended motion trajectory

Figure 16.2. A horizontally extended motion trajectory

zontally extended (connecting point A with point B, as in Figure 16.2), as evidenced for instance in the Platonic cosmology *Timaeus*. Hence, the motion
associated with time was not conceptualised in terms of the paths followed by
humans (which often are horizontally extended straight lines), but rather with
the motion associated with heavenly bodies, which is typically cyclical rather
than straight (or at least perceived as such) in nature.

A number of scholars suggest that the linear view of time (as exemplified in
Figure 16.2) dominant in the modern Western world derived via Christianity
from the Hebrew tradition (Bennett 1998; Coveney & Highfield 1990; Turetzky
1998; Whitrow 1988). Turetzky summarises this position as follows:

> The decline of the classical world and the introduction of Christian themes ini-
> tiated profound changes in the philosophy of time. The Christian conscience
> places the highest priority on personal spiritual progress occurring within its
> historical narrative of creation, fall, divine incarnation, and redemption. The
> Christian notion of salvation depends upon this narrative of spiritual progress.
> Consequently, it must deny cyclical theories of time. For were time an endless
> cyclical return of events the incarnation could not retain the significance of a
> unique saving event. (Ibid.: 56)

In the modern world, some cultures still retain a cyclical view of time, e.g., the
Indian tradition (Whitrow 1988), the Malagasy of Madagascar (Dahl 1995),
etc., and there is abundant evidence that earlier cultures, e.g., the Aztec of
South America held a cyclical as opposed to a linear view of time (Whitrow
1988). Indeed, cultural constructs such as the calendar are firmly rooted in
earlier cyclical conceptions of temporality, as attested by an expression such as:

Christmas has come around again, implicating cyclical as opposed to straight linear motion.

We must also be careful to distinguish temporal experience and structure from spatial experience and structure. For instance, Shinohara (1999), a conceptual metaphor scholar, has suggested that time is structured in terms of motion because just as linear motion is one-dimensional so too time is inherently one-dimensional. She summarises this position as follows, "[T]ime itself is nothing but the "order" of recognized events. If this is the case, it is quite natural that time is conceived as one-dimensional, since it seems impossible to think of an "ordinal structure" which is more than one-dimensional" (Ibid.: 155–156). However, it is important to avoid confusing the fact that temporality can be modelled in terms of a one-dimensional line (or linear motion), with the view that temporality is inherently one-dimensional, i.e., it is in essence constituted by ordinal structure. As I have argued in detail, the sequential nature of temporal experience results from the experience and mechanisms responsible for duration. Temporality is fundamentally durational in nature, and all else follows from this.

Indeed, at the perceptual level temporality is experienced in terms of durational 'episodes' configured by virtue of perceptual moments. These durational episodes are related in memory such that they can be chronologically sequenced. However, while chronological sequencing correlates with spatial (i.e., geometrical) sequences – tracing points on a line correlates with successive temporal 'moments' – such a correlation does not imply that temporality is fundamentally one-dimensional or ordinal in the manner supposed, nor that it shares any inherent similarity with spatial structure, contra the position advocated by Shinohara (1999). Duration and chronological sequencing constitute a wholly subjective aspect of experience and simply cannot be considered to be one-dimensional in the way that geometrical properties derived from spatial points can be. Accordingly, it is erroneous to believe that time is itself ordinal and so one-dimensional.

Nevertheless, it is widely assumed in modern physics that time can be described in geometric terms properly reserved for spatial experience (either in Euclidean geometric properties employed since the time of Galileo, or more recently in the non-Euclidean properties associated with the spacetime perspective of Minkowski and Einstein). The view of time in modern physics will be addressed in Chapter 19.

16.2 Motion and concept elaboration

Given the importance of vision in primates it is natural that the experience of motion should be such an important and salient diagnostic for a change in the world-state. Accordingly, motion serves to elaborate a range of distinct concepts, other than the temporal concepts considered in this book.

An important consequence of the correlation uncovered between occurrences and motion is that this predicts that any lexical concept, which can be said to occur, should be able to be elaborated in terms of deictic motion phenomena. Indeed, this is exactly what we find, as attested by the following:

(16.1)   a.   I have a headache coming on
         b.   Disaster is approaching
         c.   He has a heart-attack heading his way

Each of the lexical concepts referenced by *headache*, *disaster* and *heart-attack*, constitutes a discrete event, which can therefore be defined in terms of occurrence (and hence non-occurrence). This being so, they are elaborated in terms of motion content, such that we understand their manifestation in terms of motion. Hence, the occurrence of a headache is understood in terms of the headache *coming*, etc.

Similarly, it is for this reason, I suggest, that other kinds of discrete events such as Christmas, Easter, graduation etc., can be elaborated in terms of deictic motion as attested by the following examples:

(16.2)   a.   Christmas is approaching
         b.   Easter is moving up on us fast
         c.   Graduation is moving closer

Equally, events which are symptomatic of a more general occurrence, such as extinction, exhibit the same pattern, as the following example illustrates:

(16.3)   The anticipated extinction of a rare Amazonian spider has finally arrived

Moreover, as we have seen, a number of temporal lexical concepts such as the Moment Sense, the Event Sense, and the Measurement-system Sense can also be elaborated in terms of motion events of this kind:

(16.4)   a.   The time for a decision has come   [Moment Sense]
         b.   Her time has come   [Event Sense]
         c.   The time is approaching midnight   [Measurement-system Sense]

This suggests that there is a generalisation to be captured, in which events which are experienced and conceptualised as being temporally discrete, and hence which are experienced as occurring and so can be distinguished perceptually from their non-occurrence, can be elaborated in terms of deictic motion events, as evidenced by lexemes such as *come, approach, arrive, get closer*, etc. This pattern I term the Moving Event mapping.

There is another pattern in which it is not the discrete event which has motion ascribed to it, but rather it is the experiencer, termed Ego, which is conceptualised as moving. In Chapter 5 I introduced this pattern with respect to our conceptualisation of temporal concepts. However, this pattern, like the Moving Event pattern, appears to apply to a wide-range of distinct lexical concepts:

(16.5) a. The Managing Director is moving towards a make-or-break decision
        b. We're approaching Christmas/Easter/graduation
        c. Several species are going extinct everyday   [BBC Radio 4][1]
        d. Western civilisation is approaching spiritual bankruptcy

While in the Moving Event pattern the (temporal) Event is conceptualised as in motion (typically with respect to a linguistically overt or covert Ego), in the Moving Ego pattern (16.4) it is the TR, i.e., *the Managing Director, we, several species* and *western civilisation*, which is in motion with respect to a particular Event.

It has been suggested that Moving Event patterns and Moving Ego patterns may be figure-ground reversals of one another (Lakoff 1993; Lakoff & Johnson 1999). While this appears to be true in principle, it is not straightforwardly the case that Moving Event and Moving Ego patterns are figure-ground reversals. There are a number of mapping gaps between what is acceptable in the Moving Event pattern and the Moving Ego pattern.

For instance, while (16.6a) is acceptable in my dialect, standard British English, (16.6b) is decidedly odd:

(16.6) a. I have a headache coming on
        b. ?I'm coming on to a headache/?I'm approaching a headache

If the Moving Ego pattern (16.6b) constitutes a straight-forward reversal of the Moving Event pattern (16.6a), we would expect the sentence in (16.6b) to be acceptable. Hence, we need to consider why certain figure-ground reversals are permitted whilst others are not. The solution to such mapping 'gaps' will be seen to centre on the relationship between motion and agency. In order to elucidate this relationship we must first consider Talmy's (1996, 2000) discussion of fictive motion.

16.3 Motion and agency

Talmy (1996, 2000) presents a detailed investigation of the way in which humans employ motion phenomena in order to elaborate events and situations which do not involve objective or veridical motion. The ascription of motion to physical entities which cannot be said to be undergoing motion, Talmy terms FICTIVE MOTION.

Fictive or apparent motion is well-known in the psychology literature. One example of this concerns what psychologists call frame-relative motion. For instance, when waiting on-board a train for its departure, if another train is sitting alongside and begins to move out of the station first, it is common for the observer to experience his or her own train to be moving, and for the train alongside to be experienced as stationary when in fact the reverse is the case.[2] There is abundant linguistic evidence which suggests that fictive motion is reflected in language, and moreover that it is a highly ubiquitous linguistic phenomenon. Linguistic examples of fictive motion include sentences such as the following:

> (16.7) a. The road goes from London to Brighton
> b. The fence crosses the field
> c. The great wall of China zigzags its way across a subcontinent
> d. The blackboard runs along the wall

in which motion is ascribed to entities which are veridically stationary. The examples in (16.7) illustrate what Talmy terms COVERAGE-PATH fictive motion, in which motion is ascribed to the 'path' covered by the entity. One explanation for such coverage-path fictive phenomena may be due to the fact that in order to trace a coverage path, humans must actually move their heads, bodies and eyes, giving rise to the perception of motion at some level.

Talmy presents a taxonomy of the different linguistic manifestations of fictive motion. In particular, he provides a detailed analysis of one kind of fictive motion which he terms EMANATION. According to Talmy, emanation involves the emergence of something intangible from an object. It is the intangible entity which exhibits fictive motion. Talmy identifies a number of emanation types only two of which will be given below:

Radiation path

(16.8)   The sun is shining into the cave

Shadow path

(16.9)   The tree threw its shadow down into/across the valley

In each of these examples emanation ascribes fictive motion to an intangible entity. For instance, in (16.8) radiation (i.e., sunlight) is held to be emanating from the sun, while in (16.9) a shadow is held to emanate from a tree. Patterns of emanation such as this led Talmy to consider why it should be that one entity rather than another is the source of emanation. For instance, why is it that the sun rather than the cave, and the tree rather than the valley are considered to be the sources of emanation respectively?

Talmy suggests that what counts as the source of the emanation is due to what he terms an ACTIVE-DETERMINATIVE PRINCIPLE. This states that the entity which is considered to be more active and/or more determinative will be conceptualised as the source of emanation. For instance, in (16.8) the sun is considered to be more active than a cave, presumably because the light associated with it can vary in magnitude at different times of the day, and because it appears to move across the sky. Similarly in (16.9), shadows are typically contingent on trees, rather than on valleys, and moreover, trees are not contingent upon shadows, but rather vice versa: shadows disappear whereas trees tend not to. Hence, a tree is conceptualised as being more determinative with respect to the presence or absence of a shadow.

Having established a plausible motivation for what counts as source of emanation, Talmy wonders why this source (the sun, and the tree respectively), should give rise to fictive motion. After all, shadows are not veridically (i.e., objectively) *thrown* across the valley by the tree. Talmy (1996) hypothesises that the active-determinative principle is a consequence of our conceptualisation of agency. That is, "[T]he individual's exercise of agency functions as the model for the source of emanation" (Ibid.:228). The model of agency which Talmy proposes is what he terms the agent-distal object pattern. This model of agency has three variants: (1) the agent moves to the distal object in order to affect it; (2) the agent extends his/her arm in order to affect it; (3) the agent propels another object at the distal object in order to affect it. In each variant, there appears to be a tight correlation between the ability to affect (i.e., agency) and motion. That is, affecting a distal object (the exhibition of agency) forms a tight correlation in experience with motion.

This experiential correlation plausibly gives rise to a conceptual association between being able to affect and motion, such that we conceptualise an agent in terms of an entity capable of motion. Entities such as the sun and a tree, both of which are considered to be active and/or determinative and thus exhibit agentive characteristics, have motion ascribed to them, due to the correlation between the experience of agency and motion. Accordingly, the properties ascribed to such agentive entities, radiation and shadows, are conceptualised as being related to the 'source' entities, i.e., the sun and the tree, via motion. We see sunlight in the cave, yet sunlight derives from the sun, hence, emanation is the result of ascribing fictive motion to the sun. Similarly, emanation ascribes fictive motion to the tree enabling it to *throw* its shadow.

The active-determinative principle, and the notion that motion correlates with the ability to affect, provides a means for understanding why (16.6a) is acceptable but the Moving Ego pattern in (16.6b) is at best marginal, reproduced below:

(16.6)   a.   I have a headache coming on
           b.   ?I'm coming on to a headache

As we experience headaches, headaches are conceptualised as being active, in the sense that they directly affect us (rather than headaches being affected by us, for instance). Hence, the human experiencer who suffers the headache is less active (with respect to the headache), being largely unable to consciously will the headache away, for instance. Consequently, the active-determinative principle predicts that, in such situations, the experiencer could not have deictic motion ascribed to him or her, while it appears natural for deictic motion to be ascribed to the headache. Thus, while the ascription of motion to events such as headaches derives from the correlation between occurrences and motion, the fact that motion cannot be ascribed to the experiencer in (16.6b) is predicted by the active-determinative principle, and the correlation between motion and the ability to affect (agency).

In sentences in which the Moving Ego pattern is felicitous, such as in (16.10a, b):

(16.10)   a.   We're moving towards a (time for a) decision
                (cf. The time for a decision is moving towards us)
           b.   We're approaching Christmas/Easter/graduation
                (cf. Christmas/Easter/graduation is approaching us)

the fact that the Moving Ego pattern is felicitous is licensed by the active-determinative principle. That is, we can construe the experiencer as being in part responsible for a particular decision, by virtue of processes of discussion and reflection, etc., which often prefigure important decisions. Similarly, the Ego can be construed as preparing for important events such as Christmas or graduation, by virtue of the preparation and hard-work involved prior to these events occurring. Indeed, in some sense such preparations can constitute a pre-requisite for particular events to take place. Expressions such as: *I didn't do Christmas this year*, uttered by someone who spent the Christmas season away from family, enjoying a tropical holiday instead, makes perfect sense, and attests to the active and determinative role of the Ego in terms of events that might typically be thought of as being beyond the Ego's control. That is, while Christmas occurs at a particular time of the year, it need not necessarily 'happen' for someone, if they choose not to participate in the behaviour typically associated with Christmas.

16.4 Conclusion

In this chapter evidence has been presented to support the view that motion elaborates a range of concepts, not just temporal lexical concepts. Two patterns were in evidence, which facilitate ascription of motion to the Ego, or to a particular Event. These patterns reflect the more specific temporal Moving Time and Moving Ego patterns first discussed in Chapter 5. The ascription of motion to Events, or the Ego respectively, appears to be determined by our construal of agency, and the tight correlation in experience between motion and agent-like behaviour. Whether a particular entity can be construed as agent-like in relation to another appears to determine whether motion can be ascribed. This conclusion has implications for the two cognitive models of time to be presented in the next chapter.

CHAPTER 17

Two complex cognitive
models of temporality

> There are certain metaphors which we commonly feel constrained to use when talking about time. We say that we are advancing through time, from the past into the future, much as a ship advances through the sea into unknown waters. Sometimes, again, we think of ourselves as stationary, watching time go by, just as we stand on a bridge and watch leaves and sticks float down the stream underneath us. Events, we sometimes think, are like such leaves and sticks; they approach from the future, are momentarily in the present, and then recede further and further into the past. Thus, instead of speaking of our advance through time we often speak of the flow of time. Sometimes we carry this line of thought further. Thus there are occasions on which we feel inclined to say that time flows at an even rate (cf. Newton), while there are other occasions on which we want to say that sometimes time flows faster than it does at other times. "To-day", we may say, "has just flown past. How different from yesterday when the time just seemed to crawl."   (Smart 1949:483)

At the outset of this book I introduced the common-place conception of time. I described this as an entity as fundamental and all encompassing as three-dimensional space, consisting of present, past and future. Yet, unlike space, our common-place conception of time is of an enigma, an unseen 'flow', strikingly described by J. T. Fraser (1987) as *The familiar stranger*. Moreover, this common-place view informs the way we think about and interpret experience, and the world around us. It imbues our language, influences our reasoning and structures the indispensable instruments we use on a daily basis in order to manage our lives: calendars, clocks, watches, timetables, etc. Moreover, it manifests itself in the philosophical models we advance when attempting to provide a metaphysics for time.

In this chapter I will argue that the common-place conception derives from (at least) two complex cognitive models of time, the COMPLEX MOVING TIME model and the COMPLEX MOVING EGO model, which while complementary, are not straight-forward reversals of one another. The purpose of this chapter is to describe these two models and show how the range of primary and secondary temporal concepts (described in Part II), together with the way in which many of these concepts are elaborated, are integrated into these two coherent models of temporality. A third complex model will be introduced in the next chapter.

17.1 Moving Time and Moving Ego as Complex Cognitive models

In Chapter 5 I introduced the notions of Moving Time and Moving Ego, which in recent versions of Conceptual Metaphor Theory (CMT) are held to constitute primary metaphors. In this chapter I will argue that Moving Time and Moving Ego constitute complex mental constructs (compound metaphors in CMT terms).

In essence, I will suggest that Moving Time and Moving Ego are culturally-constructed complex cognitive models. In order to make this point explicit, and to distinguish these models from the putative primary metaphors, in this chapter I will refer to what I term Complex Moving Time, and Complex Moving Ego respectively. I will argue that these models do not constitute a pairing of primary source and target concepts (as discussed in Chapter 5), but rather consist of independently-motivated sets of temporal lexical concepts, and the elaborations associated with this range of concepts. The range of temporal concepts which participate in the Complex Moving Time and Ego models can be distinguished based on putative universality versus cultural-specificity. Those lexical concepts that appear to relate to phenomenologically-basic aspects of human experience constitute concepts that are likely to be universal and thus may be evident in a cross-linguistically robust way. Concepts of this kind may include the lexical concepts of Duration, Temporal Moment, Temporal Event, and in addition, the lexical concepts Present, Past and Future. I have referred to lexical concepts of this kind as primary temporal concepts.

Temporal concepts which appear to be more culture-specific, I have referred to as secondary temporal concepts. Such lexical concepts may be derived from primary temporal concepts. Examples of this second set may include the Matrix Sense, the Commodity Sense, the Time-measurement Sense and lexical concepts such as Christmas, Graduation, Summer, Her Prime, etc.

Accordingly, Complex Moving Time and Complex Moving Ego are complex in that they may include both primary and secondary temporal concepts, replete with a subset of the range of conventional elaborations associated with the lexical concepts which constitute them. Moreover, these concepts and their elaborations must be integrated in a way which is coherent. Hence, the Complex Moving Time and Ego models may be motivated by virtue of relatively complex grounding scenarios (to be explicated; see Moore 2000), which are humanly relevant.[1]

Finally, what makes the Complex Moving Time and Complex Moving Ego models distinct is how the entities in a particular scene are construed with respect to the active-determinative principle, discussed in the previous chapter. Complex Moving Time assigns temporal concepts an agentive construal in effecting the 'passage' of time, while Complex Moving Ego privileges the experiencer.

17.2 Evidence for Complex Moving Time

In Part II of the book I presented evidence for treating the semantic pole of the lexeme *time* as subsuming a category of distinct but related lexical concepts. However, simply demonstrating that there are a range of distinct temporal lexical concepts does not by itself provide evidence that these concepts form a complex cognitive model. For this to be demonstrated, it must be shown that they are integrated into a mental 'account' or 'theory' which is coherent. There are (at least) two lines of evidence that a range of primary and secondary temporal concepts are integrated into such a Complex Moving Time model.

First, evidence that English users have a coherent conception of Complex Moving Time comes from the way in which this conception can be explicitly articulated. For instance, consider part of J. C. C. Smart's (1949) description of time, from the quotation above, reproduced here, "[W]e think of ourselves as stationary, watching time go by, just as we stand on a bridge and watch leaves and sticks float down the stream underneath us. Events, we sometimes think, are like such leaves and sticks; they approach from the future, are momentarily in the present, and then recede further and further into the past. Thus...we often speak of the flow of time."

This articulation encapsulates a relatively complex conception which would be a familiar and 'natural' way of accounting for time for most native speakers of English. The fact that a particular conception can be articulated and compared to other complex and unified scenarios, such as the complex behaviour associated with objects borne along on bodies of water, suggests that there is a relatively complex and unified conception to be articulated in the first place.

The second line of evidence for Complex Moving Time relates to linguistic examples such as the following:

(17.1)   Time flows by

In Chapter 11 I invoked linguistic examples involving the ascription of motion which is continuous and ongoing in order to provide evidence for the Matrix Sense. Moreover, there I suggested that this sense does not invoke a deictic centre (cf. *Time flows on forever*). However, in (17.1) the use of the spatial particle *by* presupposes a deictic centre. That is, time "flows **by**" something or someone. An informal survey suggests for native speakers of English, in a sentence such as this, the deictic centre is assumed to be facing Moving Time, such that as a portion of the Temporal Matrix passes, it comes to be 'located behind' the Ego. That is, the Ego and time are aligned in something akin to a mirror-image format, deriving from what Clark (1973) terms the canonical (human) encounter (see discussion in the next chapter). Yet, there is nothing in the sentence which might provide such a reading as the landmark past which the "flow" of time proceeds is not encoded linguistically, and as such its orientation with respect to Moving Time cannot be established based on linguistic evidence. The fact that native speakers of English appear to consistently derive a mirror-image reading from examples such as this is highly suggestive that they are applying a conventional schema or cognitive model in order to interpret this sentence. In other words, there is a cognitive model beyond the Matrix Sense – the Matrix Sense encodes nothing regarding deictic centres or landmarks – that facilitates our understanding of examples such as (17.1), in which a deictic centre is assumed.

17.3 The Complex Moving Time model

Complex Moving Time involves the integration of at least the following concepts: Present, Future, Past, the Duration Sense (subsuming the canonical experience of duration as well as its two variants: 'temporal compression' and 'protracted duration'), the Matrix Sense, the Moment Sense, and the Event Sense. Yet what is integrated constitutes the patterns of elaboration associated with these concepts in a way which is coherent with the inferences and entailments resulting from the various sets of elaborations.

The Complex Moving Time model is diagrammed in Figure 17.1. In this model the Ego correlates with the concept of Present. The lexical concept Present is elaborated in terms of locational structure which is proximal or co-locational with the Ego, e.g., *From my vantage point here in 2003, the Middle Ages seems like a bleak place.* Hence, in Complex Moving Time, the Ego's lo-

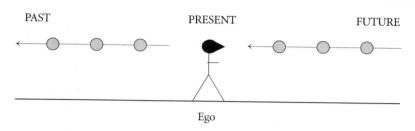

PAST   PRESENT   FUTURE

Ego

Figure 17.1. The Complex Moving Time model (for English)

cation (the deictic centre) constitutes the Present. While the concepts of Future and Past also appear to be universally elaborated in terms of locational structure, there are logically two possible elaborative configurations. Many languages (including English), elaborate the concepts Future and Past in terms of locations ahead of and behind the deictic centre respectively, e.g., *She has a bright future ahead of her*; *Don't look back, the past was bleak* (as illustrated in Figure 17.1). Some languages (e.g., Aymara)[2] elaborate these concepts the other way round, such that the Future is structured in terms of locations behind the Ego, and the Past as in front of the Ego (recall the discussion in Chapter 15).

As we saw in Chapter 11, the Matrix Sense relates to an entity which is ongoing and infinite in nature, the event subsuming all others. It is by virtue of the temporal Matrix that we understand change in the world-state as becoming apparent; the temporal Matrix is conceived as a 'frame' against which change can be ascertained. Moreover, the temporal Matrix is elaborated in terms of non-terminal and non-deictic motion.

As in this model the Ego is stationary (due to agency being ascribed to temporal concepts), a consequence of the ongoing motion associated with the temporal Matrix is an awareness of change in the world-state. As the Matrix 'moves' from what has not yet transpired (Future), towards what is transpiring (Present) and on towards what has transpired (Past), and moreover, as Future and Past are elaborated in terms of locations in front of and behind the Ego respectively, this elaboration provides the orientation frame for the direction of motion. That is, the direction of motion associated with the Matrix in the Complex Moving Time model is from the future towards the Ego, which faces the future, and then on behind the Ego into the past, as indicated by the arrows in Figure 17.1. This then accounts for the construal of something akin to mirror-image alignment in sentences such as (17.1) in spite of such not being explicitly coded by linguistic elements.[3]

It is worth noting at this point that a language such as Aymara which conceptualises Past as in front of the Ego and Future behind will presumably integrate the motion elaborations associated with other temporal concepts in the reverse direction. That is, time will 'move' from behind the Ego before emerging in front (see Miracle & Yapita Moya 1981 for discussion of Aymara). This would provide further evidence that the Complex Moving Time model (as diagrammed in Figure 17.1) is a culturally-grounded cognitive model.

Let's now consider how the remaining temporal lexical concepts are integrated in the Complex Moving Time model. The Event Sense is also integrated into the model. This lexical concept brings with it the notion of temporal Events, which are elaborated in terms of deictic motion. As the temporal Matrix constitutes the event subsuming all others, temporal Events are conceptualised as being embedded within the temporal Matrix which in 'conveyor-belt' fashion brings the temporal events along with it. Events are diagrammed in Figure 17.1 as small spheres embedded in the temporal Matrix.

Like temporal Events, temporal Moments are conceptualised as discontinuous and iterative in nature. Accordingly, just as temporal Events are embedded in the temporal Matrix, so too Moments of time can be borne along (hence temporal Moments are also represented by the small spheres in Figure 17.1). Accordingly, *The young woman's time* [=child birth], or *A time for a decision* can both be said to be 'approaching'. Both lexical concepts are hence elaborated in terms of deictic motion.

Finally, the 'temporal compression' and 'protracted duration' meanings derived from the Duration Sense are integrated into this model. Accordingly, rapid motion of the temporal Matrix (or of Temporal Events or Moments) past the Ego results in the conceptualisation of 'temporal compression' – time passing abnormally quickly. Conversely, slow motion of the Temporal Matrix (or of temporal Events or Moments) past the Ego results in time being conceived as passing abnormally slowly. This results in the inference that the normal state associated with the 'passage' of time is steady-state motion.

Indeed, it is perhaps easy to forget that this is in fact a way of modelling and thus elaborating a fundamentally subjective experience. That is, whatever it is that time is and does, it presumably does not literally undergo locomotion. Yet, both philosophers and scientists often appear to take the cognitive models we employ everyday, in order to understand time as physical fact. For instance, Newton, took the inference regarding steady-state motion associated with Complex Moving Time, which he termed 'absolute time', as a central axiom in his theory of mechanics.

In sum, I present below the conventional patterns of inference which result from (i) the range of temporal concepts integrated in the Complex Moving Time model, and (ii) the patterns of elaboration associated with the concepts which constitute this model. I refer to these patterns as ELABORATIVE CONSE-QUENCES. That is, a consequence of these particular integrated patterns of elaboration is the range of inferences derived. In other words, the information on the left hand side of the arrows relates to the nature of the integrated elaborations, e.g., in (17.2a) the integration of motion associated with the temporal Matrix and the Ego as constituting the experience of the present, and the information on the right hand side, again in (17.2a), as relating to the inference derived from this integration.[4]

(17.2) a. motion of the temporal matrix (and   → awareness of 'passage'
            hence embedded times and events)   of time
            past the ego
        b. rapid motion of events past the ego → temporal compression
        c. slow motion of events past the ego   → protracted duration
        d. steady-state motion of events past   → experience of normal
            the ego   duration
        e. events in front of the ego   → future
        f. events co-located with the ego   → present
        g. events behind the ego   → past
        h. an event approaching the ego   → imminent   occurrence
                                                    of the event
        i. arrival of an event at the ego   → occurrence of the event

As noted above, the Complex Moving Time model also accounts for a range of other secondary temporal concepts, as lexicalised by *Christmas, Easter, graduation, her prime, my favourite part of the piece*, etc. which can all be integrated with this model. Their integration is licensed (i) by application of the active-determinative principle, which ascribes deictic motion to them, and (ii) by virtue of their constituting temporally-framed events. Hence, their integration is both motivated by, and coherent with, the model as a whole. Hence, expressions such as: *Christmas is getting closer (to us)*, can be accounted for based on (17.2e) and (17.2h). Accordingly, by virtue of 'getting closer', the occurrence of Christmas is understood as imminent. That is, all secondary temporal concepts can be integrated into the model such that the inferences deriving from the Complex Moving Time model can be applied to them.

17.4 Evidence for the Complex Moving Ego model

As with the Complex Moving Time model, one important line of evidence for positing a Complex Moving Ego model is that language users articulate, in a consistent and reliable fashion, a particular conception of temporality in which it is the experiencer (rather than time) which undergoes motion. For instance, in the quote provided at the outset of this chapter Smart observed that we can "say that we are advancing through time, from the past into the future". Moreover, in this model it is our 'passage' over a temporal 'landscape' which relates to our understanding of temporality.

The second line of evidence for claiming that there is a Complex Moving Ego model is linguistic in nature. For instance, consider the following examples:

(17.3) a. We're approaching full-time
        b. Arsenal saved face with an Ian Wright leveller five minutes from time.   [BNC]⁵

In these sentences a familiar temporal concept is apparent: the Event Sense, e.g., the event of the final whistle being blown on a soccer-match. Yet, while this lexical concept can be elaborated in terms of motion in (17.3a), for instance, motion is being ascribed to the referent of *we* (the Ego), rather than the referent of *time*. Accordingly, the temporal Moment is being conceptualised as a location which serves as the end-point for the motion attributed to the Ego. In (17.3b) we ascribe motion to the Ego (and not the temporal Event), and thereby understand that the Event in question, namely *(full)-time*, is about to take place. This leads us to consider why it should be that motion ascribed to the Ego results in a reading in which imminent occurrence is ascribed to the temporal event. That is, how can the temporal Event, which is not elaborated in terms of motion, still be conceptualised as about to occur? This point highlights the way in which this conception is distinct from the Complex Moving Time model in which the Ego is stationary and time moves.

The reason for this divergence in behaviour is the result of the Complex Moving Ego model. By virtue of integrating a moving Ego with temporal concepts, the latter are conceptualised as locations with respect to which the Ego moves. The ascription of motion to the Ego, as before, is motivated, I suggest, by the active-determinative principle. In this model it is the conceived active and determinative role played by the Ego in manifesting events which is being emphasised. After all, many events that we experience are related, to some degree, to the actions of human agents. For instance, referees, time-keepers, and the human-devised conventions of a football match determine when 'time' (i.e., the blowing of the final whistle) occurs, i.e., at the end of 90 minutes of play; moreover, 'time' is signalled by a human agent: the referee, who employs an instrument expressly carried for this purpose: the whistle. Being agentive and hence responsible, to a large extent, for the occurrence of a particular event, the active-determinative principle ascribes motion to the Ego, such that lexemes which refer to ego-like lexical concepts, such as *we* in (17.3a), are elaborated in terms of motion content. This conception is integrated with particular locational elaborations associated with temporal concepts resulting in a Complex Moving Ego model.

17.5 The Complex Moving Ego model

The Complex Moving Ego model is presented in Figure 17.2. In Figure 17.2 the 'location' of the Ego at any particular time constitutes the Present. The Past is 'located behind' the Ego and the future 'in front'. Moreover, the Ego 'moves over' or 'across' the temporal 'landscape'. The motion of the Ego is signalled by the arrows, while the temporal landscape is captured by the bold line upon which the Ego is standing. Temporal Events (the spheres shaded in grey) are 'located on' the temporal landscape and constitute 'locations'. The Ego moves 'towards' and then 'past' these temporal Events.

The lexical concepts which are integrated into this model are similar to those integrated in the Complex Moving Time model. However, as we saw there, a consequence of the way the active-determinative principle applies results in different kinds of elaborations being integrated. The fundamental difference is that whereas in Complex Moving Time elaborations relating to the motion of temporal concepts were integrated, in Complex Moving Ego, the elaborations integrated relate to non-motion content.

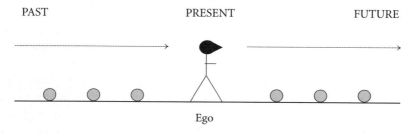

Figure 17.2. The Complex Moving Ego model (for English)

In addition to the lexical concepts of Present, Past and Future, the other temporal concepts integrated in the Complex Moving Ego model include the Matrix Sense, the Event Sense, the Moment Sense and the Duration Sense.

It will be recalled from Chapter 11 that a conventional means of elaborating the Matrix Sense is in terms of a straight linear path. This elaboration provides the temporal 'landscape' elaboration which is integrated into this model. A consequence of integrating the Event and Moment Senses with the temporal 'landscape' conception is that these senses, both of which are discrete with respect to the on-going temporal Matrix, are conceptualised as discrete locations embedded within the temporal 'landscape'. Integration of the Duration Sense, in which duration can be elaborated in terms of length (recall the discussion in Chapter 7), results in the distance between events being conceptualised as 'lengths' of duration. Hence, an important consequence of the integration is that the temporal landscape can be quantified, and that this quantification results from temporal Events being embedded as 'locations' within a temporal Matrix conceptualised as 'landscape'.

Accordingly, the nature of the elaborations integrated, and the way in which they are integrated, provides a number of elaborative consequences deriving from the Complex Moving Ego model. These are detailed in (17.4):

(17.4) a. motion of the ego across the tempo- → awareness of the 'pas-
          ral landscape   sage' of time
       b. locations   → events (and moments
                                                of time which correlate
                                                with events)
       c. distance between events   → magnitude of duration
       d. the landscape in front of the ego → future
       e. the landscape behind the ego   → past
       f. the landscape in the proximal vicin- → present
          ity of the ego
       g. ego approaching a location   → imminent occurrence
                                                of an event
       h. arrival of ego at location   → occurrence of an event
       i. motion of ego past a location   → an event's occurrence
                                                being past

As noted in the discussion of the Complex Moving Time model, there are a massive number of secondary temporal concepts instantiated in the conceptual system. These lexical concepts can also be integrated with Complex Moving Ego such that the consequences detailed in (17.4) occur. Some examples are provided in (17.5):

(17.5) a. We're moving up on Christmas/Easter/graduation
        b. We're approaching my favourite part of the piece
        c. She's passed the deadline
        d. We'll have an answer within two weeks
        e. The meetings were spread out over a month

17.6 Complex Moving Time versus Complex Moving Ego

In this section I briefly compare the Complex Moving Time and Moving Ego models. I noted above that the two models are not straightforward reversals of each other. This follows due to the slightly different elaborative consequences which emerge from each model. In Complex Moving Time the active-determinative principle motivates elaborations in terms of motion being integrated in the model. Hence, 'abnormal' duration (qua 'protracted duration' and 'temporal compression') can be elaborated in terms of slow or rapid motion respectively. This also gives rise to the elaboration, a consequence of the complex model itself, that 'normal' duration is associated with steady-state motion.

This inference is not a conventional elaboration associated with any of the independently-motivated lexical concepts integrated in the model. After all, we do not have in English a single lexical item that specifically means 'normal duration'. Flaherty introduces the term 'synchronicity' in order to capture this concept, while Newton employed the term 'absolute time'. Yet, while other technical terms employed by Flaherty, for instance, *protracted duration* and *temporal compression*, are conventionally indexed by the lexeme *time*, *synchronicity* (or *absolute time*) is not. This suggests that the particular meaning Flaherty associates with the term 'synchroncity', and Newton with 'absolute time', is not a conventional lexical concept, thus necessitating the coining of a new term (or in the case of Flaherty the application of a new meaning to an existing term).

Of course, to say that 'normal' duration is not a distinct lexical concept (at least for many if not most speakers of English), is not to deny that a 'normal' duration CONCEPTION cannot be indexed. However, that it can be, and that scholars such as Flaherty can employ existing forms in novel ways in order to denote such a conception, is evidence that the conception derives from, and relates to, a larger cognitive model. Hence, conceptions are concepts which while they can be symbolised via language do not have the same level of conventionalisation in language that lexical concepts have.

Steady-state motion, metaphorically conveying 'normal' duration, is a consequence of rapid and slow motion being integrated as representing two extreme kinds of 'abnormal' duration. Accordingly, the 'normal' duration conception results from the Complex Moving Time model. The way it is elaborated, in terms of steady-state motion, can be viewed as an elaborative consequence of the patterns of elaboration associated with 'protracted duration' and 'temporal compression'. As 'temporal compression' is elaborated in terms of rapid motion, and 'protracted duration' is elaborated in terms of slow motion, it is natural that Newton should claim that 'absolute time', for instance, is characterised by "equable" motion.

In contrast, in the Complex Moving Ego model the notions of 'protracted duration' and 'temporal compression' are completely absent. In their stead we have the notion of magnitude of duration, which is the closest this model comes to Flaherty's notion of 'synchronicity'. We can describe a particular interval as *long* or *short*, but these elaborations simply tell us how much duration there is, rather than whether the lived duration is 'abnormal'. We could obviously lexicalise a duration as 'longer than normal' or 'shorter than normal' and begin to get at the experiences of protracted duration and temporal compression. However, these elaborations do not fall out of the Complex Moving Ego model as self-evidently as their counterparts, employing motion content, do from the Complex Moving Time model.

Further evidence for the integration of temporal lexical concepts in complex models of temporality comes from sentences of the following kind:

(17.6)   A lot of time has passed/flowed by

This sentence involves a complex conception in which time is at once a substance which can be quantified, an entity which passes or flows, and one involving a deictic centre or Ego. In other words, a number of distinct lexical concepts, including the Commodity Sense, the Matrix Senses, and the concept of Present are involved. Hence, much of the way in which we ordinarily think and talk about time derives from relatively complex conceptions which derive from complex cognitive models for time.

17.7 Levels of conceptual organisation

At this point it is worth making explicit the two levels of conceptual organisation that have been adduced, namely lexical concepts versus cognitive models, and the way they are structured in terms of other lexical concepts by virtue of concept elaboration.

A lexical concept, as defined in Chapter 1, relates to the conventional meaning associated with a particular lexeme (or collocation). As has emerged in this chapter, cognitive models are distinct from lexical concepts (or senses) and their conventional elaborations, while they are constituted by both. A consequence of organisation at the level of a cognitive model is that certain conceptions result from the integration of lexical concepts (and their elaborations) not explicitly provided by the sum of the parts. For instance, the integration of 'protracted duration' and 'temporal compression' readings in Complex Moving Time has resulted in a conception of 'normal duration'. Evidence for this conception is that it can be indexed by virtue of a (somewhat novel) lexicalisation, e.g., *synchronicity*, or *absolute time*. Moreover, an elaborative consequence of the integration is that this conception can be elaborated in terms of steady-state or equable motion.

Hence, cognitive models appear to constitute a more generalised level of conceptual organisation, relating sets of lexical concepts and their elaborations. As such, such models are inferred by virtue of the novel conceptions which can be articulated via language. Accordingly, it is this level of conceptual organisation which evidences processes of the following kind: abstraction, inferencing, prediction and the modelling of complex temporal relations. It appears then that much of our understanding about, and reasoning in terms of, temporality is likely to relate to the level of temporal cognitive models.

Finally, the structuring of lexical concepts and conceptions is facilitated by concept elaboration. Elaboration can be conventional or novel, and serves to highlight some aspect of the lexical concept or a particular conception associated with a cognitive model. For instance, elaborations employing adjectives commonly highlight some attribute associated with a particular lexical concept (or conception). Elaborations employing verbs highlight what it is that the lexical concept 'does'. By way of illustration consider the following:

(17.7) a. The relationship lasted only a short time
        b. The time for a decision is approaching

In (17.7a) the lexical concept indexed by *time* is the Duration Sense. This lexical concept is elaborated by the verb *last* and by the adjective *short*. From this we know that what this lexical concept 'does' is endure, and that an attribute of the lexical concept in this context is that the duration, relatively speaking, is not of great magnitude. Hence, the lexical concept is conventionally lexicalised by *time*, and elaborated by the lexical concepts indexed by *last* and *short*.

In (17.7b) the lexical concept referenced by *time* is of a temporal moment, which is to say it relates to an entity which is punctual in nature and is considered without respect to a period of duration. It is elaborated in terms of motion content, the lexical concept indexed by the form *approach*. A consequence of this elaboration is that we conceptualise its occurrence as imminent.

Finally, it is worth pointing out that while elaborations do appear to, in large measure, constitute particular lexical concepts, such elaborations do not 'create' the experiences which give rise to primary temporal concepts. After all, primary temporal concepts relate to directly perceived phenomenological experience. This level is held to antecede enrichment via elaboration, and to provide a rudimentary level of conceptual structure which serves as the 'target' for patterns of concept elaboration via conceptual projection.

17.8 Primary scenes and grounding scenarios

It will be recalled from Chapter 5 that primary metaphors are grounded by virtue of clear and direct experiential correlations. These sets of correlations constitute what have been termed PRIMARY SCENES, which relate recurring and relatively simple aspects of experience (Grady 1997a). The present analysis reveals that as the cognitive models under consideration in this chapter are comprised of a number of distinct and independently-motivated temporal concepts, involving different types of elaboration, they cannot constitute primary metaphors. On the present view, the integration of the Complex Moving Time and Moving Ego models is not effected by primary scenes, suggesting that these two models should be conceived as complex metaphoric mappings.

I noted above that whether time, or the Ego, is construed as undergoing motion derives from which is being construed as agentive and/or determinative in terms of our experience of time. That is, we can construe time or Ego as being agentive resulting in two distinct models. However, what might motivate these two distinct construals?

Moore (2000) has proposed two GROUNDING SCENARIOS which plausibly motivate the two construals of agency in question. In terms of construing Complex Moving Time as agentive, and hence privileging elaborations of temporal concepts involving motion, Moore suggests that the correlation between an object moving towards the experiencer, and the anticipated arrival time of the object, motivates our conceptualisation of time as moving from the future located in front of the experiencer towards the experiencer. Similarly, Moore has proposed that construing the Ego as agentive, resulting in privileging elaborations of temporal concepts involving non-motion content, is motivated by the correlation between the experiencer's anticipation of arriving at a particular location, and the fact that arrival correlates with a future (anticipated) time. In other words, ubiquitous scenarios involving motion and change of location correlate with anticipated and actual arrival. As human agents can move, and we anticipate our arrival at a particular location (the future) with respect to our present location (the present), and as objects can move towards us, and we anticipate their arrival (the future) at our current location (the present), these two scenarios may contribute to grounding the Complex Moving Time and Complex Moving Ego models respectively.

We must be careful, however, not to attribute too much to grounding scenarios such as these. While it is likely that such scenarios motivate our ability to construe time or the Ego as agentive, it is less likely that these scenarios motivate all of the complexity associated with the two cognitive models adduced in the present chapter. After all, the motion apparent in the grounding scenarios of Moore primarily relates to deictic motion (the motion of an object towards an experiencer, or the experiencer's motion towards a particular location). In an important sense, the range of temporal concepts apparent in the Complex Moving Time and Moving Ego models relate to experience which is ongoing and infinite in nature. This is presumably due to the integration of the Matrix Sense into both these models.

While aspects of the two cognitive models under consideration are likely to be universal, given that they are structured, in part, by primary temporal concepts, these primary temporal concepts may be elaborated in culture-specific ways (as suggested in Chapter 15). This may result in cultural differences in terms of cognitive models for temporality. Moreover, these models are also constituted of a range of secondary temporal concepts which are likely to be more culture-specific, especially in terms of their elaborations.

A clear example of this is the lexical concept akin to the Matrix Sense which shows up in many languages. While in some cultures something approximating this lexical concept is conceptualised as undergoing linear motion, in other cultural traditions it is cyclical. For instance, Aion in the Greece of late antiquity was the god of indefinitely extending time. Aion was closely linked with the single unchanging Kosmos (Oxford Classical Dictionary). Hence, as the celestial spheres which were held to manifest the behaviour associated with the Kosmos were conceptualised as undergoing cyclical motion, indefinitely extending time was characterised as being cyclical in nature.

Consequently, while Moore's grounding scenarios may motivate ascription of agency to time and the Ego respectively, licensing application of the active-determinative principle, the complexity of the models themselves results from the range and nature of the lexical concepts and elaborations integrated, and consequently the conceptions and elaborative consequences derived.

17.9 Conclusion

In this chapter I have argued that the Moving Time and Moving Ego models are complex cognitive models rather than primary metaphors (in the sense of Grady 1997a). This follows as these models are constituted of a range of independently-motivated lexical concepts, involving a range of distinct elaborations, including elaborations in terms of a prescribed set of motion content and non-motion content. Moreover, these models may have culture-specific distinctions and nuances. I further suggested that the integration of the range of lexical concepts, and their elaborations in a particular model, is motivated by application of the active-determinative principle, which is construed as relating to time or the Ego. That the active-determinative principle can be construed as applying to either time or the Ego may be motivated, in part, by Moore's grounding scenarios.

Not only does the present perspective offer a way of testing whether putative sets of mappings in the CMT framework constitute primary or compound metaphors, but in addition, this approach also allows us to see the way in which different levels of conceptual organisation are integrated in order to build up complex cognitive models. A consequence of studying temporality from this perspective is that a richer and more elaborate understanding of how time is conceptualised and organised is achieved. In more general terms, the present approach provides methodology for employing linguistic evidence as a way of investigating conceptual structure, and criteria for formulating and evaluating theories of conceptual organisation.

Chapter 18

A third complex model of temporality

In addition to the two complex cognitive models described in the previous chapter, English (and indeed other languages) exhibit(s) a third cognitive model of temporality, which like the previous models is a complex model in the sense defined. This follows as it serves to integrate a range of distinct lexical concepts. This model constitutes what I have already termed the COMPLEX TEMPORAL SEQUENCE MODEL (see Chapter 15), and has previously been most extensively articulated in the literature by Moore (2000). However, unlike the previous two models considered, the hallmark of the Complex Temporal Sequence model is that it does not conventionally include integration of the lexical concepts Present, Past and Future. Rather, this model serves to integrate temporal events of various kinds, such that they can be related as being earlier or later with respect to one another. Hence, the essential relation which derives from integrating the temporal concepts involved in this model, and their patterns of elaboration, typically involving following or preceding deictic motion, is that the temporal events are sequenced with respect to one another.

18.1 Sequencing relations

Moore (2000) and Traugott (1978) have observed that temporal sequencing is, in principle, independent of the concepts of Past and Future. For instance, Traugott has made the point that in sentences of which the following are indicative:

(18.1)   a.   In a soccer match half-time precedes full-time
           b.   In Britain's antiquated pub licensing laws, the calling of time follows the bar tender's ten minute warning that time will be called

(18.2)   a.   February is/comes after January
           b.   Spring is/comes before Summer

the only information we need is relative sequencing, rather than notions of Past and Future. For instance, in (18.1a) we understand that in a soccer match, full-time is sequenced later with respect to half-time, without needing to know whether the two events are Past, Present or Future. Indeed, the concepts of Past and Future will necessarily be tied to the human experiencer, related as they are (or at least as I have suggested in Chapter 15), to the perceptual moment and hence the human experience of the present, and do not affect our understanding of two events being sequenced with respect to one another.

Moore (2000) has observed that there is a tight correlation in experience between earlier/later relations and being in-front/behind. For instance, in terms of a race, the winner (the earliest arrival) is located in front of the runner-up, while the runner-up (the later arrival) is located behind the winner, such that sequence of arrival correlates with relative location of the contestants with respect to one another. Moore suggests that it is this experiential correlation which takes an event in the sequence as the deictic reference point, rather than the experiencer, which motivates our conceptualisation of event sequences in terms of before/after or preceding/following relations, as in the examples above. On this view, it is the elaboration of temporally-framed events such as the Event Sense lexicalised by *time*, in terms of locational content, rather than the use of the Past/Future concepts, which are evident in these examples.

This discovery enables us to account for a puzzling fact. Lakoff and Johnson (1980: 41) observed that on first inspection there appears to be a contradiction in expressions such as the following:

(18.3)   a.   In the weeks ahead of us   (future)
         b.   That's all behind us now   (past)

(18.4)   a.   In the following weeks   (future)
         b.   In the preceding weeks   (past)

The contradiction is that in (18.3) concepts relating to the 'future' are conceptualised as being ahead and concepts relating to our experience of the 'past', as behind, while in (18.4) the 'future' is being conceptualised as behind (i.e., following), and the past as being ahead (i.e., preceding). While Lakoff and Johnson correctly note that in (18.4) temporal events are being sequenced with respect to each other, rather than with respect to an experiencer, we can also now observe that the expressions in (18.4) do not relate to the concepts of Past and Future at all. This is not to say that we cannot, and indeed do not, construe such sentences from our own conceptual vantage point, and hence impose a past/future matrix on our event-sequences (e.g., as I write these sentences, today is Tuesday, hence Wednesday lies in the future with respect to my temporal vantage point). However, what this does mean is that the use of locational content in sentences such as (18.3) is due to the fact that an earlier/later relation is being construed, rather than the concepts Past and Future. This is achieved by virtue of a highly conventional Complex Temporal Sequence model, which allows us to understand temporal events being sequenced with respect to one another, such that the earlier event is the one located ahead or in front of the later event.

18.2 The Complex Temporal Sequence model

This model integrates all those temporally-framed lexical concepts which can be conceptualised as discrete and hence as being capable of elaboration in terms of deictic motion, i.e., motion with respect to a particular deictic centre. However, as this model does not involve the integration of the concepts Present, Past and Future, the deictic centre is not the Ego which is apparent in the models discussed in the previous chapter, but rather another temporal event with respect to which the event in question is sequenced. Moreover, the nature of the motion untaken by events in this model is unidirectional, exhibiting what following Hill (1978) I will refer to as IN-TANDEM ALIGNMENT (see also Tyler & Evans 2003:Ch. 6).[1] A motion event of this kind is one in which the entities involved in the motion event are travelling in the same direction such that they are sequenced with respect to one another. This is diagrammed in Figure 18.1. The Complex Temporal Sequence model is diagrammed in Figure 18.2.

In Figure 18.2 the shaded circles represent temporal events of various kinds. These include, but are not limited to, the Event Sense, the Moment Sense, and temporally-framed events such as days of the week, months of the

Figure 18.1. In-tandem alignment

LATER   EARLIER

Figure 18.2. The Complex Temporal Sequence model

year, seasonal holidays such as Christmas, sub-events of particular events, e.g., half-time and full-time in a soccer match, etc. Following the Moving Event pattern described in Chapter 16, each of these events can be elaborated in terms of deictic motion. A consequence of their integration in the Complex Temporal Sequence model is that an in-tandem alignment is imposed on the various temporal events, as signified by the arrow which designates orientation.

Accordingly, these events are conceptualised in terms of their sequence with respect to each other, resulting in an assessment of an earlier/later relationship. That is, an assessment of an earlier/later relationship is a consequence of the complex cognitive model.

Evidence for this comes from the fact that the verbs *follow* and *precede* and the prepositions *before* and *after* are compatible with this model, while these lexical items are not otherwise employed with the individual lexical concepts which are integrated in this model. For instance, while verbs of deictic motion such as *come, draw near, arrive, approach*, etc., are conventional ways of elaborating, for instance, the Event Sense, as in the following:

(18.5)   a.   The young woman's time [=labour] is approaching/coming/drawing near
         b.   The young woman's time has arrived

the lexical items *precede/follow* or *before/after* are not conventional ways of elaborating this lexical concept, as evidenced in (18.6):

(18.6)   a.   ?The young woman's time is following
         b.   ?The young woman's time is preceding
         c.   ?The young woman's time is/comes before/after

In none of the sentences in (18.6) do we derive a reading in which it is understood that childbirth is imminent. This follows as the verbs *precede/follow* and the prepositions *before/after* are only compatible with the Event Sense when it is integrated in the Complex Temporal Sequence model. This model serves to relate one event to another by virtue of imposing an in-tandem motion event.

Interestingly, other prepositions which are related to *before* and *after*, namely *in front of* and *behind* (*in back of* in American English) are not compatible with the Complex Temporal Sequence model:[2]

(18.7)   a.   ?February is behind January
              (cf. February is after January)
         b.   ?January is in front of February
              (cf. January is before February)

This follows as prepositions such as *in front of* and *behind* relate elements in static spatial scenes. Hence, they are incompatible with spatial configurations which also involve motion. As the temporal lexical concepts which are integrated in the Complex Temporal Sequence model are already elaborated in terms of deictic motion, then we would expect that prepositions of this kind would be incompatible with this model, which is what we find.

By way of summary, the elaborative consequences resulting from integration in the Complex Temporal Sequence model are as follows:[3]

(18.8) a. sequence of temporal events → chronology of events
       b. temporal events located before or preceding other events → earlier events
       c. temporal events located after or following other events → later events
       d. motion of temporal events with respect to other temporal events → awareness of the "passage" of time

18.3 The Complex Temporal Sequence model in Hausa

I now turn to a brief examination of the West African language Hausa, which offers an interesting contrast in terms of the way temporal events are integrated into the Hausa equivalent of the Complex Temporal Sequence model. As with the discussion of Aymara in Chapter 15, the point here is to illustrate that different languages can elaborate related concepts, or complex models, in slightly different ways, by virtue of different patterns of elaboration available in the language, and different ways of construing similar humanly-relevant scenes.

Hill (1978) argues that native speakers of Hausa, in some situations, elaborate the earlier event in a temporal sequence in terms of *after/behind* while the later event in a sequence is elaborated in terms of *before/in front of*. This pattern contrasts with the way assessments relating to earlier or later are elaborated in English, as observed above. The Hausa pattern is attested by the following examples drawn from Hill (Ibid.: 528), where *gaba* is 'before/in front of', and *baya* is 'in back of/after'.

(18.9) a. ranar Talata gaba da ranar Littinin
            'Tuesday is in front of/before Monday'
        b. ranar Littinin baya da ranar Talata
            'Monday is in back of/after Tuesday'

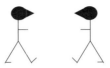

Figure 18.3. Mirror-image alignment

What we see in the examples in (18.9a) is that Tuesday which follows Monday in the temporal sequence is elaborated in Hausa as being 'before'. In English Tuesday would be described as being 'after' Monday. Similarly, in (18.9b) Hausa describes the relation in which Monday precedes Tuesday as one in which Monday is 'after' Tuesday. In English this relation would be described such that Monday is 'before' Tuesday.

Hill suggests that this elaboration may be due to the privileging by Hausa speakers of one form of locational relationship between two entities with unmarked front/back axes over another, and its projection onto temporal relations. Hill suggests that there are two common locational relationships deriving from spatial interaction and experience. In one, which concerns MIRROR-IMAGE ALIGNMENT, two entities are located such that they face each other, as in Figure 18.3.

In the other, in-tandem alignment introduced and discussed earlier, recall Figure 18.1, two (or more) entities are oriented in the same direction such that they do not face each other.

Hill suggests that these two forms of alignment derive from "two basic perceptual patterns in which physical entities conceived as possessing an intrinsically marked front/back axis are oriented in contrasting ways (Ibid.: 525; see also Heine 1997). Hence, while we commonly experience mirror-image alignment, as when engaged in conversation with an interlocutor, we also commonly experience in-tandem alignment, such as standing in a queue in a bank or post-office for instance. Hill observes that in Hausa there is a tendency by experiencers to employ in-tandem alignment to conceptualise spatial situations involving entities lacking an inherent front/back asymmetry, e.g., a rock and a tree. For instance, Hill reports that in a study, a significant majority of Hausa speakers identified a more distant object as being located 'in front of' the nearer one and the nearer one as being located 'behind' the further one. This tendency, he suggests, is extended to the expression of temporal sequential relations, as evidenced in the examples in (18.9).

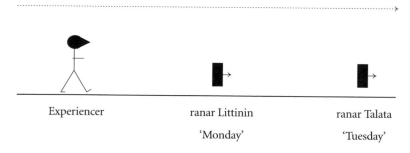

Figure 18.4. An in-tandem alignment applied to a temporal sequence in Hausa

However, this cannot be the whole story, as English speakers also appear to employ an in-tandem alignment in relating temporal sequential relations and yet elaborate earlier/later relations in distinct ways from Hausa.

The different pattern exhibited by Hausa, with respect to English, is suggested by Hill's finding that in terms of spatial relations, Hausa speakers impose an in-tandem relation on entities lacking inherent front/back asymmetry when they are actually perceiving a particular scene. That is, the orientation of the in-tandem alignment is a consequence of the experiencer being present and imposing his or her own orientation on entities in the scene which otherwise lack an inherent front/back axis (see Heine's 1997 discussion of what he terms 'single-file' and 'face-to-face' models). In other words, the experiencer forms part of the in-tandemly aligned spatial relationship. This situation is then projected onto temporal sequential relations as depicted in Figure 18.4.

In Figure 18.4, the dashed arrow refers to orientation. An in-tandem construal is imposed on the relation holding between the temporal events *ranar Littinin* 'Monday' and *ranar Talata* 'Tuesday, by virtue of the experiencer being conceived as forming part of the sequence which is aligned in in-tandem fashion. From this it follows that *ranar Littinin*, the earlier event, which is accordingly closest to the experiencer, is conceptualised as being after or behind the later event, *ranar Talata* and conversely *ranar Talata* is conceptualised as being in front or before the earlier event *ranar Littinin*.

This situation contrasts with English. While English imposes an in-tandem alignment on the temporal events which form the event sequence, as we saw in Figure 18.2, these events are construed with respect to an experiencer who is in a mirror-image alignment with respect to the moving events. This is depicted in Figure 18.5.

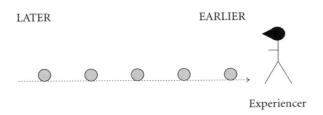

Figure 18.5. The Revised Complex Moving Time model for English

Figure 18.5 is similar to the Complex Temporal Sequence model depicted in Figure 18.2 except that an experiencer has now been added, depicted by the figure icon. While the temporal events are oriented with respect to one another, as indicated by the dashed arrow, the experiencer is oriented in mirror-image alignment with respect to the in-tandemly sequenced temporal events. The experiencer's orientation is represented by the arrow extending from the figure's head. A consequence of this arrangement is that the earlier event, as with Hausa is closest to the experiencer, but unlike in Hausa, is, from the perspective of the experiencer, before (rather than after) the later event. Similarly, the later event is after, rather than before, the earlier event.

However, Hill points out that in some instances, Hausa employs mirror-image alignment as in English. For instance, in the following sentence, the application of mirror-image alignment akin to English results in a temporal event sequence being elaborated in similar fashion to English:

(18.10)   Dauda zai zo bayan Saratu ta fita
          'David will come after Sarah leaves'

In (18.10) the form *bayan* 'after/in back of' is employed in order to denote a 'later than' relationship. Hill suggests that in this event-sequence the relation is holding between two events, as opposed to events in a larger sequence (e.g., days of the week). He describes such a relation between two temporal events as one which is CLOSED, and a relation between events comprising a larger event sequence as OPEN. He suggests that Hausa speakers follow the pattern as in a language such as English, i.e., an 'earlier' temporal relation is elaborated in terms of before/in front of content and a 'later' relation in terms of after/in back of content, when the event-relation is 'closed'.

What emerges from this discussion of Hausa is that the choice of locational content imposed by a particular complex model is in part influenced by conventionalised patterns of deictic construal entrenched in the linguistic system (see Heine 1997 for further discussion; see also Moore 2000).

18.4 Earlier/later and the vertical axis

Finally, there is evidence that some languages employ the vertical axis, and up/down relations, in their particular version of the Complex Temporal Sequence model.

Some of the clearest evidence thus far documented for this pattern of elaboration comes from Mandarin (Yu 1998), and from Japanese (Shinohara 2000b). For instance, consider the following examples drawn from Shinohara (Ibid.:2):

(18.11) a. ima kara sanbyaku-nu sakanoboru to, Edo-jidai dearu
        now Abl. 300-years ascend-back Conj. Edo-era be
        'Ascending 300 years from now is the Edo era'

      b. Kamakura-jidai kara yonhyaku-nen kudaru to, Edo-jidai
        Kamakura-era Abl. 400-years descend Conj. Edo-era
        dearu
        be
        'Descending 400 years from the Kamakura era is the Edo era'

In these examples it is the relation between two particular periods in history which are being elaborated in terms of the vertical axis. Motion downwards results in a later event with respect to an earlier event which is located higher on the vertical axis.

Some examples for Mandarin are provided by Yu (Ibid.:110) and include the following:

(18.12) a. shang-ban-tian (upper-half-day) "morning; forenoon"
      b. xia-ban-tian (lower-half-day) "afternoon"

(18.13) a. shang-ban-yue (upper half of the month) "the first half of the month"
      b. xia-ban-yue (lower-half month) "the second half of the month"

As with the Japanese data, these sentences evidence an elaboration of assessments relating to earlier/later relations in terms of locational content relating to up/down. While earlier events, e.g., the morning or the first half of the month are conceptualised as being higher, the afternoon, or the second half of the month, which are later, are conceptualised as being lower.

Moore (2000) and Shinohara (2000a) have both proposed that the motivation for elaborating assessments of earlier/later relations in terms of up and down locational content respectively is motivated by our experience of slopes. That is, when we are on a slope, we are compelled by gravity to move in a

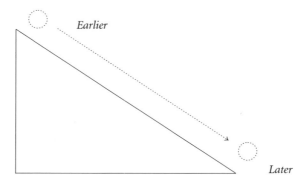

Earlier

Later

Figure 18.6. The slope model (adapted from Shinohara 2000b: 5)

downward direction, hence there is a tight correlation between being located higher on a slope and an earlier point in an object's trajectory, due to the fact that being further down the slope correlates with a later point in the trajectory. Shinohara terms this the Slope Model, depicted in Figure 18.6.

18.5 Conclusion

In this chapter I have presented evidence for a distinct Complex Temporal Sequence model in English. While this model integrates a range of distinct lexical concepts, it does not serve to integrate concepts such as Present, Past and Future. Nevertheless, as we have seen, it does conventionally involve a particular deictic viewer, an experiencer, which provides a particular alignment, mirror-image in the case of English. Hence, in English, while the temporal events are aligned in an in-tandem fashion with respect to each other, they are aligned in a mirror-image fashion with respect to the experiencer, which provides the viewpoint from which they are viewed, and hence the nature of the locational and sequential content in terms of which they are elaborated. In Hausa, by contrast, both the event sequence and experiencer are aligned in an in-tandem fashion, such that the nature of the locational content which elaborates earlier/later relations is often (although not always) the inverse of the situation in English. Hence, we have further evidence both for complex cognitive models for temporality, in the sense defined in Chapter 17, and for their cultural distinctiveness.

CHAPTER 19

Time in modern physics

In this chapter we turn to a consideration of the treatment of time in modern physics. We do so in the light of special and general relativity, as developed by Einstein (1950, [1916] 1961). After all, if special and general relativity have the status of being plausible accounts of the physical structure of the world – the predictions pertaining to time made by special relativity have been verified experimentally many times (Coveney & Highfield 1991; Davies 1995; Sklar 1974) – then any investigation into the nature of our experience of time must take stock of how time is treated in such theories.

19.1 The rise of relativity

The rise of relativity began with the pre-relativistic world-view inherited from Newtonian classical mechanics in the 17th century. Essentially, the mechanics of Newton, enshrined in his three laws, rested upon the hypothesis that material entities move through space in predictable ways, and are acted upon by forces subject to invariant physical laws (Einstein [1916] 1961). As Davies (1995) observes, "From this belief emerged the picture of the cosmos as a gigantic clockwork mechanism, predictable in every detail. The clockwork universe enshrined time as a fundamental parameter in the workings of the physical world" (Ibid.: 31). Newton described his view of absolute time in the following way:

> Absolute, true, mathematical time, of itself, and from its own nature, flows equably without relation to anything external, and by another name is called duration: relative, apparent, and common time, is some sensible and external (whether accurate or unequable) measure of duration by the means of motion, which is commonly used instead of true time; such as an hour, a day, a month, a year. (Newton; cited in Turetzky 1998: 73)

As noted earlier, for Newton time flows equably regardless of the state of the world. Consequently, time flows at the same rate irrespective of what velocity an entity is moving at. It is external to consciousness, and hence is of eternal duration. This view treats time as some fixed and eternal matrix stretching across the whole of existence, by which events can be measured and assigned a temporal value. For Newton absolute time was co-existent with God upon whom it depended.

It was Galileo (1564–1642) who first symbolised time geometrically by means of marking a line at regular points. Such a representation suggests the comparison of time with space. Hence, for Newton, motion can be defined in terms of distance travelled per unit time. In this sense, time is an experiential (and theoretical) primitive, employed in order to understand motion (Akhundov 1986; Coveney & Highfield 1990; Davies 1995; Einstein 1950, [1916] 1961; Sklar 1974; Turetzky 1998).

The problem for the Newtonian world-view began to emerge in the middle of the 19th century with the advent of electromagnetic theory. Scientists gave uniform speeds for the propagation of electromagnetic radiation, light being one such form. According to classical mechanics, uniform motion is relative.[1] Hence, the speed of light should vary according to the speed of the observer relative to the beam of light.[2] As electromagnetic radiation has wave-like properties, and as in the 19th century it was assumed that a wave could only travel with a uniform speed through an isotropic medium, it was widely assumed that the cosmos was filled with an invisible aether.[3] Consequently, it was with respect to this aether that light was propagated at a constant speed, just as sound waves, for instance, travel at a constant speed through the air (Einstein [1916] 1961).

Towards the end of the 19th century two scientists, Michelson and Morley, designed an experiment in order to assess the speed at which the Earth travelled through the aether. They chose to measure the Earth's speed by measuring the speed of light in different directions relative to the Earth. Classical mechanics predicted that the speed of an entity, such as electromagnetic radiation, should vary according to the speed of another entity, in this case an observer. As the Earth travelled at some speed through the aether, then by splitting a single beam of light, and sending it in different directions relative to the direction of motion of the Earth, the split light beams, when reflected back to their source, should arrive at different times. Michelson and Morley split a beam of light into two pulses. One they sent in the direction of the Earth's motion (the laboratory being an inertial frame of reference relative to the Earth), and one they sent perpendicular to the Earth's motion. They then reflected the two pulses, using mirrors, back to the origination of the split, and then back to the source. They measured the times of arrival of the two pulses. Michelson and Morley expected to find that the pulse sent in the direction of the Earth's motion would arrive back at the source later than the pulse sent perpendicular to the Earth's motion. This was because as the Earth travels through the aether, the aether is in motion relative to the Earth. Hence, a pulse of light travelling against the direction of aether relative to the Earth would travel more slowly than a pulse of light travelling perpendicular to and hence across (rather than against) the direction of the aether relative to the Earth.

However, the Michelson-Morley experiment failed to find any significant difference in arrival times between the two pulses of light. Put another way, the speed of light was constant irrespective of the relative motion in the frame of reference. If then there were an aether, this finding implied that the Earth was at rest in it, leading to the unpalatable conclusion that the Sun must be moving around the Earth rather than the other way around (Coveney & Highfield 1991; Davies 1995; Einstein [1916] 1961).

19.2 Time in special relativity

The difficulty then with classical mechanics lay in its notion of relative motion as it applied to electromagnetic radiation. The Michelson-Morley experiment had found that the speed of light was invariant with respect to the motion of the frame of reference. So, the difficulty lay in reconciling relative motion with the finding that this relativity principle breaks down when applied to electromagnetic radiation.

In his resolution of this problem, Einstein ([1916] 1961) employed the notion of relative motion between two entities in uniform motion and the constancy of the speed of light, as the two founding principles of a completely new theory termed SPECIAL RELATIVITY.[4] However, as we have seen, asserting that the speed of light is constant regardless of the velocity of the observer violates the principle of relativity. The reconciliation Einstein adopted was the proposal that time and space are themselves relative (Einstein [1916] 1961). Put another way, for an observer in motion and an observer at rest both to experience the speed of light as being constant, i.e., as moving at the same speed (300, 000 km/s) relative to their (differing) motion, then something else must give. Einstein proposed that it was the nature of space and time which had to be reappraised. He argued that for two observers, one at rest and in motion, to experience light as travelling at a constant velocity relative to their respective frames of reference, then each observer must have a different experience of space and time relative to one another; put another way, space and time are themselves relative. Einstein summarises the position as follows:

As a result of an analysis of the physical conceptions of time and space, it became evident that *in reality there is not the least incompatibility between the principle of relativity and the law of propagation of light*, and that by systematically holding fast to both these laws a logically rigid theory could be arrived at. (Ibid.: [1916] 1961: 23–24; original emphasis)

With respect to the Newtonian view then, for Einstein, time is not some absolute entity flowing equably irrespective of the motion of particular entities, being the same for all observers. On the contrary, time is itself relative, flexible and malleable, depending upon the speed of the particular observer (the frame of reference) in question.

A number of important consequences or effects emerge from this relativistic view of time. Perhaps the most important concerns the notion of simultaneity. As time is relativised to the motion of a particular observer, each observer occupies a unique frame of reference. That is, without the notion of absolute time to relate different frames of reference, we can no longer be sure that the now that I experience is the same as the now that an observer in a different frame of reference experiences.[5] This dramatically affects the notion of simultaneity; under special relativity we must abandon the common-sense view that observers in two different systems of reference, (e.g., one in motion and one at rest), experience particular events simultaneously, or share the same time. For instance, Einstein ([1916] 1961) provides the example of a train moving through an embankment. In this example there is a long train moving in the direction of the arrow indicated in Figure 19.1. The centre of the train is indicated by M'.

Passengers on the train will take the train to constitute their frame of reference. Einstein also points out that every event which occurs on the train correlates with a point along the embankment. Accordingly, every event occurring

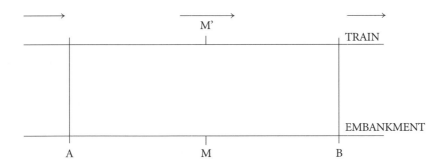

Figure 19.1. Adapted from Einstein (1961: 29)

on the train also takes place at a particular point on the embankment. As such, simultaneity is the same whether we take the train or the embankment as our system of reference. Einstein then points out that for two events which are simultaneous with regard to the embankment, they will not be simultaneous with regard the train. He gives the example of two flashes of lightning occurring at points A and B. He observes that if there are two observers, one at M on the embankment, and one at M' on the train, and if the observers are provided with two mirrors angled at 90 degrees, so that they could simultaneously observe points A and B, then if the lightning flashes occur when M and M' are simultaneous, the two events will not be seen as simultaneous by M' although they will be seen as simultaneous by M. As the observer on the train at M' is borne along by the train, then he or she is moving towards the flash propagated at B, while moving away from the flash at A. Hence, for the observer on the train the flash emitted from B will be seen prior to the flash emitted from A and the two events will not be seen as simultaneous. However, for the observer at M on the embankment, the two flashes will arrive at the same instant, and so be judged to be simultaneous. Einstein argues that,

> Events which are simultaneous with reference to the embankment are not simultaneous with respect to the train, and *vice versa* (relativity of simultaneity). Every reference-body (co-ordinate system) has its own particular time; unless we are told the reference-body to which the statement of time refers, there is no meaning in a statement of the time of an event.
>
> (Ibid.: 30–31; original emphasis)

The startling consequence to emerge from this, then, is that simultaneity, what counts as now, is distinct depending not only on relative motion with respect to another reference-body, but also on the location of the reference-body. As Einstein (1950) points out, this "reduces the concept of simultaneity of spatially distant events to that of simultaneity of events happening at the same place (coincidence)" (Ibid.: 7).

Even more startling effects result from the view of time adopted in special relativity. One of these effects is referred to as TIME DILATION. Special relativity predicts that for a system S' in motion relative to a system S, time becomes warped. The closer to the speed of light one gets the more warped time becomes. In essence then, for system S' in motion, clocks will run more slowly (i.e., time slows down) relative to a system S which remains at rest. However, this is purely a relativistic phenomenon. Special relativity predicts that for an observer in S' it will appear that it is system S which is in motion and that system S' is stationary, and hence it is the clock in S which is running slow. As one approaches the speed of light the slower time will go, relative to a frame of reference at rest.

While Einstein's proposals were based on a chain of mathematical reasoning, the time dilation effect has subsequently been verified experimentally. According to Davies (1995:56), the first 'direct test' of time dilation only occurred in 1941. Since then, time dilation has been verified on a number of occasions involving particle accelerators, which are able to accelerate particles up to speeds approaching that of light (see Coveney & Highfield 1991; Davies 1995). Davies reports that the time dilation effect has also been verified involving atomic clocks. He describes an experiment which took place in 1971, in which four atomic clocks were flown on commercial airliners around the world. Relative to a clock at rest, a 'home' clock, with which the other atomic clocks had been synchronised prior to their departure, the time dilation effect was indeed observable. However, as Davies observes, "As airliners travel at less than one-millionth of the speed of light, the timewarp on board was very small indeed – about a microsecond per day's flying" (Ibid.:57). Nonetheless, even a discrepancy this small can still be reliably detected by modern atomic clocks.

But if time dilation is a real-effect it should apply to any kind of clock, not just those used by physicists to measure time. Put another way, it should also apply to biological mechanisms. According to special relativity time dilation is experienced by people. The way this has been framed in the literature is in terms of the TWINS PARADOX.

The paradox proceeds as follows. There are two twins, A and B. Twin A is propelled into space on board a rocket, while twin B remains at home on the Earth at rest. If twin B had a powerful telescope and could monitor the ship's clock on board the rocket, it would appear that time were running more slowly on board the rocket (A's system of reference), relative to twin B's system of reference, at rest on the Earth. Accordingly, it would appear to twin B that the twin on board the rocket would also be ageing more slowly. For twin B, upon returning to Earth twin A would appear to be younger than twin B, i.e., to have aged more slowly relative to twin B. However, for twin A the situation would be reversed. From A's perspective on board the ship it appears that it is twin B' system of reference which is in motion, and hence in which time is running more slowly. Hence, upon A's arrival back on Earth, it would be B who has aged more slowly. The paradoxical nature of this concerns the fact that special relativity appears to be predicting that both twin A and twin B can be younger than each other which is clearly contradictory.

In fact however, there is no paradox, as the experiences undergone by the two twins are not symmetrical. Twin A has undergone absolute motion (e.g., accelerating away from the Earth, breaking, de-accelerating, and then re-accelerating back towards the Earth. That is, the motion experienced by A has not been uniform relative to B's system of reference and the principle of relativity applies to uniform motion). Accordingly, it will be twin A on the rocket who has aged less upon arrival back on Earth. Nevertheless, the twins paradox presents a stark illustration of the effects attendant upon special relativity. In essence, two observers, here twins A and B, 'experience' different intervals of time between the same two events, A's departure from Earth and A's return to Earth, both of which are simultaneous for both twins, as these events are coincident.[6]

19.3 Spacetime

One of the most counter-intuitive consequences to emerge from Einstein's theory of time in special relativity concerns the notions of past, present and future. After all, if simultaneity is relative, then events in the past potentially have the same status as those in the present and as those in the future. If twin A on the rocket experiences a different interval of time between departure and arrival relative to the interval of time experienced by twin B on Earth, then clearly, what constitutes now for twin A, at any point during the journey, cannot correspond with twin B's experience of now. The conclusion which emerges from this is that both events and times may exist all at once. That is, the distinctions between past, present and future are in effect illusions, as times like space, are given all at once, rather than being things which occur in succession.

The view that time, like space, is simply 'out there', rather than something waiting to happen reinforces the spatialisation of time foreshadowed by the application of geometry to time by Galileo, and subsequently by Newton's notion of absolute mathematical time. The spatialisation of time as a consequence of special relativity was first mooted by Herman Minkowski (Einstein ([1916] 1961).[7] His proposals for a union between space and time, namely SPACETIME, were developed by Einstein in his theory of general relativity, which sought to extend the insights of special relativity to gravitation (Einstein [1916] 1961).[8] In order to grasp Minkowskian spacetime, it will be useful to contrast the notion of spacetime with the notions of space and time in classical mechanics.

According to Sklar (1974), the pre-relativistic view treated events as being analysable into two distinct components, a spatial location and a temporal moment. That is, space and time were clearly distinct entities and wholly analysable as such. Moreover, for Newton, the structure of space was based on the Euclidean notion of flat three-dimensional space. As a result of the relativity of simultaneity, Minkowski proposed a union between space and time, namely spacetime. On this view, it no longer becomes meaningful to separate space from time, events into locations and instants, as an event, on this view, becomes a function of both space and time, which is to say space and time are treated as inseparably fused components of the event. Hence, while the pre-relativistic theories treated the structure of space and time as the product of Euclidean three space and mathematical time (the one dimensional real-line), Minkowskian spacetime treats time and space as a continuum, in which time is an inseparable fourth dimension of spacetime (Sklar 1974).[9]

In his theory of general relativity, Einstein ([1916] 1961) proposes that gravity can be equated with the metric structure of spacetime. This led to the proposal that spacetime could, in effect, be equated with the distribution of matter and energy in the spacetime. As Einstein put it, "[S]pace-time is not necessarily something to which one can ascribe a separate existence, independently of the actual objects of physical reality" (Ibid.: vii).[10] Such a view attempts to equate spacetime with the physical fabric of the cosmos. According to Sklar (1974), this kind of scientific enterprise,

> attempts to show that the relation between what we take to be matter and what we take to be spacetime is such that for each distinct kind of matter we can describe, the spacetime region occupied by that matter has its own characteristic spacetime structure – its own characteristic intrinsic geometry that is. If we knew the full spacetime structure of a region, then, we would already know what kind of matter occupied that region. This suggests that we can do without the matter as a separate individual and simply identify a particular kind of spacetime region as that kind of matter.   (Ibid.: 223)

On this view, time as a constituent of spacetime does form part of the physical fabric of the cosmos, and hence becomes both a theoretical and an empirical primitive.

The consequences of having relativised the whole of physics are clearly far-reaching. An important consequence is that due to the abandonment of a single universal time shared by everyone, we have a plurality of times, leading to the postulation of spacetime, a physical aspect of the universe, laid out all at once in its entirety. Clearly this view of time is at odds with the phenomenological view of time presented in Chapter 2. There I argued that time is characterised by the notion of succession, and derives fundamentally from internal perceptual mechanisms founded on duration. I suggested that time is fundamentally experienced, it is lived, rather than being an external attribute of the universe.

Before attempting to reconcile the phenomenological view of time proposed in this book with the treatment of time in Einsteinian relativity, it is worth examining some consequences of the Einsteinian view of time which are at odds with everyday experience. One of the fundamental problems with time, as it emerges from the Einsteinian world-view, concerns the directionality of time. That is, as Coveney and Highfield (1991) have shown in detail, there is no principled way of explaining irreversible processes, such as the fact that coffee sitting in a cup, if left to its own devices, will cool, snowmen will melt, we age, etc. We would be very surprised in the extreme if a cold cup of coffee could somehow warm up again all on its own, or if people could grow younger (rather than older). Yet, as the metric structure (i.e., the geometrical properties) of spacetime gives rise to equations in which motion is unchanged regardless of whether a positive value for time is replaced by a negative value, a later event could in principle be the cause of an earlier event. In other words, rather than time being an asymmetric 'arrow', it becomes symmetric and hence reversible (Coveney & Highfield 1990; see also Davies 1995).

Another related problem associated with the Einsteinian view of time, as already intimated, is that the notions of past, present and future lose their meaning. As time is simply there, a fourth dimension of spacetime, we have no means of distinguishing past, from present from future. These notions become essentially meaningless, despite what we intuitively may believe, feel, and actually experience, the notion of becoming has been eliminated. As Bergson observes, this leads to us

> taking the unfolding of the whole past, present, and future history of the universe for a mere running of our consciousness along this history given all in one stroke in eternity; events would no longer file before us, it is we who would pass before their alignment. ([1922] 1999: 107–108)

Davies (1995) describes the situation in this way,

> Einstein's time is seriously at odds with time as we human beings experience it. All this leads me to believe that we must embrace Einstein's ideas but move on... [his] account of time frequently leaves us stranded, surrounded by a welter of puzzles and paradoxes. In my view, Einstein's time is inadequate to explain fully the physical universe and our perception of it. (Ibid.: 10)

19.4 Bergson's view of Einsteinian time

How is the Einsteinian view of time to be reconciled with the view of time as phenomenological in nature, relating to subjective experience, structured at the conceptual level in terms of complex cognitive models? One attempt to reconcile the former view of time (as a physical component of the cosmos) with our everyday experience emerges from the work of Bergson ([1922] 1999).

Bergson argues compellingly that a crucial difficulty with the theory of special relativity is that it fails to account for what it is that makes time fundamentally temporal. By reconciling the objective measurable time employed by Einstein with the temporal nature of time, Bergson argues that some central paradoxes within the theory can be overcome, and moreover, that the theory, if interpreted in this way, concurs with our everyday experience of time.

Accordingly, a fundamental question that Bergson asks is: what makes time temporal? The answer, he suggests, is the presence of consciousness. As time derives from the "continuity of our inner life", real time is both perceived and lived. Time in this sense, Bergson argues, informs our notion of conceived time, that is, the notion of time we attribute, objectify and measure. Hence, for Bergson, "we cannot conceive a time without imagining it as perceived and lived" (Ibid.:33). In other words, time can be measured not because time is an objective property of the world, but because events correlate with (and hence are simultaneous with), states of duration (i.e., internal time).[11] Based on this definition of temporality, which relates measurable time (the objectified time of the physicist) to internal real time, Bergson argues that special relativity, properly understood, will support the thesis not that there are a plurality of times (relativity of simultaneity), but rather that there is a single "time common to all things" (Ibid.:32).

In order to illustrate his view that measurable time originates in internal time, Bergson describes the action of drawing a line. The line, he suggests, represents the continuity of consciousness, which is co-extensive with the action of drawing. Hence, not only is the line an external symbol of inner time or duration projected into space, as the line can be measured, so it is also a means of objectively measuring the duration with which it is co-extensive. Hence, to assume that time is first and foremost a measurable entity fails to correctly understand that the temporality associated with time results from the correlation of internal time with external events, and moreover, that the ability to measure events is derived from their correlation with internal time. Similarly, simultaneity results from objects of consciousness being assigned a temporal value by virtue of their simultaneous correlation with internal time. As temporality is co-extensive with consciousness, without consciousness there can be no temporality.

For Bergson there is a fundamental paradox which obscures a correct understanding of special relativity. He argues that by relating the measurable time of special relativity to that of real time, the paradox will thereby be removed. The paradox concerns Einstein's claim that there are a multiplicity of times, which follows from the claim that simultaneity is itself relative. As internal time, i.e., consciousness, grounds measurable time, it would be genuinely paradoxical, Bergson argues, to suggest that there could exist a multiplicity of equally real times. This follows as for a physicist to posit multiple times, it is entailed that the physicist possesses a multiplicity of consciousnesses.

In essence then, Bergson's argument bears on Einstein's fundamental epistemological assumption in deriving his view of relativity of simultaneity. For Einstein, simultaneity can only be asserted if two events can be directly observed to be simultaneous, what he terms coincidence. This being so, an observer cannot claim simultaneity for another system of reference, precisely because the observer cannot directly observe events in any system except his or her own. Analogously, Bergson holds that "we cannot speak of a reality that endures without introducing consciousness there" (Ibid.: 33). Hence, while Bergson admits that it is possible for the physicist to claim that there are a multiplicity of times, only where consciousness can be found to co-exist can any of these times be claimed to be real. Put another way, just as the physicist cannot derive any information pertaining to simultaneity in any other system of reference, precisely because he or she cannot observe events in such a system, there can be no consciousness in such a system as the physicist remains in his or her own system. Thus, Bergson claims that while admitting a multiplicity of times, special relativity, properly interpreted, suggests that there exists just "a single real one among them" (Ibid.: 20).

For instance, in analysing the twins paradox, Bergson observes that the time experienced by the twin on the rocket ship is not real as it is not lived through. The physicist on Earth attributes a time to the twin physicist on the rocket. But this attributed time reflects the fact that the physicist has taken the motionless Earth as his or her frame of reference. Moreover, in so doing the physicist has placed the rocket in a state of motion. Yet, the rocket is still connected to the physicist's system of reference, and the slower time attributed to it by the physicist is a reflection of the difference in the degree of motion of the rocket relative to the zero motion of the system of reference, the Earth. Put another way, this time is conceived as opposed to being perceived. It represents a mathematical means of signifying a change in frames of reference by a physicist on Earth who takes Earth as his or her inertial system of reference. The attributed time to an imaginary twin physicist on the rocket can be contrasted with the real time experienced by the physicist at rest on Earth. From this it does not follow that a real physicist on the rocket would experience a different time to that of a real physicist on the Earth. At each location the laws of physics are the same, and thus, Bergson maintains, each physicist would experience the same time.

Bergson's point is that by allowing an inertial system of reference to be related to any frame of reference in the universe (i.e., by precluding the view that there is a single privileged frame of reference), the proposition of multiple times in relativity actually presupposes a single real time. As multiple times presuppose an inertial system of reference (other frames of reference, e.g., a rocket, are in motion relative to an inertial system of reference, e.g., the Earth), then all other frames of reference predicated on the inertial system of reference, will necessarily derive their temporality from the consciousness of the observer inhering in the system of reference. Bergson summarises this position in the following way,

> [I]n the system in which I live and which I mentally immobilize by conceiving as a system of reference, I directly measure a time that is mine and my system's; it is this measurement which I inscribe in my mathematical representation of the universe for all that concerns my system. But in immobilizing my system, I have set others moving, and I have set them moving variously. They have acquired different speeds. The greater their speed, the further *removed* they are from my immobility. It is this greater or *lesser distance* of their speed from my zero speed which I express in my mathematical representation of other systems when I assign them more or less slowed times... The multiplicity of times which I thus obtain does not preclude the unity of a real time; rather it presupposes it.   (Ibid.: [1922] 1999:53, original emphasis)

19.5 Conclusion

The phenomenological view of time advocated in this book, on first inspection, differs from the view of time offered by special relativity (the relativity of simultaneity), and the notion of spacetime in general relativity. In the latter, time can be seen to be a physical attribute of the universe, principally because special relativity reveals that there is not a single time experienced by all, but rather a multiplicity of times. That is, time is relative to a particular frame of reference. Yet given the position that meaning is embodied (recall Chapter 4), ultimately the questions science can ask, and the possibilities it can conceive are necessarily dependent on the nature of our embodiment, tied to and viewed through the lens of conscious experience. Failing to relate putative aspects of the world at large to the human observer, in a thoroughgoing way, will lead to discrepancies and paradoxes which ultimately will undermine any theory.

This point was made by Bergson ([1922] 1999), who argued that the paradoxes that remain in special relativity resulted from special relativity not being relativistic enough. Vestiges of an objectivist world-view remained. By recognising that multiple times can only be conceived as they are tied to the conceptualisation of a unique observer, an inert system of reference, Bergson argues that special relativity correctly interpreted reduces to the position that there can only be a single real time, while the multiplicity of times are mathematical signifiers of a change in reference frames. That is, such times are fictive and contingent upon a single conscious observer, occupying a particular location. This treatment, also, I suggest, reflects the embodiment thesis developed in Chapter 4. Our world of experience, the world for us, is mediated by the nature of our bodies, and in this sense there can be no mind-independent objectivist world in which there are multiple times.

CHAPTER 20

The structure of time

There is no doubt but that for us time is at first identical with the continuity of our inner life. What is this continuity? That of a flow or a passage, but a self-sufficient flow or passage, the flow not implying a thing that flows, and the passing not presupposing states through which we pass; the *thing* and the *state* are only artificially taken snapshots of the transition; and this transition, all that is naturally experienced, is duration itself. It is memory, but not personal memory, external to what it retains, distinct from a past whose preservation it assures; it is a memory within change itself, a memory that prolongs the before into the after, keeping them from being mere snapshots and appearing and disappearing in a present ceaselessly reborn.   (Bergson [1922] 1999: 30)

Time has structure. It serves to distinguish the present from the past, and allows us to anticipate the future. Time emerges from perceptual mechanisms which correlate with the dynamic nature of consciousness, undulating from focal state to focal state. It provides a means of segmenting and so analysing experience, processing raw perceptual data into events and states, into change and stasis, experiences which can be encoded in language. It has perceptual, conceptual and external sensory dimensions. Yet, despite the conceptual models and language we employ to make sense of it, our experience of time is not a thing which can be pointed to and observed, but rather derives from a process (or processes) which form(s) the bedrock of our cognitive architecture. Paradoxically, time provides structure to our experience, and yet we relentlessly ascribe structure to it, formulating concepts and models of time as if it had none of its own. We think of it as a quantity, as valuable, as a person, as an indefinitely extending matrix, as duration, as a point, and so on. In this final chapter we consider some of the implications of the present study for our understanding of the structure of our pre-conceptual experience of time, and of our concepts of time, structure both inherent and ascribed.

20.1 Two problems of time

The problem with which this book began constituted the so-called metaphysical problem of time. While we intuitively experience time there appears to be nothing tangible in the world which can be pointed to and identified as time. The status of time has been complicated by its objectification via language. This constitutes what I termed the linguistic problem. Time often appears to employ language (and hence conceptual structure) that derives from domains which are not purely temporal in nature, such as space. One solution to the metaphysical difficulties associated with time has been to view time as inhering in the physical world. On this 'physicalist' view, the reason language employs spatial 'metaphors' for time, e.g., *a long time*, is that time is (in some sense) part of the fabric of existence and hence enters into everything. After all, time is an essential ingredient of processes which take place in three-dimensional space, such as motion, standing still, etc. Indeed, even length is processed 'in time', and hence has a temporal component to it.

An alternative view is the 'mental achievement' position, in which time is considered an abstraction based on event-comparison. On this view, the spatial (and motion) metaphors are conceptual, motivated by the experiences in which time, as mental construct, is grounded.

However, viewing the metaphysical problem as resolving into a bifurcation between 'physicalist' and 'mental achievement' positions presents a false dichotomy, ignores much of the richness associated with our experience of time, and leaves subjective (i.e., phenomenological) experience and its relationship with neurological antecedents and external sensory perception out of the picture altogether.

20.2 A richer view

This book has attempted to sketch a richer view. Time is not a unitary phenomenon, and so any account which privileges a physicalist, a mental achievement or a phenomenological perspective will necessarily exclude essential ingredients of this phenomenon. Moreover, such exclusion is fundamentally arbitrary, as all these elements are inextricably linked in our conceptualisation of time.

20.2.1 The inherent structure of time: Time as process

The phenomenological experience of time relates to a number of cognitive processes which appear to enter into the judgements and evaluations we make on an ongoing basis. Such processes include our ability to assess duration, to distinguish the present from the past, to anticipate the future based on present and past experience, to judge simultaneity, to relate events held in memory in a chronological sequence, etc. Indeed, these processes provide structure to our conscious experience such that experience is segmented in a multitude of ways (see Chafe 1994).

In so far as the processes described relate to experiences of the self, they are phenomenological. Yet, such phenomenological experience crucially relates to antecedent perceptual processing, which is itself, in part, a response to the external sensory world of experience. Hence, our subjective experiences are constructed perceptions of the external world.

Perceptual processing is a consequence of both innate mechanisms, such as the perceptual moment, but also the external world, which perceptual mechanisms have, in part, evolved in response to, and continue to model during the course of an individual's lifetime. Hence, like all other organisms, humans need to take account of an external environment which is subject to change. Such an ability requires perceptual apparatus which can monitor and assess change.

However, an ability to perceive change does not guarantee complex adaptive processes during the course of an individual organism's lifetime such as learning. For this to occur perceptual experience must be subject to further processes such as chronological sequencing, which allows us to distinguish between present and past experience and so anticipate the future. This constitutes the "memory within change itself" described by Bergson.

20.2.2 The ascribed structure of time: Time as object

Our conceptual systems allow us to model the phenomenological experiences that constitute temporal awareness. Via language these models are indexed and elaborated in service of our functional, communicative, and cultural needs. Primary temporal concepts, which relate to fundamental aspects of phenomenological experience, can give rise to new conceptions which through conventionalisation can become entrenched as distinct lexical concepts subject to enrichment via elaboration. Hence, our ability to assess duration, and to distinguish discontinuous moments of time, ultimately facilitates an ability to coordinate social interaction.

Time-reckoning devices which rely on external periodicities make use of ready-made 'time-keepers' in the physical world in order to enrich a subjective experience which, if successfully co-ordinated, provides great functional utility. The ability to co-ordinate social activities of almost every kind (meetings, arrival at work, bus/train schedules, the start of a soccer match, the end of a soccer match, etc.), requires an ability to co-ordinate an otherwise subjective experience of time. Yet, it is at the level of conceptual structure that such experiences are modelled, enriched and constituted, in part by patterns of concept elaboration, which supply conceptual content from diverse (primarily non-temporal) domains of experience. Hence, at the conceptual level, time emerges as a thing which can be measured, which can thereby affect us, which can bring about change, which co-occurs with conscious experience, a thing which resides in the world and ultimately serves as a template by which we measure our lives, extending indefinitely before and behind us.

At the cognitive level, time is highly complex. But this does not deny that the concepts and cognitive models we construct relate to an antecedent phenomenological experience. Nor does this deny that such experience constitutes a response, both at the level of the species (in terms of hard-wiring), and at the level of the individual organism, to an environment which is structured the way it is. Hence, in a fundamental sense, time constitutes a response to the world we inhabit, a world that rarely stands still.

However, it is at the conceptual level that time achieves its apotheosis. Here it reaches the intricacy and beauty attested by the lexical concepts and cognitive models for time uncovered in this book. Only at this level of detail could time, a rich and elaborate intellectual feat, be enshrined in modern physics as physical fact. The conceptual alchemy partially obscures from view the phenomenological basis of time, directly perceived, an adaptive response to a mutable and ephemeral world of experience.

Notes

Chapter 1

1. The view that time is internal in origin is related to a tradition in philosophy, psychology and neuroscience which can be traced back to the views of St. Augustine (354–430).

Chapter 2

1. Of course, this is not to say that temporal experience is not an essential aspect of motion events. Langacker (1987) for instance suggests that time constitutes what he terms a BASIC DOMAIN, which structures other concepts such as motion. Nevertheless, this does not in itself explain why time should be elaborated in terms of structure from motion events through three-dimensional space (and locations in three-dimensional space), rather than other kinds of purely temporal structure. After all, what ever it is that time does, it presumably does not manifest veridical motion.

2. Some languages, e.g., Inuktitut, the language of the Inuit, spoken in Canada and Greenland, do not have a lexical item corresponding to the English concept of time. It is worth pointing out that this does not entail that they do not have the concept, but rather that they lexicalise this concept in different ways, based on a fine-grained distinction in the seasons and other environmental markers (see MacDonald 1999:92–95).

3. For detailed discussion of the phenomena of protracted duration and temporal compression see Flaherty (1999).

4. As with the examples in (2.1), the examples in (2.3) show that temporal concepts are being elaborated in terms of motion events, without precluding the position that such concepts may also be constituted by virtue of more subjective kinds of experiences. This position is developed during the course of this chapter.

5. Ecological psychology emphasises environmental sources and experience (the perceptual world), rather than subjective experience, in the origin and development of concepts (see Gibson 1986).

6. Grady's views are presented in Chapter 5.

7. Flaherty (1999:60).

8. Ibid.:52.

9. Pöppel (1994) has suggested that as perceptual processing appears to only be able to unify experiences within a temporal window with an outer limit of between 2–3 seconds, temporal compression may be the result of "temporal leakage", in which "successive information disintegrates into parts, if longer lasting stimulus sequences have to be processed" (Ibid.: 194).

10. Varela et al. (1991) have observed that it appears to take 0.15 seconds to form an identifiable percept.

11. In spite of the foregoing, I must emphasise that I am not claiming that a neurologically instantiated temporal code forms the basis of our conception of temporality. Clearly, features of cognitive processing at this level cannot be said to form the basis of experiences, let alone conceptualisations pertaining to temporality. However, in so far as temporal experience must ultimately derive from neurological processes, evidence of cognitive mechanisms and processes of this kind are suggestive that temporality is internal rather than external in origin, and may ultimately be traceable to specific cognitive apparatus and processes.

12. Chafe (1973) notes some ways in which anticipation mirrors memory.

13. A Necker cube, due to the Swiss naturalist and mineralogist Louis Necker (1786–1861) constitutes a drawing of cube where the parallel lines have the same length so that an observer appears to be looking down at the top or up at the bottom depending on the perspective reversing (cf. the Gestalt image of the vase/face which reverses with a changed perspective).

14. For an overview of the constant and variable aspects of conscious experience see Chafe (1994: Ch. 3).

15. Chafe's transcription conventions are as follows: pauses are marked by sequences of dots and measured times, terminal contours are marked by full-stops (sentence-final falling pitch), question marks (an interrogative terminal contour) and commas (a terminal contour which is not sentence-final), primary accents are marked by acute accents and secondary accents by grave accents, and lengthening of a preceding segment is marked by an equals sign.

16. Chafe suggests that evidence for peripheral consciousness is provided by the notion of discourse TOPIC (see Chafe 1994: Ch. 10, for discussion and elucidation of this construct).

17. Proposals of this kind fail to fully recognise that meaning cannot be divorced from the perceptual mechanisms which serve to mediate and construct the nature of our bodily experience, and moreover, that such experience crucially includes internal subjective experience.

18. In a darkened cell I would still be aware of the passage of time. In such a situation it would appear to pass painfully slowly, as I would be focusing on temporal experience rather than external events (Flaherty 1999).

Chapter 3

1. This is not to deny of course that we do have quite elaborate linguistic and extra-linguistic means to convey emotional states. For instance, since at least Darwin (1872) it has been

recognised that facial expressions convey emotional states in a consistent way, a trait common to other species. Moreover, in terms of language, prosody provides rich information concerning a speaker's emotional state.

Chapter 4

1. Here by 'meaning' I have in mind a notion far broader than semantic structure (i.e., meaning at the linguistic level). In this sense, I am equating meaning with the nature of our environment. Clearly, the nature of our environment, including on-going changes, has non-trivial consequences for our survival, and in this very general sense, the nature of our environment is meaningful. This notion will be developed in greater detail throughout this chapter.

2. Despite characterising concepts as mental representations, strictly speaking concepts are not representations of anything. They do not, after all, re-present (Varela et al. 1991). Rather, they constitute what is meaningful for us, and in this sense they **are** our reality (see Fauconnier 1997; Jackendoff 1983, 1990, 1992; Langacker 1987, 1991b; Marmaridou 2000; Torey 1999; Varela et al. 1991).

3. The present approach differs significantly from formal analyses of meaning, which in general terms, assume that concepts are internal representations of an external verifiable reality. The formal tradition (see Portner & Partee 2003) owes much to the work of the analytic philosopher Frege ([1892] 1975). Frege argued for a distinction between what he termed SENSE and REFERENCE. While sense corresponds to an internal concept, reference corresponds to the external objective entity indexed by the sense. In this chapter I will argue in detail that as human consciousness only has direct access to the conceptual system, it is erroneous to assume that there can be a pre-given objective (and hence mind-independent) reality to which concepts refer.

4. Scholars who take the mental nature of meaning seriously have suggested that there are conceptual/semantic "parts of speech" such as PATH, PROCESS, etc. These conceptual categories can be contrasted with the logical categories of truth-conditional approaches, e.g., variables, predicates, quantifiers, etc., which as Jackendoff (1992:34) notes, have little in common with each other.

5. How language expresses conceptual ideas almost certainly has to be constrained by the conceptual system. If language represents the means of externalising concepts, then it can only encode those concepts contained within the conceptual system. Nonetheless, the fact that language externalises meaning is not to say that language is simply a one-way "conduit", which conveys meaning without in any way affecting the nature of the conceptual system. On the contrary, I will suggest that through the correlation between language use and a situationally-implicated meaning component, "new" meanings come to be instantiated within the conceptual system. This process, following Traugott (1989), Hopper and Traugott (1993), and the work on PRINCIPLED POLYSEMY by Tyler and Evans (2001b, 2003), I will label PRAGMATIC STRENGTHENING (see Chapter 6). This view is suggestive that language plays a role in mediating the development of new conceptual structure. In this way, language

not only expresses a set of lexical concepts, but can itself increase, decrease and modify this set of concepts, and the meanings which constitute these concepts.

6. The notion of embodied meaning is increasingly being advocated by a number of scholars. For some related views and treatments see Edelman (1992), Johnson (1987), Lakoff (1987), Lakoff and Johnson (1999), Langacker (1987), Putnam (1981), Sweetser (1990), Talmy (1983), Turner (1991), Tyler and Evans (2003), Varela et al. (1991).

7. The term PERCEPTUAL RESEMBLANCE is due to Grady (1997a, 1999a).

8. I am using the term IMAGE as employed in cognitive psychology, referring to patterns of mental experience, not exclusively visual.

9. See Jackendoff e.g., (1983) in particular, for a related perspective on this point.

10. This position is consonant with Lakoff's (1987) view that mental imagery constitutes a different level of organisation from perceptions which are far richer in detail. See also Palmer (1996: Ch. 5).

11. In terms of the concept of Containment, this presumably derives by virtue of conceptualising a functional relationship holding between an entity contained and the properties of the container (e.g., a bottom and sides).

Chapter 5

1. Image concepts are held to constitute concepts redescribed from sense-perceptory processing. Hence, they relate to experience derived from external reality, e.g., motion (Grady 1997a). See Mandler (1992, 1996) for some suggestions on how this process of redescription may occur.

2. Response concepts are held to constitute concepts redescribed from body-states such as emotional experience, e.g., love, anger, and also time. Such concepts relate to experience which is subjective in nature (see Grady 1997a).

3. In fact this is one of many ways in which temporal concepts can be elaborated. For instance time can be elaborated in terms of a commodity (e.g., *Time is money*), as a bounded landmark (e.g., *in time, through time*), etc., as we will see in Part II.

4. This distinction is important not least as it has, for the most part, been adopted by subsequent studies in CMT (notably Lakoff & Johnson 1999; Moore 2000).

5. Theories are conceptually complex in that they constitute composite structures, consisting of axioms, proofs, entailments and complex knowledge systems.

6. Some examples of primary target concepts proposed by Grady include Similarity, Importance, Existence, and Quantity.

7. Examples of primary source concepts provided by Grady include Itch, Hunger, Warmth, Large, Near, Motion.

8. Recall the discussion of experiential correlation in Chapter 4.

9. 1997a: 269.

10. 1997a: 270.

11. To make the notion of experiential correlation explicit, we do not invent new theories, or discuss theories etc., only when we are in buildings. That is, we do not find a tight co-occurrence in experience between theorising and being located in or near buildings. Compare this with the very tight correlation between experiencing an increase in quantity and an increase in vertical elevation, as when water is poured into a glass, or more items are added to a pile.

12. Grady (1997a) suggests that THEORIES ARE BUILDINGS is comprised of the primary metaphors: PERSISTING IS REMAINING ERECT, and ORGANIZATION IS PHYSICAL STRUCTURE.

13. These patterns have been noted by a wide range of scholars e.g., Clark (1973), Fleischman (1982), Grady (1997a), Lakoff (1990, 1993), Lakoff and Johnson (1980, 1999), Moore (2000), Radden (1997), Shinohara (1999), Smart (1949) Traugott (1978), Yu (1998).

14. While assuming that the Moving Time and Moving Ego mappings may be primary metaphors, Grady does observe that there may be reasons for thinking that these mappings may not be primary (in the sense defined). First, he notes that it may be the case that some of the correspondences which serve to constitute the Moving Time and Moving Ego mappings may be "independently motivated" (Grady 1997a: 122). For instance, the concept of Present may be structured in terms of "the physical situation in which we find ourselves...even in the absence of any understanding of time as motion" (Ibid.: 122), as evidenced by examples such as: *Christmas is here.* Second, Grady points out that the motion in terms of which time is metaphorically structured cannot be of any kind, as he illustrates with the following:

(a) ?Christmas is falling

(b) ?We are just south of Christmas

15. The concepts of time and motion are held to inhere in distinct conceptual domains: TIME and MOTION.

16. This position revises the earlier (received) view in CMT (e.g., Lakoff & Johnson 1980; Gibbs 1994) that what motivated metaphoric mappings was their utility in understanding putative abstract concepts and conceptual domains in terms of more concrete concepts and domains.

17. This intuition is formalised in modern physics which takes time to be an empirical and a theoretical primitive (Akhundov 1985; Einstein [1916] 1961).

18. Moreover, the linguistic evidence they use to support the conceptual metaphors they propose (e.g., Moving Time and Moving Ego/Observer mappings) relates to a change in the world-state. For instance, a sentence such as *Christmas has arrived*, relates to a change by virtue of which we understand that the occurrence of the festival known as Christmas can be contrasted with a previous state held in memory in which Christmas had not occurred.

19. Neuroscientists refer to the phenomenon whereby information from different parts of the brain is integrated so as to provide a coherent percept as *binding*. As is well-known, in each modality, for instance in the visual system, "the sensory representations of the various qualities of an object are arrayed over an enormous expanse of cortex" (Stryker 1991:252). The problem is to discover how the brain manages to integrate the sensory information associated with spatially-dislocated neuronal assemblies into a coherent percept, given that there is no single place in the brain where such sensory stimuli are integrated. This has been termed the *binding problem.*

20. Moreover, the fact that the primary target concept is elaborated in terms of a range of distinct motion events, as we will see, suggests that the putative primary source concept in the Moving Time and Ego mappings does not constitute a single unified concept either.

21. The notion of heterogeneity of temporal lexical concepts and the apparent coherence in how they are elaborated in terms of Motion, etc., will be explored in Part II of the book.

22. Ibid.: 1999:143.

23. On the face of it, it might seem reasonable to suggest that the temporal Matrix reading (in 5.13) and the Duration reading associated with the examples in (5.11) are somehow similar. However, there are a number of reasons for thinking that the experiences which underpin these concepts are quite distinct. It will be recalled from Chapter 2 that Ornstein (1997) found that durational experience appeared to correlate with the amount of memory required to store the particular experience. While this is hardly surprising, what is surprising is that more complex events appear to require greater memory capacity, and hence provide an experience of greater duration, even when duration remains constant (i.e., a less complex event is experienced which lasts for the same amount of time as measured by a clock). While our experience of duration thus correlates with 'storage space' in episodic memory, to experience an unbounded elapse of time is clearly a physical impossibility, not least because such assumes immortality, as well as an infinite mental storage capacity. However, Lakoff and Núñez (2002) have suggested that the concept of infinity derives from abstraction over iterative (i.e., what they term imperfective) processes. That is, the concept of infinity may well derive from durationally-bounded events, but ones which form part of an on-going cycle. Experiences of this type may give rise to the concept of an unbounded temporal elapse, by virtue of being repeated, and hence forming part of inherently unbounded processes. What this suggests is that the experience of duration, while grounded in mental storage capacities and the concomitant experience resulting from memory processing, may be distinct from the concept of temporal unboundedness, as in the temporal Matrix reading of time in (5.13), which derives from observing iterative processes. A consequence of this may be that while the concept of duration may relate to the phenomenological experience of time, and thus be inherently subjective in nature, the concept of a temporal Matrix, which relates to observing iterative events, may be closer to the concept that Lakoff and Johnson (1999) took to be the fundamental aspect of time. In other words, by virtue of there being a number of distinct temporal lexical concepts, different scholars may be assuming a wholly different concept of time, which would account for the divergent claims and conclusions adduced.

24. The term MATRIX is meant to get at the idea that this temporal concept relates to an entity conceived of as unending and all-encompassing, as in Newton's notion of *absolute time* (propounded in his *Principia Mathematica*), and at least one version of the so-called common-place view of time, claimed to be held by ordinary language users (see Langone 2000).

25. 1997b:Ch. 4.

26. 1997b:Ch. 4.

27. In so far as the Moment and Event senses relate to occurrences (i.e., both moments and events, by virtue of being discontinuous, occur), they are conceived independently of their duration. This phenomenon is reflected in language more generally. For instance, an event, such as a concert, can be conceived independently of its duration, e.g., *The concert will take place on Thursday*. However, this is not to say that events in general cannot be conceived in terms of durational units, e.g., *The concert will last for one hour*. Nevertheless, both the temporal Moment and Event Senses associated with *time* do appear to be conceived independently of their duration (e.g., *Her time* [=*labour*] *has arrived*, prompts for the onset of labour and not labour in its entirety).

28. In using the term *deictic motion*, I have in mind motion which presupposes a particular deictic centre with respect to which motion occurs.

29. Boroditsky (2000) for instance, has made a promising start in this vein.

Chapter 6

1. I will use the term 'sense' interchangeably with 'lexical concept'.

2. From this it does not follow that the Sanctioning Sense will constitute the most frequent sense. An informal survey indicates that the citation sense for the English lexeme 'fuck' is 'to have sex', even though the invective and swearing usages are far more frequent.

3. See Tyler and Evans (2003: Ch. 3) for a discussion of the notion of primariness.

4. Rice et al. (1999) demonstrate empirically that the temporal meanings associated with certain English and Dutch prepositions tend to no longer be seen as related to their spatial meanings by native speakers.

5. Reasons for the disjunctive behaviour of examples such as (6.11) and (6.12) in terms of the Concept Elaboration Criterion and the Grammatical Criterion will be examined in Chapter 7.

6. This does not mean, of course, that it is not possible to derive an interpretation for the example in (6.14). However, a conventional interpretation does not immediately suggest itself.

7. This is analogous to Tyler and Evans' (2001b) criterion of grammatical predictions.

8. However, there is some evidence that the historically earliest sense may not always relate to the synchronically most central (see Michaelis 1996; Tyler & Evans 2003: Ch. 6).

9. Although this criterion, which relates to frequency of a particular sense, may be a useful indicator of psychological predominance for language users, there is some evidence that this may not be the most important (or is not the sole) factor. Recall the earlier discussion of the lexeme 'fuck'.

10. However, it is by no means inevitable that the historically earliest sense will remain the Sanctioning Sense. For instance, Michaelis (1996) based on a survey of *still* argues that the historically earliest sense of this lexeme is no longer central.

11. Advert for Equitable Life, October 22nd, 2000.

12. The notion of pragmatic strengthening as I am presenting it here is consonant with the process of DECONTEXTUALIZATION described in Langacker (1987).

Chapter 7

1. As on-going perception can be preserved by virtue of memory, humans have the means to conceptualise events which are no longer actually being perceived. This allows us to construe temporal relations (i.e., intervals) of varying degrees of complexity, and so reanalyse certain intervals as subsuming others etc. The phenomenon whereby certain intervals are construed as subsuming others is termed TIME EMBEDEDNESS by social psychologists.

2. The Sea, The Sea (Vintage [1978] 1999:71).

3. Henry IV Part I. V. ii. 8. In the first line of this quotation Shakespeare treats time as prompting for an interval of bounded duration, the sanctioning sense. In the second line he evokes the notion of time as a commodity which can be spent. I will deal with this sense, which I term the Commodity Sense in Chapter 14.

4. British National Corpus: FYV 3375.

5. Ibid.: GT6 1277.

6. According to the OED, the earliest attested appearance of a 'duration' sense is lexicalised by the archaic form *tide*, and is found in Beowulf around 700 AD.

7. The origin of the expression: *Time and tide wait for no one*, was originally: *The tide tarrieth (for) no man*. Due to alliterative reduplication it became: *Tide nor time tarrieth (for) no man*. According to the OED, from the 16th century *tide* lost its earlier meaning of 'time', and has been interpreted as meaning 'tide of the sea'. The original expression has been superseded by *time and tide*, as opposed to *tide and time*.

8. Ibid.:KP6 1200.

9. Ibid.: G2C 1140.

10. To recap, Flaherty (1999) has studied in detail phenomenological experiences such as protracted duration and temporal compression. He has observed that "[p]rotracted duration is experienced when the density of conscious information processing is high...temporal compression is experienced when the density of conscious information processing is low" (Ibid.:112–113). The density of conscious information can be said to be high when the subject is attending to more of the stimulus array. The density of conscious information can be said to be low when the subject is attending to less of the stimulus array. Flaherty provides a taxonomy of the various kinds of experiences which give rise to high and low densities of conscious information processing. For instance, experiences which give rise to a higher density of information processing, and hence in which time appears to pass more slowly (protracted duration), include suffering and intense emotions, violence and danger, waiting and boredom (experiences which I referred to as "empty" in Chapter 2), concentration and meditation, and shock and novelty. As the subject is consciously attending to the stimulus array, a greater density of information processing occurs. Given that our experience of duration appears to correlate with the amount of memory taken up (Ornstein [1969] 1997), then if more of the stimulus array is attended to, more memory is required to store and pro-

cess what is being attended to, and consequently it is to be expected that we should actually experience the duration as being more protracted, which is what we find. Flaherty suggests that experiences which produce a lower density of information processing, and hence in which time appears to "pass more quickly" (temporal compression) include those which exhibit what he terms ROUTINE COMPLEXITY, i.e., activities which while potentially complex, through routine practice give rise to "an abnormally low level of stimulus complexity brought on by the near absence of attention to self and situation." Habitual conduct results in little of the stimulus array being attended to, resulting in low density of information processing. Accordingly, time seems to have passed "quickly".

Chapter 8

1. British National Corpus: CBF 12610.

2. Ibid.: B34 22.

3. Ibid.: FBN 2148.

4. Ibid.: ABD 1080.

5. OED (second edition): Tide, 2, 64. Circa 1430, R. Gloucester's Chronology.

6. Ibid.: Time, II, 13a, 102. Circa 1391, Chaucer.

7. Ibid.: Time, I, 1b, 100. 1827, G. S. Faber.

8. British National Corpus: JY7 2329.

9. *Down-time* prompts for an interval characterised by rest, inactivity, or a general slowing-down in proceedings.

10. The provenance of the division of the day into 24 hours, 12 hours for the day, and 12 for the night derives from ancient Egypt (Barnett 1998; Whitrow 1988).

11. British National Corpus: CF4 1375.

Chapter 9

1. Ibid.: K5A 2740.

2. Ibid.: CBG 9709.

3. Ibid.: B20 3017.

4. Ibid.: JYF 1603.

Chapter 10

1. Ibid.: CH3 3819.

2. Ibid.: HRB 912.

Chapter 11

1. Other secondary temporal concepts include the Agentive Sense (Chapter 12), the Measurement-system Sense (Chapter 13), the Commodity Sense (Chapter 14), and lexical concepts indexed by forms such as: *Christmas, Summer, Graduation, her prime*, etc.

2. Newton's view of absolute time, cited in Turetzky (1998:73).

3. 'Tis Pity She's a Whore, V. v.

4. Newton (1642–1727) enshrined his view of mechanics in his great work *Principia Mathematica*. Classical mechanics stood firm until the advent of Einstein's work on special and general relativity at the beginning of the twentieth century.

5. It is worth noting in passing that this concept of Time resonates with the common-place view of time, a physically real entity discussed in Chapter 1.

6. Psalms xc.

7. The Future.

8. Meditations, IV. 43. Marcus Aurelius was Roman Emperor from 161–180 AD, and was also an influential Stoic philosopher.

9. Walden, 'Where I lived and what I lived for'.

10. Geoff Dyer in The Observer Review, 12th Nov., 2000.

11. Turner suggests that, "A genealogy is a lineage, a line, conceived of spatially, yet the line is a time line, a spatial conceptualization of chronology" (1987:193).

12. Romeo and Juliet, I. iv. 78.

13. Langone (2000:27).

14. Psalms xc.

15. It should be noted that while a dictionary based on historical principles, such as the OED, may be indicative, it is only accurate if we assume that the sample it has consulted is representative. Clearly, the OED can only reference written works, having no access to spoken discourse. Moreover, earlier written usages of *time* in its eternal sense may have existed, but not survived.

Chapter 12

1. Endymion, Book. I, Chapter 81.

2. Essays: 24, Of Innovations.

3. Childe Harold IV, cxxx.

4. Sonnet: On being arrived at the age of twenty-three.

5. Metamorpheses: XXV. 234.

6. The Comedy of Errors: II. ii. 71.

7. Time, You Old Gipsy Man.

8. The Hobbit: 1951:82 [1937].

9. Sonnet 16.

10. Troilus and Cressida, III. iii. 165.

11. Sonnet 116.

12. As You Like It. III. ii. 328.

13. Note that the Agentive Sense is like the Event Sense in that it cannot undergo determination by an article. However, the Event Sense requires an NP modifier in subject position (e.g., *The young woman's time is approaching*), whereas the Agentive Sense does not.

14. Meditations: IV. 43.

Chapter 13

1. OED (second edition). Time: 11, 102.

2. Ibid.

3. OED (second edition). Time: 12, 102.

4. Ibid.

5. Ibid.

6. OED (second edition). Time: 10, 102.

7. Ibid.

8. Ibid.

9. British English.

Chapter 14

1. Advice to Young Tradesmen.

2. The Observer on-line: "The Mad Rush to Save Time" 3rd October, 1999 [www.newsunlimited.co.uk/observer/focus/story/].

3. Ibid.

4. British National Corpus: K4H 50.

Chapter 15

1. Chafe (1973) presents linguistic evidence for what he terms SURFACE MEMORY, SHALLOW MEMORY and DEEP MEMORY. He suggests that these distinctions are mirrored by the following categories: SURFACE EXPECTATION, SHALLOW EXPECTATION and DEEP EXPECTATION, all of which relate to the notion of EXPERIENTIAL TIME.

2. Moreover, in expressions such as: *the here-and-now,* the notion of the present, as lexicalised by the form *now,* is conventionally associated with the spatial deixis marker *here.*

3. I reject Gibson's (1975) assertion that the concept of present itself derives from proprio-ception. To assume this, we have to assume that perceptual processes at the cognitive level play no part in the development of concepts, but only external sensorimotor information. As I have been arguing throughout this book, I believe this assumption to be false. While the elaborated concept of the present is structured in terms of such content, it is erroneous to suggest that, at base, the concept of present is wholly derived from external sensorimotor experience.

4. This observation was also made by Grady (1997a). He argued for a primary metaphor termed NOW/PRESENT IS HERE, structured in terms of (static) Locational content rather than motion content. Indeed, the putative existence of this metaphoric mapping, with its corollaries FUTURE IS (LOCATED) AHEAD, and PAST IS (LOCATED) BEHIND was one of the reasons that he equivocated as to whether Moving Time and Moving Ego constitute pri-mary metaphors. If Moving Time and Moving Ego are, at least partially, structured by independently-motivated mappings, then they cannot be primary. Indeed, this position ap-pears to be the one adopted by Lakoff and Johnson (1999) who assume an orientational metaphor (akin to NOW IS HERE), which contributes to what they take to be compound (they use the term 'composite') Moving time and Moving Ego metaphors (see Chapter 18 for dis-cussion of how the lexical concept of Present is integrated with the other lexical concepts considered in order to give rise to these complex models for time).

5. Lakoff makes the point that just because translation between two different languages may be impossible due to languages possessing distinct conceptual systems, from this it does not follow that understanding is impossible. To assume such is to fail to recognise that humans have what he terms a 'conceptualizing capacity'. This allows us to learn and understand other languages, with their unique conceptual systems, even if one can still not translate one's original language precisely into the learned language.

6. See also Shinohara (2000a) who presents a methodology for assessing whether a partic-ular language structures the concepts of Past and Future along the lines of the 'Aymara' or 'English' pattern.

Chapter 16

1. This example was heard on BBC Radio 4's Today programme 14th April 2000.

2. This phenomenon was first observed by Galileo, and later enshrined in classical me-chanics by Newton as his relativity principle. Later this relativity principle was extended by Einstein to cover the whole of physics (see Chapter 19 and references therein).

Chapter 17

1. In other words, the experiential scene(s) which motivate the integration of lexical con-cepts resulting in Complex Moving Time are likely to be more complex that the primary scenes of Grady (discussed in Chapter 5).

2. The way in which many non-Indo-European languages elaborate temporal concepts remains a huge and largely uncharted territory. Given the current rate of language death, this is an area awaiting the urgent attention of linguists.

3. Crucially, the direction of motion is not due to the pattern of concept elaboration associated with the Matrix Sense. Rather, it is due to its integration with other temporal lexical concepts and their elaborations.

4. Hence, the information presented in (17.2) should not be confused with the representation of a metaphoric mapping, in the sense of, for instance, Lakoff and Johnson (1999). After all, I am not presenting a mapping between a SOURCE and TARGET. The patterns adduced are distinct from cross-domain mappings, e.g., from a 'concrete' to an 'abstract' domain, such as motion of objects → 'passage' of time. This is because the cognitive model being dealt with involves primary and secondary temporal concepts being integrated (together with their elaborations) which are already at a relatively abstract level of conceptualisation on the left hand side. The right hand side of the arrow depicts the 'elaborative' consequences attendant upon integration in the complex model.

5. British National Corpus: CH3 3819.

Chapter 18

1. Hill (1978) uses the term 'prototype' rather than 'alignment'.

2. See Tyler and Evans (2003: Ch. 6) for a discussion of the complexity, and distinct semantic character associated with prepositions of this kind.

3. As noted in Chapter 17, the elaborative consequences presented in (18.8) do not represent a metaphoric mapping in the sense of conceptual metaphor scholars. This follows as the information presented in (18.8) relates to concepts which are already metaphorically complex, e.g., the description on the left hand side of the arrows concerns temporal events elaborated as moving objects, etc.

Chapter 19

1. Since the time of Galileo it has been recognised that motion is relative. This notion of relative motion is enshrined in classical mechanics. Hence, if two bodies are moving in uniform motion relative to each other, it is impossible to tell the difference between motion and being at rest, the experience is the same. Hence, to a passenger in a moving plane, unless the passenger looks out of the window, it feels exactly the same as if the plane were stationary (cf. Einstein [1916] 1961; Coveney & Highfield 1990; Davies 1995).

2. This predicts that the speed of light varies depending upon whether an observer is racing towards a beam of light, or whether the observer is at rest.

3. It was inconceivable that light could travel through nothing, i.e., a vacuum.

4. The theory was 'special' as it only applied to bodies in uniform motion, and did not deal with issues such as gravitation. It was in his theory of general relativity that Einstein sought

to extend the applicability of the insights from special relativity to a wider range of physical phenomena. Einstein's first relativity paper was written and published in 1905.

5. Newton had hypothesised that an ideal state of absolute rest might constitute an ideal reference frame for motion, which leads to the spectre of absolute space (Einstein ([1916] 1961). Einstein (1950) summarises the position as follows, "The name "theory of relativity" is connected with the fact that motion from the point of view of possible experience always appears as the *relative* motion of one object with respect to another (e.g., of a car with respect to the ground, or the earth with respect to the sun and the fixed stars). Motion is never observable as "motion with respect to space", or as it has been expressed, as "absolute motion". The "principle of relativity" in its widest sense is contained in the statement: The totality of physical phenomena is of such a character that it gives no basis for the introduction of the concept of "absolute motion"; or shorter but less precise: There is no absolute motion" (Ibid.: 5).

6. Davies (1995) points out that the twins effect "has nothing to do with the effect of motion on the aging process" (Ibid.: 59). That is, it is not motion per se which somehow slows down biological processes of ageing. Rather, the prediction made by special relativity is that twin A actually experiences a shorter interval of time, relative to twin B, a consequence of the fact that time is relative.

7. Minkowsi made proposals concerning spacetime in 1908 (Davies 1995).

8. Einstein developed his theory of general relativity from 1909 to 1916 (Coveney & Highfield 1991; Davies 1995).

9. In the view of spacetime proposed by Einstein ([1916] 1961) in general relativity, Einstein adopts the notion of Riemannian curved geometry, proposing that spacetime is curved, rather than flat in the Euclidean sense (see Sklar 1974). As Coveney and Highfield (1990) observe, while Euclidean geometry works well on a small-scale, it breaks down on a larger scale. For instance, to a cricketer on a cricket pitch the ground appears flat. From the perspective of an astronaut in space, the ground appears curved.

10. See Sklar (1974).

11. Recall that events, as I have defined them are 'constructed' by virtue of temporality and then ascribed veridical status, held to inhere in an objectively real world. In this sense, our experience of duration correlates with 'external' events.

References

Augustine (1907). *The confessions*. Translated by E. B. Pusey. London: J. M. Dent and Son.

Alverson, Hoyt (1994). *Semantics and experience: Universal metaphors of time in English, Mandarin, Hindi, and Sesotho*. Baltimore: The Johns Hopkins University Press.

Akundov, Murad (1986). *Conceptions of space and time: Sources, evolution, directions*. Translated by Charles Rougle. Cambridge, MA: MIT Press.

Bach, Emmon (1989). *Informal lectures on formal semantics*. State University of New York Press.

Barlow, Michael & Suzanne Kemmer (2000). *Usage-based models of language*. Stanford, CA: Center for the Study of Language and Information.

Barnett, Jo (1998). *Time's pendulum*. San Diego, CA: Harcourt Brace.

Barsalou, Lawrence (2003). Situated simulation in the human conceptual system. *Language and Cognitive Processes*. Special issue on semantic and conceptual representation, *5/6*, 513–562.

Bergson, Henri ([1922] 1999). *Duration and simultaneity*. Manchester: Clinamen Press.

Bietel, Gibbs & Sanders (1997). The embodied approach to the polysemy of the spatial preposition *on*. In H. Cuyckens & B. Zawada (Eds.), *Polysemy in Cognitive Linguistics: Selected papers from the fifth international cognitive linguistics conference* (pp. 241–260). Amsterdam: John Benjamins.

Bloomfield, Leonard (1933). *Language*. New York, NY: Henry Holt.

Boroditsky, Lera (2000). Metaphoric structuring: Understanding time through spatial metaphors. *Cognition, 75*(1), 1–28.

Brisard, Frank (1999). A critique of localism in and about tense theory. Doctoral dissertation, University of Antwerp.

Brugman, Claudia & George Lakoff (1988). Cognitive topology and lexical networks. In S. Small, G. Cottrell, & M. Tannenhaus (Eds.), *Lexical ambiguity resolution* (pp. 477–507). San Mateo, CA: Morgan Kaufman.

Bybee, Joan, Revere Perkins, & William Pagliuca (1994). *The evolution of grammar: Tense, aspect and modality in the languages of the world*. Chicago, IL: Chicago University Press.

Cann, Ronnie (1993). *Formal semantics*. Cambridge: Cambridge University Press.

Chafe, Wallace (1973). Language and memory. *Language, 49*, 261–281.

Chafe, Wallace (1994). *Discourse, consciousness and time: The flow and displacement of conscious experience in speaking and writing*. Chicago, IL: The University of Chicago Press.

Chierchia, Gennaro & Sally McConnell-Ginet (2000). *Meaning and Grammar: An introduction to semantics* (2nd ed). Cambridge, MA: MIT Press.

Chomsky, Noam (1995). *The minimalist program*. Cambridge, MA: MIT Press.

Comrie, Bernard (1985). *Tense*. Cambridge: CUP.

Coveney, Peter & Roger Highfield (1990). *The arrow of time: A Voyage through science to solve time's greatest mystery*. New York, NY: Ballantine.

Clark, Herbert, H. (1973). Space, time, semantics and the child. In T. E. Moore (Ed.), *Cognitive development and the acquisition of language* (pp. 27–64). New York, NY: Academic Press.

Crick, Francis (1994). *The astonishing hypothesis*. New York, NY: Simon and Schuster.

Crick, Francis & Christof Koch (1990). Towards a neurobiological theory of consciousness. *Seminars in the Neurosciences, 2*, 263–275.

Crick, Francis & Christof Koch (1998). Consciousness and neuroscience. *Cerebral Cortex, 8*, 97–107.

Cuyckens, Hubert & Britta Zawada (2001). *Polysemy in Cognitive Linguistics*. Amsterdam: John Benjamins.

Cuyckens, Hubert, Dominiek Sandra, & Sally Rice (1997). Towards an empirical lexical semantics. In B. Smieja & M. Tasch (Eds.), *Human contact through language and linguistics* (pp. 35–54). Berlin: Lang.

Croft, William (1998). Linguistic evidence and mental representations. *Cognitive Linguistics, 9*, 151–173.

Croft, William (2000). *Explaining language change: An evolutionary approach*. Harlow, Essex: Longman.

Croft, William (2001). *Radical construction grammar: Syntactic theory in typological perspective*. Oxford: OUP.

Cruse, D. Alan (1986). *Lexical semantics*. Cambridge: Cambridge University Press.

Damasio, Antonio (2000). *The feeling of what happens: Body, emotion, and the making of consciousness*. London: Heinemann.

Darwin, Charles (1872). *The expression of the emotions in man and animals*. London: John Murray.

Davies, Paul (1995). *About time: Einstein's unfinished revolution*. New York, NY: Simon and Schuster.

Deacon, Terrence (1997). *The symbolic species: The co-evolution of language and the brain*. New York, NY: W. W. Norton and co.

Dennett, Daniel (1991). *Consciousness explained*. Boston, MA: Little Brown and Co.

Disciullo, Anna-Maria & Edwin Williams (1987). *On the definition of word*. Cambridge, MA: MIT Press.

Edelman, Gerald (1992). *Bright air, brilliant fire: On the matter of mind*. New York, NY: Basic Books.

Einstein, Albert ([1916] 1961). *Relativity: The special and the general theory*. New York, NY: Three Rivers Press.

Einstein, Albert (1950). *The theory of relativity and other essays*. New York, NY: MJF Books.

Engel, Andras, Peter König, & Thomas Schillen (1992). Why does the cortex oscillate? *Current Biology, 2*(6), 332–334.

Engel, Andreas, Peter König, Andreas Kreiter, Thomas Schillen, & Wolf Singer (1992). Temporal coding in the visual cortex: New vistas on integration in the nervous system. *TINS, 15*(6), 218–224.

Evans, Vyvyan & Melanie Green (2006). *Cognitive linguistics: An introduction*. Edinburgh: Edinburgh University Press.

Evans, Vyvyan & Andrea Tyler (2004a). Spatial experience, lexical structure and motivation: The case of *In*. In G. Radden & K. Uwe-Panther (Eds.), *Studies in linguistic motivation* (pp. 157–192). Berlin: Mouton de Gruyter.

Evans, Vyvyan & Andrea Tyler (2004b). Rethinking English "prepositions of movement": The case of 'to' and 'through'. *Belgian Journal of Linguistics, 18*, 247–270.

Fauconnier, Gilles (1994). *Mental spaces*. Cambridge: Cambridge University Press.

Fauconnier, Gilles (1997). *Mappings in thought and language*. Cambridge: Cambridge University Press.

Fauconnier, Gilles & Mark Turner (2002). *The way we think: Conceptual blending and the mind's hidden complexities*. New York, NY: Basic Books.

Fillmore, Charles (1982). Towards a descriptive framework for spatial deixis. In R. Jarvella & W. Klein (Eds.), *Speech, place and action* (pp. 31–59). London: John Wiley.

Flaherty, Michael (1999). *A watched pot: How we experience time*. New York, NY: New York University Press.

Fleischman, Suzanne (1982). The past and the future: Are they coming or going? *Berkeley Linguistics Society, 8*, 322–334.

Fraser, J. T. (1987). *Time: The familiar stranger*. Amherst, MA: University of Massachusetts Press.

Frege, Gottlieb ([1892] 1975). On sense and reference. In D. Davidson & G. Harman (Eds.), *The logic of grammar* (pp. 116–128). Encino, CA: Dickenson.

Gibbs, Raymond, Jnr. (1994). *The poetics of mind: Figurative thought, language, and understanding*. Cambridge: Cambridge University Press.

Gibbs, Raymond, Jnr. & Teenie Matlock (1997). Psycholinguistic perspectives on polysemy. In H. Cuyckens & B. Zawada (Eds.), *Polysemy in Cognitive Linguistics: Selected papers from the fifth international cognitive linguistics conference* (pp. 213–239). Amsterdam: John Benjamins.

Gibbs, Raymond, Jnr. & Gerard Steen (1999). *Metaphor in cognitive linguistics*. Amsterdam: John Benjamins.

Gibson, James (1975). Events are perceivable but time is not. In J. T. Fraser & N. Lawrence (Eds.), *The study of time II* (pp. 295–301). New York, NY: Springer-Verlag.

Gibson, James (1986). *The ecological approach to visual perception*. Hillsdale, NJ: Lawrence Erlbaum.

Goldberg, Adele (1995). *Constructions: A construction grammar approach to argument structure*. Chicago, IL: Chicago University Press.

Gell, Alfred (1992). *The anthropology of time: Cultural constructions of temporal maps and images*. Oxford: Berg.

Grady, Joseph (1997a). Foundations of meaning: Primary metaphors and primary scenes. Doctoral dissertation, U.C. Berkeley.

Grady, Joseph (1997b). THEORIES ARE BUILDING revisited. *Cognitive Linguistics, 4*(4), 267–290.

Grady, Joseph (1999a). A typology of motivation for conceptual metaphor: Correlation versus resemblance. In R. Gibbs & G. Steen (Eds.), *Metaphor in cognitive linguistics* (pp. 79–100). Philadelphia, PA: John Benjamins.

Grady, Joseph (1999b). *Cross-linguistic regularities*. Paper presented at the annual meeting of the LSA, January 1999, Los Angeles, California.

Grady, Joseph (no date). *Foundations of meaning*. Unpublished manuscript.

Grady, Joseph, Sarah Taub, & Pamela Morgan (1996). Primitive and compound metaphors. In A. Goldberg (Ed.), *Conceptual structure, discourse and language* (pp. 177–187). Stanford, CA: Center for the Study of Language and Information.

Grady, Joseph, Todd Oakley, & Seana Coulson (1999). Blending and Metaphor. In R. Gibbs & G. Steen (Eds.), *Metaphor in cognitive linguistics* (pp. 101–124). Amsterdam: John Benjamins.

Gumperz, John (1982). *Discourse strategies*. Cambridge: Cambridge University Press.

Haiman, John (1980). Dictionaries and encyclopedias. *Lingua, 50*, 329–357.

Heine, Bernd (1993). *Auxiliaries: Cognitive forces and grammaticalization*. Oxford: Oxford University Press.

Heine, Bernd (1997). *Cognitive foundations of grammar*. Oxford: Oxford University Press.

Hill, Clifford Alden (1978). Linguistic representation of spatial and temporal orientation. *Proceedings of the fourth annual meeting of the Berkeley linguistics society*, 524–538. Berkeley, UC: Berkeley Press.

Hopper, Paul & Elizabeth Closs Traugott (1993). *Grammaticalization*. Cambridge: Cambridge University Press.

Husserl, Edmund ([1887] 1999). A phenomenology of the consciousness of internal time. In D. Welton (Ed.), *The essential Husserl*. Bloomington, IN: Indiana University Press.

Jackendoff, Ray (1983). *Semantics and cognition*. Cambridge, MA: MIT Press.

Jackendoff, Ray (1987). *Consciousness and the computational mind*. Cambridge, MA: MIT Press.

Jackendoff, Ray (1990). *Semantic structures*. Cambridge, MA: MIT Press.

Jackendoff, Ray (1992). *Languages of the mind*. Cambridge, MA: MIT Press.

Jackendoff, Ray (1996). The architecture of the linguistics-spatial interface. In P. Bloom, M. Peterson, L. Nadel, & M. Garrett (Eds.), *Language and space* (pp. 1–30). Cambridge, MA: MIT Press.

Jackendoff, Ray (1997). *The architecture of the language faculty*. Cambridge, MA: MIT Press.

Jackendoff, Ray (2002). *Foundations of language: Brain, meaning, grammar, evolution*. Oxford: Oxford University Press.

James, William ([1890] 1950). *The principles of psychology*, Vols I and II. New York: Henry Holt.

Johnson, Mark (1987). *The body in the mind*. Chicago, IL: Chicago University Press.

Johnson, Christopher (1999). Metaphor vs. conflation in the acquisition of polysemy: The case of *see*. In M. Hiraga, C. Sinha, & S. Wilcox (Eds.). *Cultural, typological and psychological perspectives in cognitive linguistics*. Amsterdam: John Benjamins.

Kövecses, Zoltán (2000). *Metaphor and emotion*. Oxford: Oxford University Press.

Kreitzer, Anatol (1997). Multiple levels of schematization: A study in the conceptualization of space. *Cognitive Linguistics, 8*(4), 291–325.

Lakoff, George (1987). *Women, fire and dangerous things: What categories reveal about the mind*. Chicago, IL: Chicago University Press.

Lakoff, George (1990). The invariance hypothesis: Is abstract reason based on image schemas? *Cognitive Linguistics, 1*, 39–74.

Lakoff, George (1993). The contemporary theory of metaphor. In A. Ortony (Ed.), *Metaphor and thought* (2nd ed., pp. 202–251). Cambridge: Cambridge University Press.

Lakoff, George & Mark Johnson (1980). *Metaphors we live by.* Chicago, IL: Chicago University Press.

Lakoff, George & Mark Johnson (1999). *Philosophy in the flesh: The embodied mind and its challenge to western thought.* New York, NY: Basic Books.

Lakoff, George & Rafael Núñez (2000). *Where mathematics comes from.* New York, NY: Basic Books.

Lakoff, George & Mark Turner (1989). *More than cool reason: A field guide to poetic metaphor.* Chicago, IL: University of Chicago Press.

Langacker, Ronald (1987). *Foundations of cognitive grammar.* Vol. 1. Stanford, CA: Stanford University Press.

Langacker, Ronald (1991a). *Concept, image and symbol.* Berlin: Mouton de Gruyter.

Langacker, Ronald (1991b). *Foundations of cognitive grammar.* Vol. 2. Stanford, CA: Stanford University Press.

Langacker, Ronald (1999). *Grammar and Conceptualization.* Berlin: Mouton de Gruyter.

Langone, John (2000). *The mystery of time: Humanity's quest for order and measure.* Washington, DC: National Geographic.

Lens, Willy & Marie-Anne Moreas (1994). Future time perspective: An individual and a societal approach. In Z. Zaleski (Ed.), *Psychology of future orientation* (pp. 24–38). Lublin: Towarzystwo Naukowe KUL.

Lipincott, Kristen, Umberto Eco, & E. H. Gombrich (1999). *The story of time.* London: Merrell Holberton.

Macdonald, John (1999). Inuit time. In K. Lipincott, U. Eco, & E. H. Gombrich (Eds.), *The story of time* (pp. 92–95). London: Merrell Holberton.

Mandler, Jean (1988). How to build a baby: On the development of an accessible representational system. *Cognitive Development, 3,* 113–136.

Mandler, Jean (1992). How to build a baby: II. Conceptual primitives. *Psychological Review, 99,* 587–604.

Mandler, Jean (1996). Preverbal representation and language. In P. Bloom, M. Peterson, L. Nadel, & M. Garrett (Eds.), *Language and Space* (pp. 365–384). Cambridge, MA: MIT Press.

Marmaridou, Sophia (2000). *Pragmatic meaning and cognition.* Amsterdam: John Benjamins.

McNeill, David (1992). *Hand and mind.* Chicago, IL: Chicago University Press.

Michaelis, Laura (1996). Cross-world continuity and the polysemy of adverbial *still.* In G. Fauconnier & E. Sweetser (Eds.), *Spaces, worlds and grammar* (pp. 179–226). Chicago, IL: University of Chicago Press.

Miller, George & Phillip Johnson-Laird (1976). *Language and perception.* Cambridge: Cambridge University Press.

Miracle, Andrew & Juan de Dios Yapita Moya (1981). Time and space in Aymara. In M. Hardman (Ed.), *The Aymara language and its social and cultural context* (pp. 33–56). Gainsville, FL: University of Florida press.

Moore, Kevin Ezra (2000). Spatial experience and temporal metaphors in Wolof: Point of view, conceptual mapping and linguistic practice. Doctoral dissertation, U.C. Berkeley.

Neisser, Ulric (1976). *Cognition and reality*. San Francisco, CA: W. H. Freeman.

Núñez, Rafael, Vicente Neuman, & Manuel Mamami (1997). Los mapeos conceptuales de la concepción del tiempo en la lengua Aymara del Norte de Chile. *Boletín de Educación de la Universidad Católica del Norte, 28*, 47–55.

Núñez, Rafael & Eve Sweetser (in preparation). In Aymara, next week is behind you: Convergent evidence from language and gesture in the crosslinguistic comparison of metaphoric models. Manuscript. Dept. of Cognitive Science, UCSD and Dept. of Linguistics, UC-Berkeley.

Ornstein, Robert ([1969] 1997). *On the experience of time*. Boulder, CO: Westview Press.

Ortony, Andrew (1988). Are emotion metaphors conceptual or lexical? *Cognition and emotion, 2*, 95–103.

Plato (1965). *Timaeus and critias*. Translated by Sir Desmond Lee (revised edition 1977). London: Penguin Books.

Pöppel, Ernst (1994). Temporal mechanisms in perception. In O. Sporns & G. Tononi (Eds.), *Selectionism and the brain: International review of neurobiology*. Vol. 37 (pp. 185–201). San Diego, CA: Academic Press.

Portner, Paul & Barbara Partee (2002). *Formal semantics: The essential readings*. Oxford: Blackwell.

Pustejovsky, James (1995). *The generative lexicon*. Cambridge, MA: MIT Press.

Putnam, Hilary (1981) *Reason, truth and history*. Cambridge: Cambridge University Press.

Quirk, Randolph, Sidney Greenbaum, Geoffrey Leech, & Jan Svartik (1985). *A comprehensive grammar of the English language*. London: Longman.

Radden, Günter (1997). Time is space. In B. Smieja & M. Tasch (Eds.), *Human contact through language and linguistics*. Frankfurt: Lang.

Reddy, Michael ([1979] 1993). The conduit metaphor: A case of frame conflict in our language about language. In A. Ortony (Ed.), *The contemporary theory of metaphor* (2nd ed., pp. 164–201). Cambridge: CUP.

Reichenbach, Hans (1947). *Elements of symbolic logic*. London: Macmillan.

Rice, Sally, Dominiek Sandra, & Mia Vanrespaille (1999). Prepositional semantics and the fragile link between space and time. In M. Hiraga, C. Sinha, & S. Wilcox (Eds.), *Cultural, psychological and typological issues in cognitive linguistics: Selected papers of the bi-annual ICLA meeting in Albuquerque, July 1995* (pp. 108–127). Amsterdam: John Benjamins.

Rock, Irwin (1984). *Perception*. New York, NY: New Scientific American.

Ruhl, Charles (1989). *On monosemy: A study in linguistic semantics*. Albany, NY: SUNY Press.

Sandra, Dominiek (1998). What linguists can and can't tell us about the mind: A reply to Croft. *Cognitive Linguistics, 9*(4), 361–378.

Sandra, Dominiek & Sally Rice (1995). Network analyses of prepositional meaning: Mirroring whose mind–the linguist's or the language user's? *Cognitive Linguistics, 6*(1), 89–130.

Shinohara, Kazuko (1999). *Epistemology of space and time*. Kwansei, Japan: Kwansei Gakuin University Press.

Shinohara, Kazuko (2000a). Typology of space-time mappings. Manuscript, Tokyo University of Agriculture and Technology.

Shinohara, Kazuko (2000b). Up-down orientation in time metaphors: Analysis of English and Japanese. Manuscript, Tokyo University of Agriculture and Technology.

Sinha, Chris & Tania Kuteva (1995). Distributed spatial semantics. *Nordic Journal of Linguistics, 18*, 167–199.

Sklar, Lawrence (1974). *Space, time and spacetime.* Berkeley, CA: University of California Press.

Smart, J. J. C. (1949). The river of time. *Mind, 58*, 483–494.

Stryker, Michael (1991). Seeing the whole picture. *Current Biology, 1*(4), 252–253.

Svorou, Soteria (1994). *The grammar of space.* Amsterdam: John Benjamins.

Sweetser, Eve (1988). Grammaticalization and semantic bleaching. *Berkeley Linguistics Society, 14*, 389–405.

Sweetser, Eve (1990). *From etymology to pragmatics: Metaphorical and cultural aspects of semantic structure.* Cambridge: Cambridge University Press.

Talmy, Leonard (1983). How language structures space. In H. Pick & L. Acredolo (Eds.), *Spatial orientation: Theory, research and application* (pp. 225–282). New York, NY: Plenum.

Talmy, Leonard (1996). Fictive motion in language and "ception". In P. Bloom, M. Peterson, L. Nadel, & M. Garrett (Eds.), *Language and space* (pp. 211–276). Cambridge, MA: MIT Press.

Talmy, Leonard (2000). *Toward a cognitive semantics.* Vols. I and II. Cambridge, MA: MIT Press.

Taylor, John (1995). *Linguistic categorization* (2nd ed.). Oxford: Oxford University Press.

Tomasello, Michael (2003). *Constructing a language.* Harvard, IL: Harvard University Press.

Torey, Zoltan (1999). *The crucible of consciousness.* Melbourne, Australia: Oxford University Press.

Toulmin, Stephen & June Goodfield (1965). *The discovery of time.* University of Chicago edition 1977. Chicago, IL: University of Chicago Press.

Traugott, Elizabeth Closs (1975). Spatial expressions of tense and temporal sequencing. *Semiotica, 15*(3), 207–230.

Traugott, Elizabeth Closs (1978). On the expression of spatio-temporal relations in language. In J. Greenberg (Ed.), *Universals of human language* (pp. 369–400). Stanford, CA: Stanford University Press.

Traugott, Elizabeth Closs (1989). On the rise of epistemic meanings in English: An example of subjectification in semantic change. *Language, 65*(1), 31–55.

Turetzky, Phillip (1998). *Time.* London: Routledge.

Turner, Mark (1987). *Death is the mother of beauty.* Chicago, IL: University of Chicago Press.

Turner, Mark (1991). *Reading minds.* Princeton, NJ: Princeton University Press.

Turner, Mark (1996). *The literary mind.* Oxford: Oxford University Press.

Tyler, Andrea & Vyvyan Evans (to appear). Applying cognitive linguistics to pedagogical grammar: The case of *over*. In M. Achard & S. Niemeier (Eds.), *Cognitive linguistics, second language acquisition and foreign language teaching.* Berlin: Mouton de Gruyter.

Tyler, Andrea & Vyvyan Evans (2001a). The relation between experience, conceptual structure and meaning: Non-temporal uses of tense and language teaching. In M. Pütz, S. Niemeier, & R. Dirven (Eds.), *Applying cognitive linguistics* (pp. 63–108). Berlin: Mouton de Gruyter.

Tyler, Andrea & Vyvyan Evans (2001b). Reconsidering prepositional polysemy networks: The case of *over*. *Language, 77*(4), 724–765.

Tyler, Andrea & Vyvyan Evans (2003). *The semantics of English prepositions: Spatial scenes, embodied meaning and cognition*. Cambridge: Cambridge University Press.

Vandeloise, Claude (1990). Representation, prototypes and centrality. In S. Tsohatzidis (Ed.), *Meanings and prototypes: Studies in linguistic categorization* (pp. 403–437). London: Routledge.

Varela, Francisco, Evan Thompson, & Eleanor Rosch (1991). *The embodied mind: Cognitive science and human experience*. Cambridge, MA: MIT Press.

Whitrow, G. J. (1988). *Time in history*. Oxford: Oxford University Press.

Wierzbicka, Anna (1996). *Semantics: Primes and universals*. Oxford: Oxford University Press.

Winifree, Arthur (1987). *The timing of biological clocks*. San Francisco: W. H. Freeman.

Yu, Ning (1998). *The contemporary theory of metaphor: A perspective from Chinese*. Amsterdam: John Benjamins.

Index

In the series *Human Cognitive Processing* the following titles have been published thus far or are scheduled for publication: